WHAT'S WRONG
WITH
AMERICA?

Other books by Jonathan Neale:

Non-fiction
Memoirs of a Callous Picket
The Cutlass and the Lash
Tigers of the Snow
You are G8, We Are 6 Billion: The Truth Behind the Genoa Protests
A People's History of the Vietnam War

Novels
The Laughter of Heroes
Mutineers

For Young People
Lost at Sea
Himalaya

WHAT'S WRONG WITH AMERICA?

How the Rich and Powerful Have
Changed America and Now Want to
Change the World

Jonathan Neale

For Ruard and Edward

First published in 2004 by Vision Paperbacks,
a division of Satin Publications Ltd.
101 Southwark Street
London SE1 0JF
UK
info@visionpaperbacks.co.uk
www.visionpaperbacks.co.uk
Publisher: Sheena Dewan

© Jonathan Neale 2004

ISBN: 1-904132-42-1

2 4 6 8 10 9 7 5 3 1

Cover photo: Getty Images
Cover and text design by ok?design
Printed and bound in the UK by
Mackays of Chatham Ltd, Chatham, Kent

Contents

Acknowledgements

I owe two major debts. The idea for this book came from Charlotte Cole, who has been a wise, careful and very supportive editor. Nancy Lindisfarne, the rock of my life, has edited every word, fiercely and precisely. Over many years her ideas have shaped my own. I thank both Charlotte and Nancy.

David Smith, my British agent, was committed to the political importance of doing this book, and represented me well. Anna Laerke did a brilliant editing job, for which I am very grateful. Anna Stenning did the proof reading well, under pressure. And I owe a long-standing debt to my father, Terry Neale, a deeply sceptical economist and a representative of the best of decent American liberalism.

I could not have done the research without the staff at the Bodleian Library in Oxford, the British Library, the library of the School of Oriental and African Studies, the University of London Library, and most especially the library staff at Bath Spa University College.

Finally, the understandings in this book come from thousands of conversations over the last three years with hundreds of my companions in the struggle, from the Socialist Workers Party, the International Socialists, Globalise Resistance, Stop the War, the Genoa Social Forum and the European Social Forum. I have dedicated the book to two of them.

Introduction

These are times that make you think. There are days, watching the television news, when the world seems hopeless. There are other days when a few hundred million people allow themselves to believe, mostly for the first time in their lives, that another world might be possible. Millions, caught in the wrong place at the wrong time, live in mortal fear for a few hours – or even years. Most people are thinking hard, trying to make sense of a changing world.

It is noticeable, too, how many people, inside and outside the United States, personally hate George W. Bush. Watching Bush on television, he is so obviously a bully, a man who enjoys cruelty. Many people think he's stupid or insane. Both are ways of saying they find it hard to believe what they are seeing and hearing. Many have decided that there is something badly wrong with the United States and it's spreading outwards around the world. Most people know it can't simply be a matter of George Bush. The rot must go far deeper than that.

This book tries to explain the process that has made a man like George Bush the most powerful person in the world. My central argument is that rich and powerful Americans are trying to treat people around the world in the same way they treat ordinary Americans.

I'm not against the American people. Ordinary Americans are decent men and women, by and large trying to be kind, caught in the same processes that make the world such an ugly place.

The United States is not some sort of uniquely Evil Empire. The people who run Iran and Zimbabwe and France and Britain are no better. It's just that at the moment the people who run the US are more powerful. So they're a bigger problem.

This book is written for people inside and outside the US. Each may find some parts redundant because they already know what needs explaining for the other. The tone may surprise Americans. Almost every writer on the American left feels under pressure to apologise. To say: Hey, it's okay, I'm an American too, I love my country, really.

I am an American myself, but there won't be much of that here.

My approach is unusual in other ways, too. There are plenty of wise and angry books about what is going on in the US, mostly by Americans – books on unions, abortion, AIDS, welfare, prison, poverty, drugs, food, education and health. I have relied on many of them for my research. The weakness of these books is that they tend to be about what the richest fifth is doing to some minority: the poor, or blacks, or addicts, or prisoners. The people in the middle, the large majority of Americans who are also being manipulated, tend to disappear.

In almost all these books, too, there's a taboo. They go so far, and no further. The forbidden words are 'ruling class' and 'capitalism'. Most Americans have learned the hard way that the country is run by the rich and powerful. But saying ruling class and capitalism makes you seem an old-fashioned Marxist lunatic. That's how the taboo works.

However, if you don't use those words, you can't see straight. If you're angry at American policy but don't blame the ruling class, then quite quickly you slide into anti-Americanism, blaming all Americans. If you don't understand that the ruling class is driven by the demands of a capitalist world economy, you can't explain what they do. You end up saying that particular individuals are stupid, ignorant or unfair. The whole picture doesn't make sense.

Besides the books on America there are the books on US foreign policy and globalisation, written by both Americans and foreigners. They're essential for understanding global politics. However, the books on foreign policy pay more attention to war and less to economics. The books on globalisation pay more attention to economics than war. Yet war and economics are two sides of the same policy. These authors also often write as if the conflicts were between countries, or between the rich North and the poor South. They ignore the fact that Americans are suffering from the same policies. They also ignore the existence of ruling classes in the poor countries with good reasons of their own for backing globalisation and American power.

This book tries to put it all together: domestic and foreign policy, war and economics, the oppression of minorities and majorities. Working on such a broad canvas, I have to assert my arguments, rather than prove them. I've used the footnotes to direct you to the books and articles I've used, so you can read them and judge for yourself. In a larger sense, though, the way to judge this book is to see if it presents a useful way of thinking. If it helps you make sense of the world, this book will be justified.

The argument

I will now summarise the argument of this book. Since the mid-1960s there has been a sharp fall in profits from industry in all the rich industrialised countries of the world, including the United States. This fall in profits from industry has been so severe that it has brought down profits as a whole. This in turn has led to slow rates of economic growth in most of the world, high rates of unemployment and much financial speculation.

Profits are critical to every corporation and national government in the world. Without sufficient profits, they cannot invest. Without investment, they cannot compete. And if they lose in economic competition, they go under. So since the 1970s the corporate and government elites in all the rich countries have concentrated their policies on trying to solve this problem over profits. To do this, they have reduced taxes on business, cut the welfare state, broken unions, held down wages, torn up environmental regulations and privatised anything that moved. This has produced a far more unequal world.

In the 1980s this process was called Reaganism in America and Thatcherism in Britain. On a world scale, it was called globalisation. Of course, we have had an integrated world economy for centuries. Think of the slave trade and the settling of the Americas. But globalisation now means specifically the way the Washington consensus is restructuring the world economy.

From the point of view of the American government and corporate elites, there are two sides to globalisation. One side tries to raise profits across the world by cutting the welfare state and letting the market rip. The other tries to ensure that American corporations and US government dominate other corporations and governments.

In the United States, the political response to falling profits took off when Ronald Reagan became president in 1981. Reagan's administration faced the legacy of previous opposition movements – the unions in the 1930s, and civil rights, anti-war marches, women's liberation and gay liberation in the 1960s. All of these, in different ways, defended equality and human need. If the rich and powerful were to build an unequal America, they needed to break that legacy.

They did this in two ways. First, they made a space at the bottom of the top table for women and African-American leaders. This produced Colin Powell, Condoleezza Rice and Oprah Winfrey. Second, they attacked the rest. They went for the unions by closing factories and breaking strikes. Well-paid blue-collar people, the heart of the old unions, were left confused and afraid. A policy of mass imprisonment pulverised the family lives and personal courage of ordinary African Americans. The elite also attacked women's liberation with a backlash of family values and left gay men to die in an AIDS epidemic. At the same time, the elite tried to change the ideas in people's heads. They argued that individuals were to blame for their problems, and that biology was to blame for racial divisions, greed, sexism, inequality, madness, violence and every other form of human suffering.

Clinton's eight years as president followed the twelve Republican years of Reagan and Bush the elder. Clinton's administration was gentler in some ways and fiercer in others. But the process of change went on. The history of economic change and social struggles from 1980 to 2000 can be written without paying much attention to who was president.

On a world scale, the first obstacles to changing the world were the socialist parties and unions in Europe and the nationalist governments in the poor ex-colonial countries. The leaders of these parties and governments accepted that the world economy was in trouble. They had no alternative to the Washington consensus on globalisation. So they enforced the dictates of the market. As they did so, they alienated the people who supported them and hollowed out their own parties. This process produced Tony Blair and Robert Mugabe.

With the fall of communism, the changes in the world system gathered pace. I hated the old dictatorships in Russia and China, as did the people they oppressed. But many people outside those countries had seen them as in some sense socialist. Now those same people felt there was no alternative. Washington's global agencies – the International Monetary Fund, the World Bank, the North American Free Trade Agreement and the World Trade Organization – seemed to sweep all before them.

To dominate the world and push up profit, the US needed economic power. At crucial moments when that didn't work, they also needed military power. While the US and Western Europe had roughly equal economies, America spent far more on the military. After 1980, the US bombed or invaded Grenada, Panama, Kuwait, Somalia, Haiti, Libya, Lebanon, Kosovo, Serbia, Afghanistan and Iraq. All these military interventions had two points. One was to display American power to the world. The other was to persuade reluctant ordinary Americans that war could be a good thing again.

There was resistance to the economic restructuring of the world all the way through the 1980s and 1990s. Sometimes it was successful. In America alone, there was the battle over legal abortion, the UPS strike, the Los Angeles riots and the solidarity gay men showed in fighting AIDS. On the global stage, two very different movements stood out. One was the turn to a form of political and nationalist Islam in the Middle East. The other was the anti-capitalist movement that exploded in Seattle in 1999 and gave rise to strikes all over Europe, uprisings in Latin America and a global anti-war movement.

Then came 11 September 2001. This was a challenge to American power. To restore that power, someone had to be punished. 9/11 was also a gift to the US elite, because for a time it rallied ordinary Americans behind military intervention. America's rulers could, they hoped, put the memory of Vietnam behind them. The invasions of Afghanistan and Iraq, however, provoked a global anti-war movement. The demonstrations of that movement gave the Iraqi resistance enough confidence to fight back after the invasion.

As I write it seems that Bush's occupation is losing the military battle and ordinary Americans are turning against war again. If Washington withdraws, they will lose control of Iraqi oil, indeed of all Middle Eastern oil. Their military and economic prestige will be significantly weakened in every part of the world. And the whole project of globalisation, the economic restructuring of the world for profit, has been entangled with American power. A defeat for Washington will be a victory for political Islam, for the anti-war demonstrators and for the anti-capitalist movement. So the American elite faces unpleasant consequences whether they leave Iraq or stay. Much is at stake.

A final note: although I talk about America and Americans, I do know there are many other countries in North and South America, and people there usually say United States and North Americans. I mean no offense to all the other Americans.

The next chapter is about what's gone wrong with profits.

1 | Profits

This chapter is about the world economy. Most of us have been conditioned to think that economics is very hard to understand. There's a reason for this. Mainstream economics, the kind taught in universities, doesn't make sense. It's not supposed to. Economics has been developed to justify the capitalist system, not explain it. If you're defending an unequal system that makes people's lives a misery, you have to conceal an awful lot about how it works.

By contrast, mainstream geology makes sense. There may be some technical terms, but the people who run the world want petroleum geologists who can find oil. Mainstream engineering also makes sense. No one wants bridges that fall down.

The closer you get to the things the rich and powerful don't want you to understand, the more confusing a discipline gets. Economics is the discipline that touches most closely on the heart of the system. So when you read mainstream economics, you keep thinking: 'But he's leaving out something important.' And: 'No, it's not like that.' And: 'This doesn't make any sense.'

You're right – it doesn't make sense. But most people don't think that. They think: 'This would make sense to someone smarter than me. I don't like feeling stupid. So I'm going to stop reading this.'

Interestingly, mainstream economics makes so little sense that business people can't use it. The ideas of mainstream economics do turn up in the editorials in the *Wall Street Journal*. But to understand their world, business people use accounting, the articles in the *Financial Times*, and the skills and analytical techniques taught at the Harvard Business School. These have little to do with mainstream economics, and they do make sense.

In what follows I have used the work of radical Marxist economists: dissident ornery folk who are trying to explain what actually happens in the world. The footnotes point you toward the more detailed arguments.[1]

Profits

From about 1965 onwards, the rate of profit in manufacturing industries – factories – began to fall in all the rich countries of the world. Profit rates have stayed low ever since. This one stubborn fact lies behind all the policies of 'Reaganism', 'Thatcherism', 'New Labour', 'neoliberalism' and 'globalisation'. Let me explain first why profits matter so much, and then give the figures.

We live in a capitalist system. There have been other systems. In feudalism, for instance, the big economic and political powers were men who owned vast estates in the countryside. Capitalism simply means the big economic powers are corporations who invest money to buy things, employ people and sell products.

The word 'capital' is confusing, because it has two different meanings. Sometimes it means the money. Other times it means 'fixed capital' or plant – the value of all the real things one company owns, like factories, machines, trucks, forklifts, offices, computers, uniforms, tools and brooms.

Competition drives the capitalist system. Corporations compete with each other to sell their products. To compete, corporations have to keep investing. New and better machines are being produced all the time. To keep up, any one company has to invest in new machines, which are often more expensive than the old ones. But these new machines make it possible for workers to produce more goods, faster, and of higher quality. After a few years, the company that does not buy new machines will find its goods are shoddier and more expensive than those of the competition. People won't buy them and the company will go bust.

So, for instance, new and better shipbuilding yards in South Korea put shipbuilding yards in Scotland out of business. This doesn't just happen in manufacturing. McDonald's invests in a whole system of production that puts family run restaurants out of business. Or supermarket chains build ever-larger and newer stores to compete with each other. Then Wal-Mart comes along and puts supermarkets, book, clothing and hardware stores out of business all at once.

Capitalist competitors can't stand still. In the long run, a company grows or it dies. So the company has to keep investing. To invest, a company needs profits. Lets take the Safeway chain of supermarkets, for instance. They pay money for fixed capital – the stores and the trucks and the shopping trolleys. They also pay for the produce they sell – bananas and cans of tuna. And they pay wages to the workers. Once Safeway have paid all this money out, they sell their products to shoppers. Their 'gross profit' is the difference between what they pay out and the money they get for selling things.

This gross profit is then divided up between the government and the rich owners involved. Some of it goes in taxes. Some is paid to shareholders. Some is paid in rent to the people who own the land. Whatever is left, Safeway can invest.

That last part – 'whatever is left' – is the really key amount. If it is enough, Safeway can make new fixed-capital investment in stores and trucks, and compete successfully. If it isn't enough, they eventually go under. Wal-Mart wins.

That's why capitalism appears to be about greed. It certainly is true that many rich people are greedy and companies are always desperate for profits. But the drive of the system is not just to get money for the rich shareholders. The drive is to get enough left over to invest again and keep competing. That's why profits matter so much.

Falling profits

We turn now to how profits fell in the 1970s and the consequences for the world economy.

The story begins in the 1930s. Most of the world was in the grip of a global depression. Then came World War II. The demands of war kick-started industrial economies across the world. The armed forces needed planes, guns, tanks, jeeps, uniforms, buckets, forks, boots and spoons. Suddenly people had jobs making these things. They spent their pay on all the other things factories made. That made more jobs. It was a virtuous circle.

When the war ended in 1945, business, governments and everyone else were terrified the world would return to depression. It didn't happen. Economists, including Marxist economists, disagree about why. To me, the most convincing argument is that military spending made the difference.[2] In response to the Cold War with the Soviet Union, the United States ran a war economy in peacetime for the first time anywhere. This level of military spending stimulated the whole world economy for the next 25 years. For several years in the 1950s and 60s, the US spent more than ten per cent of its gross national product on defence.

For a time, America dominated the world. It was not just military might. In 1945 the US was responsible for more than half of all the industrial production in the world.[3] However, the US, the Soviet Union and Britain were spending a lot on the military. That meant they had less left over to invest in new machines and factories. The countries that had lost World War II, Japan and Germany, were forbidden to build up armies. They had more left over to invest and their economies grew more rapidly. The less they spent on guns, the more they could spend on machines to make butter.

In the 25 years after 1945, profits rose and the world economy grew quicker than at any other time in history. In the West and Japan, almost everyone who wanted a job had one. The poor economies were growing too. Sometimes that was easy to miss, because people were so poor to start with. But in Africa and India the majority of people were doing better.

In 1973 the industries of the world were producing three times as much as in 1953. Japan and Germany, without the drag of military spending, were doing best. In 1970, Germany was producing five times as much as in 1949. Japan was producing thirteen times as much as in 1949. They were now serious competitors with the United States. Back in 1957, 74 of the top 100 corporations in the world were American. By 1972, it was down to 53 of the top 100 corporations. That was still American domination, but other countries were catching up.[4]

Then industrial profits went down in all the rich countries of the world. This happened sometime between 1965 and 1970 – economists disagree about the date, and it depends on how you do the accounts. But the numbers are startling.[5]

During the 21 good years, from 1948 to 1969, manufacturing corporations in the US – factories and the like – were making 25 cents a year for every dollar they invested. During the next ten years, the 1970s, manufacturing corporations were making 15 cents for every dollar. In the 1980s they made 13 cents for every dollar.[6]

Thirteen cents is barely over half of 25 cents. American industrial corporations were now making half the profits they had made in the good years.

This was not just an American problem. In Germany, profits in the good years of the 1950s and 60s averaged 23 per cent. In the bad years from 1970 to 1993, they averaged 11 per cent – less than half. In Japan, profits were fantastic in the good years, roughly 40 per cent. In the bad years, 1970 to 1993, they averaged 20 per cent. Again, profits had fallen by half.

The same was true for the rest of the 'G7' countries – Britain, France, Italy and Canada. Taking the seven countries as a whole, their industrial profits fell from 27 cents a year for every dollar invested in the good years to 16 cents a year in the bad years.[7]

None of these numbers are very precise.[8] But what the comparisons tell us is that industrial profits went down across the world sometime at the end of the 1960s.

Of course, even in the rich industrial countries not all profits came from manufacturing – factories, steel plants, textile mills, mines, construction and so on. There are more people working for private 'service' companies – things like shops, restaurants, media, communication, office cleaning and child-care. Profits in this service economy were falling too, though not as steeply. In any case, profits in the service economy had always been lower than in industry. After the fall, they were still lower. And industry was a big enough part of the economy that the fall in profits there hurt profits for the rich as a whole.

The effects of falling profits

To understand the effect of this fall in profits, we have to go back to why profits matter. When profits fall, companies have trouble investing and then can't compete. With falling profits, competition suddenly became much more acute.

When the world economy was growing nicely, from 1945 to 1970, the long run could be put off for a very long time. The Chrysler car corporation wasn't doing as well as Ford in the US. Chrysler's machines for making cars were getting old and their new models were not as competitive. Ford wasn't doing as well as Honda and Volkswagen. But everybody was doing okay, and Chrysler could limp on.

Then the rate of profit crashed. The response of corporations and banks was to invest less in industry. For G7 countries taken as a whole, the amount invested on fixed plant increased by an average of 5.5 per cent each year from 1960 to 1973. For the years 1979 to 1989, that figure had fallen by almost half, to 3.25 per cent annually. The rate of increase in manufacturing output had been 6.4 per cent. It fell to less than a third of that, to 2.1 per cent.

Of course, investment and manufacturing output were both still growing, but more slowly. The companies still had to buy new machines. The new machines could produce better goods with fewer workers. So even in the good years, when investment was growing at 5.5 per cent, the number of workers in manufacturing had only been growing at just over 1 per cent a year. In the 1980s, with investment slowing down, the number of manufacturing workers in the G7 was decreasing at just over 1 per cent a year.[9]

This point is important. When things got bad in the United States, many people said it was because factory jobs were moving to other countries. This was part of the reason. But the main thing was that fewer manufacturing workers in the US were producing more goods.

As manufacturing jobs slowed down, the whole economy suffered. Workers who lost their jobs couldn't buy the goods and services other workers provided. Corporations became wary of opening new factories to make goods they probably couldn't sell. From 1960 to 1973 unemployment had averaged 3 per cent in the G7 countries. By the 1980s it was over 6 per cent, and stayed there through the 1990s. Gross domestic product of goods and services was growing at 4.6 per cent in the US in the 1960s, but at only 2.9 per cent by the 1980s. For the G7 countries as a whole, gross domestic product was increasing at just over 5 per cent in the 1960s, but at only 3 per cent in the 1980s.[10]

In other words, the world economy was still growing, but more slowly. Corporations were still making profits, but less than before. Workers were losing their jobs. And competition was biting harder.

There was another new problem – recession. For at least 150 years there had been a 'business cycle' in capitalist countries. Every five to eight years there would be a boom. The economy would grow quickly. Then there would be a recession for a year or two, when the economy slowed down or stopped growing. After that, the economy would pick up again and head towards a new boom. The cycle continued during the good years after 1945. But since the economy generally was doing well, the boom years were really good and the recession years were not that bad. 1958, for instance, was a recession year in the US. Few people remember 1958 because it wasn't that bad.

Once profits fell, the good years in the bad time were worse than the bad years in the good time. Unemployment was higher during booms than it had been in 1958. The recession years brought real trouble.

There were recessions in the United States, and most of the rest of the world, beginning in 1973, 1979, 1989 and 2001. These recessions saw massive job losses. Many small businesses folded and even big corporations went bust. All the averages conceal a lot of variation between different companies. In the 25 years after World War II, when profits were 25 cents on the dollar, some corporations were making a lot more than 25 cents and some were making less. But even the least competitive corporations were making some profits. Later, when average profits were 13 cents on the dollar, a lot of corporations were making very small profits and some were losing money.

Chrysler had been okay in the good years. Now in a recession, weak companies like Chrysler faced bankruptcy. Competition was suddenly worse for every corporation. When each recession hit, that competition suddenly became acute and many corporations were in serious trouble.

International competition was particularly fierce. German and Japanese companies had been investing more than American companies and were producing better goods more cheaply. So American companies could export less industrial products – like cars, steel and shoes – because people in other countries weren't buying them. The US started importing more, because Americans too wanted to buy good, cheap cars and shoes.

In the 1980s and 90s, the balance of power would shift round. The United States started doing better and Japan worse. But international competition remained fierce. For some countries, it was devastating. In the 1960s, ordinary Africans had been richer than people in India. From the 1970s on, companies stopped investing in much of Africa. By 2000, ordinary Africans were much poorer than Indians.

International competition was particularly important in industry. The main things people spent their money on in any one country were services – hamburgers, cleaners, transport, entertainment and the like. But the main trade between countries was in industrial goods. If Ford put up their prices too much, the competition from Volkswagen and Honda would crucify Ford. So Ford, Volkswagen and Honda all had to keep their prices down. That squeezed profits for all three industrial manufacturers.

Because international trade was largely industrial, the competitive health of the whole national economy depended on industry. It wasn't just Ford that had to worry about selling cars. Pizza Hut and McDonalds and Citibank had to worry about whether Ford sold cars.

When the first serious recession hit in 1973, the people who ran corporations and government were not sure what to make of it. They spent the 1970s debating. When the next recession hit in 1979, they knew they were in trouble. Something had to be done.

Where profits come from

Their first problem was that they had no idea why profits were falling. To this day, they still don't have much explanation.[11] Radical economists do. Chris Harman follows Marx in arguing that there was a long-term tendency for the rate of industrial profit to decline. American military expenditure had delayed this fall during the long boom, but could only put off the day of reckoning for so long. Robert Brenner argues that it was competition from Germany and Japan that drove profits down. And David Harvey says the decisive factor was that industry had developed so much on a global scale that it was producing more than people could buy.[12]

All of these explanations are partially valid. These arguments matter, and I will come back to them later. The important thing here is that all of them point to structural problems in the whole capitalist system. In 1980 the mainstream economists and corporate executives couldn't look at the causes of the problem. To do that, they would have to question the whole system. But they could look at how to fix the symptoms.

What they had to do was get the rate of profit back up in their part of the system.

First, the corporations had to squeeze workers because profits come from workers. This is a key point. Gross profits are the difference between what the company makes by selling things and what they spend on fixed capital, materials and wages. The gross profits of a company are shared out between taxes, the shareholders, rent, interest to banks and what's left to invest.

On the surface, those gross profits often seem to come from the company being clever, buying cheap and selling dear. In fact, at every stage of the process, the profits come from the workers. Let's take the bananas sold in a Spanish supermarket. The banana plantation in Panama employs workers to grow, harvest and pack the bananas. The plantation owner gets money from a banana company, pays a share to the workers and keeps the rest. Then the banana company employs dockers and seafarers to take the bananas to Europe. The company sells the bananas, pays a share to its workers and keeps the rest. The supermarket chain buys the bananas at the dock in Spain. It pays truck drivers to take the bananas to a warehouse and then on to the stores. It employs workers to put them on the shelves, clean the store and sit at the check out. Then it sells the bananas, pays part of what it made to the truckers and shop workers, and keeps the rest.

The supermarket chain owns the trucks too. It buys trucks from a company that employs factory workers and office workers to make the trucks. That company sells the trucks, pays its workers and keeps the rest of the money.

The company making the trucks buys steel from a steel plant. That steel plant employs workers to make steel. When it sells the steel, it pays part of the proceeds to the workers and keeps the rest. The steel plant gets its iron ore from a mine, somewhere abroad. The mine company pays miners and supervisors and accountants to get the iron out of the ground. When the mining company sells the iron, it pays its workers and keeps the rest of the money.

The supermarket chain owns the store too. It pays a firm of architects to design it. That firm pays part of the money to its architects, receptionists and tea ladies, and keeps the rest.

The supermarket also pays building contractors to build the store. They in turn pay part of the money to building workers and keep the rest. The building contractors buy wood from a timber merchant, who pays part of the money to lumberjacks and the clerks who sold the wood, and keeps the rest.

And so on, right through the economy.

If you look at the accounts of any one company, paying its own workers usually doesn't seem the main expense. But if you put all the companies together, you can see that all their gross profits are coming from what they don't pay the workers.

Corporations have to compete to survive. To compete, they have to invest. To invest, they have to make profits. And to make profits, they have to squeeze the workers. They do this by keeping down wages and making people work hard. This explains the constant pressure from the management we see in our daily working lives. It explains why the supervisor gives you that look when you're six minutes late. It explains why the company constantly tries to cheat on health and safety, why they ask you to work an extra hour for free when the rush is on, why they try to shorten the tea break. The pressure is on the company to compete; it has to invest and it needs the profits that you produce.

When the corporations were forced by the fall in profits to compete harder, this pressure increased. The increased pressure meant the corporations drove down wages where they could. Where that wasn't politically possible, they tried to hold wages steady. For this they needed two things. First, a good dose of unemployment so workers would be afraid of losing their jobs. Then workers without a union would have to take whatever they were offered. Workers with a union would be less likely to fight back. Second, the employers had to weaken the unions. Where possible, they simply broke the unions. Where that wasn't possible, the corporations or the government would provoke a big strike, hold firm and defeat the strikers. That would scare the rest of the union movement into line.

Employers could also get more out of workers by driving them harder. Again, the corporations needed weak unions and frightened workers to do that. Getting rid of government regulations about health and safety would help too. Those regulations cost money. The same went for environmental regulations. The employers also wanted to cut any direct benefits they paid workers, such as health and other insurance.

And corporations wanted to cut taxes. From the corporation's point of view, almost all the different kinds of taxes were a drain on profits.

Direct taxes on corporate profits obviously cut profits. So did taxes on the rich. If the rich paid less taxes on their dividends, the corporations could pay out less in dividends, and the owners would still be happy. Corporations also had to match the amount their workers paid in social security taxes. That was a drain. So were the taxes the workers paid. If the company could get a cut in the amount of tax workers paid, then workers would have more money in their take home pay. Then the company could pay them less.

To cut all these taxes, the government would have to spend less. In most countries of the industrialised world, including America, those taxes were mainly spent on things workers needed – health care, education, pensions, housing and welfare. So the companies wanted social spending cut.

The other strategy was to find new ways to make profits. One way to do this was privatisation. In many countries, government-owned companies were responsible for some or all of the railways, the airlines, buses, electricity, natural gas, water, telephones, the post office and television stations. In some countries the government also owned oil companies, steel plants, airplane manufacture, car factories and mines. Almost all of these made money for the government. But if they could be sold off cheaply into private hands, that would increase the share of the national income going to private profit.

Some nationalised companies, like railways in most countries, were making losses. They were sold off with a continuing government subsidy. Taxpayers were subsidising the private company.

Then there were the services it was politically impossible to privatise immediately, like social work, schools and hospitals. Here the corporations wanted partial privatisation. The service remained in public hands. But many bits of it were leased out to private companies, who would run a hospital, the local schools or the cleaning contract for government offices. Again, public spending went to increase private profits.

All over the world, from about 1975 on, companies and governments began pursuing policies to hold down wages, cut public spending and privatise.[13] This happened not just in the United States, but across the world. It was a response of the rich and powerful in every country to the falling rate of profit.

It went hand in hand, however, with an increasing attempt by American corporations to ensure that they got a larger share of the global cake. This was called 'globalisation'. The instruments of American corporate policy were the US Government, the International Monetary Fund, the World Bank, the North American Free Trade Agreement and the World Trade Organization. These bodies all encouraged governments outside the US to cut social spending. They also worked to reduce customs barriers so that the US could export more. They involved agreements to allow and protect foreign investment, so that US companies could take over markets in other countries. I will describe this process in more detail later in the book.

The word 'globalisation' was increasingly used to describe both the way workers and public services were squeezed and the way American corporations tried to squeeze out their competitors.

Endless pressure

To summarise, the strategy of the rich and powerful in almost every country from the 1970s on was to drive up unemployment, reduce taxes, cut social spending and 'globalise'.

It wasn't easy. These polices made the world a much more unequal place. They had to be forced through, often in democracies where people could easily organise and fight back. So the corporations and governments had to break resistance, whether from strikers, women marching for abortion rights or of gay men kissing each other. They had to stamp out the idea that fighting back wins. They also had to contend with a widespread feeling that inequality was bad and that society should meet the needs of human beings. So along with squeezing workers for profits went the advance of right-wing political ideas around the world.

The elite could never declare victory, because the economic squeeze did not solve their problems. In the United States there was some recovery in industrial profits in the 1990s. The figures are suspect, however. During the 1990s, American corporations wanted to make their profit figures look good to drive up their share prices. So they began changing their accounting systems, and lying outright, to inflate their reported profits. The figures became unreliable. On the most generous estimates, American industrial profits recovered half what they had lost. But that is only true if you compare the best years of the 1990s for profits with the average years of the 1960s. If you compare best years with best years, the recovery in profits was only a quarter. All we can say for sure is that profits recovered between a quarter and a half in the US.[14] In the rest of the industrialised world they did not recover at all. By the 1990s, the American economy was even more closely tied by trade and debt to the other industrial economies of Europe and Japan. A recovery in the United States alone could not last unless it became more general. In so far as the policies of squeezing and globalisation were at the heart of the recovery in US profits, the American corporations knew they had to keep squeezing.

These policies, however, could not solve the underlying problem in the world system. Employers on a global scale faced the same problem a sweatshop owner faces. If you own a rundown building and 20 sewing machines in Naples, you are still competing with massive factories in Indonesia and China. In the long run, the only way you can compete is to invest the kind of money the big factories put in. However, the small owner in Naples does not have that kind of money. What he does have is 20 women working for him. So he 'sweats' them – pays them little, works them long hours and threatens to turn them in to immigration if they complain. Instead of investing capital, he squeezes. This makes sense to him, because for a time the sweatshop owner maintains profits. But in the long run it offers no solution and the sweatshop fails.

This, in essence, was the problem on a world scale. Earlier I mentioned that radical economists had three different explanations for the fall in industrial profits. Each explanation points to structural problems in the system that cannot be solved by sweating the workers.

One school of radical economists, led by Robert Brenner, holds that the problem is international competition. [15] The corporations and national economies were all competing with each other. As one employer or government drove their own people down, the others were doing the same. This meant there were fewer people able to buy goods and the market shrank. No one could get ahead in the race to the bottom.

David Harvey and Patrick Bond say the central problem is that there is too much capital in the world already, too many factories and shipyards.[16] They cannot sell their goods. Any increased investment only makes it more difficult to sell the increased production. This problem also remains.

Chris Harman speaks for a third group of radical economists.[17] He argues, following Marx, that industrial capitalism faces a basic contradiction. The more industry develops, the more corporations have invested in fixed plant. Their profits, however, come from what they do not share with workers. If fixed plant is only a small part of their expenses, then there is a large cake left for them to split with the workers. Once fixed plant is a large part of their expenses, there is only a small cake to split with the workers. This creates a continuous downward pressure on wages. But they still have to invest more in plant in order to compete. That only drives profits down further. Simply squeezing workers will not alleviate this pressure in the long term.

As to which of these processes is more important, I agree with Harman. The point, however, is that all three schools of opinion argue that the policies governments and corporations have followed will not solve their underlying problems. Whether or not these economists are right in the details of their theories, it is the case that globalisation and sweating the workers have not solved the problem of falling industrial profits. Nor has there been a rise in other sorts of profits.

Sweating the world did not solve the problem. The capitalists still don't know how to get profits back up. So the pressures that changed the world in the 1980s and 90s continue to bear down in the new century.

That sweating and its consequences are what is wrong with America, and the world. The rest of the book will trace this process in detail.

Speculation and bubbles

But first we have one last question – 'If profits were in trouble, why did stock markets boom?' The answer is that stocks boom *because* profits are in trouble, and corporations and the rich don't want to invest in industry. So instead of investing money, they put their money into the stock market and financial speculation.

The word 'investment' is confusing here. The investment I have been talking about up to now is the money a company spends on fixed capital, materials and wages. But when most people think of investment, they think of buying shares. Now, if I have an idea for a company and I sell you shares in that new company, I will use the money to buy plant, materials and workers. You are giving me money to invest in the 'real economy'.

Buying shares in an established company is different. If someone sells you shares in Ford, then you get the shares. Later you get regular dividend payments from Ford. The person who sold you the shares gets the money. Ford doesn't get anything. You are investing, all right. But Ford itself doesn't get any more dollars to invest in the 'real economy.'

This is speculation. There is the same difference between the new company that spends money to build office buildings and the real estate companies who simply buy and sell buildings that already exist.

Likewise, a whole corporation can decide to invest their money in buying new machines and factories. Or they can spend it in buying up other companies. Again, that doesn't give the new companies any more money to invest in buying real things.

There are many other sorts of speculation – gold, diamonds, paintings by old masters, currency options, trades in the future prices of steel, oil, corn or hogs. Because industrial profit rates are in trouble, more and more money has flowed into such speculations. All of them produce bubbles.

The bubbles work like this. People buy property because the price of houses and offices is going up. The more people buy property, the faster the price rises. That feeds a speculative craze. One fine day the smart money realises the price of property is way out of line with the rents people can pay.

The same craze happens in the stock market. People buy shares because they will rise in value. On another fine day, the smart money realises the price of shares is far greater than is justified by the dividends companies can pay. Again, the smart money gets out quickly. A few hours or days later, the bubble bursts and the stupid money lose their shirts.

The stupid money is usually the small investor. Overall, no one has made any money on real productive investment. The money has just moved around and the ownership has been rearranged. The speculation has done nothing to solve the problem of falling rates of profit for the economy as a whole.

The next chapter is about the class system in America.

2 | Class in America

The United States, like the rest of the world, is currently divided between a ruling class that wants to restore profits and a working class they have to squeeze. Putting it that way, I run up against the American taboo against saying 'ruling class' and 'working class', and the European myth of rich Americans. So this chapter will explain what I mean.

There are two ways of talking about class. One emphasises hierarchy, the other power.

The hierarchical model divides people into ranked social groups. Sometimes people are divided into three categories: upper class, middle class and lower class. Or people can be divided in terms of money: into rich, middle class and poor. Or you can think in terms of lifestyle. Then the upper class are Rockefellers and Bushes, the middle class are the characters in *Friends* and the lower class are Homer Simpson and Joe Sixpack. This is the way that the media usually talks about class in America.

The other way of dividing people looks at class as a relationship of power.[1] There is a ruling class. They own almost everything and run the corporations and government. There is a working class. They have to work for the ruling class. In between there's a middle class who pass on orders from the top. The point here is not how people are ranked, but the way they relate to one another.

Looking at class as a relationship fits with the way I talked about profits in the last chapter. The ruling class have to make profits. The working class have to produce profits.

The working class

The American working class looks a lot like the working class in Europe. People in Europe and the US do the same jobs, in pretty much the same proportions.

The way I have defined the working class, in terms of power at work, it includes a lot more people than the Homer Simpsons. Slightly less than half of Americans are now blue-collar workers. But these figures don't count many service workers whose lives are not that different from blue collar workers – firefighters, supermarket checkout workers, hotel employees, security staff, McDonald's workers and so on. If you include these people in the working class, about 60 per cent of Americans are working class.[2]

I would also include all the other people who have to work to live and have to do what they're told when they go to work. This includes many people doing professional and white-collar jobs. According to US government figures, in 1996, 82 per cent of private sector employees were 'non-supervisory.'[3] The proportions in the public sector are not much different.

All these workers, professional, white collar and blue collar, may well have a mortgage and own a car. They may even own a few shares and a pension. But they don't have enough wealth to live on. To survive, they have to work. If they can't work, they have to go on welfare, beg, borrow or steal to survive. I would include in this group most teachers, civil servants, nurses, secretaries, librarians, social workers and the like. Many of these people think of themselves as middle class. But this obscures their relationship to the economic and social power. I will say more about the middle class later. For the moment, the point is that librarians and nurses don't earn much more than a skilled union factory worker or a plumber, and often earn less. All these working class people have to do what they're told at work. If profits have to be increased, they are the people who get it in the neck. When there's bullying at work, it happens to them.

These people make up roughly 80 per cent of Americans. They overlap with the 82 per cent who do non-supervisory jobs, and the almost 80 per cent who earn less than the average wage. They are the same sort of people who join unions in Europe. They used to be richer than Europeans. They're not now.

If you take simple income per person, Americans are a poorer than the Japanese and the Germans. But prices are lower in the US. If you adjust the figures for what an income can buy, the average American is richer than anyone in the world. Here are some adjusted annual income figures per person:

United States	$36,836
Ireland	$31,267
Canada	$30,060
Japan	$27,267
Germany	$26,267
France	$25,363
United Kingdom	$23,889[4]

In other words, people in Japan made an average real income three quarters of that of Americans, and British people made two thirds. But these figures are averages. The figures for the really high earners pull up the average. This happens everywhere, but America is the most unequal country in the industrialised world, so the rich people pull up the average more. In 2000, about 79 per cent of Americans made less than the average wage.[5]

Second, Americans keep up their family incomes by working harder. Full-time employees work more hours a year than people in any of the other industrialised 'OECD' countries – Canada, Western Europe, Australia, New Zealand and Japan.[6] This is partly because Americans work longer each week, and partly because most of them get only two weeks holiday a year. And a higher proportion of women work than in any other rich country – 58 per cent, compared to 53 per cent in Britain, 45 per cent in Germany, 44 per cent in France.[7]

So to get a real idea of how Americans are doing, you have to look at what the hourly wages of an ordinary worker can buy. Let's take the figures for 'manufacturing production work-ers' – ordinary factory workers – in several countries. If you look at what their hourly wages could buy in 2000:

- **Workers were getting more than the American wage in Germany, Canada, Austria, Belgium, Finland and the Netherlands.**
- **Workers were getting at least 90 per cent of the American wage in Sweden, Switzerland, Denmark, Norway and Australia.**
- **British workers were getting 81 per cent of the American wage.**[8]

Even these figures overstate the actual incomes of Americans. Americans in the military and those over 65 have a government health service. The rest have to pay for private health insurance. America has the highest medical costs in the world and when people get sick they find their insurance covers only part of the cost. Most Americans have cars, but they have to own cars to get to work. They pay more for higher education and far more for childcare.

Even more important, when working Americans fall out of luck they discover there is no floor under them. Less than half of people who lose their jobs can claim unemployment insur-ance. Forty-seven million people are not covered by health insurance. Most of those are low-paid workers and their chil-dren. Welfare is small and increasingly hard to claim. At $1,000 or more a day in hospital, a serious illness can be a personal and family catastrophe.

In short, the average French worker is doing about as well as the average American. Germans, Australians, Canadians, Belgians, the Dutch, the Irish, Austrians, the Swiss and Scandinavians are doing better than Americans in terms of buy-ing power, health and welfare support. The British worker is doing slightly worse.

The ruling class

At the other extreme, the ruling class are the small group of people who make the decisions.[9] In 1995 there were 16,000 businesses in the US employing more than 500 people. Each had a board of directors that included the owners, the chief managers and other rich people. There were roughly 200,000 of these directors.

A smaller group of the 1,000 largest corporations includes the leading companies in every sector of the economy. Among their directors are about 1,500 people, mostly men, who sit on more than one board of directors. These people tie the different companies together. Each board of directors meets every month. The chief executive officers of major corporations typically sit on the boards of several companies. The big banks, for instance, almost all include the chief executives of several major industrial corporations. This creates a dense network of people. Over the course of a month, a few thousand men will have hundreds of thousands of conversations in the boardroom, the clubhouse and on the golf course. Over the space of a few months, those conversations can make a collective policy.

These people are in regular touch with overlapping networks of top government administrators, important lawyers, leading lobbyists, university presidents, foundation presidents, senior judges and senior generals. The media and opinion makers are tied in with this network. The media are owned by corporations, and the senior editors are part of this world. So are other opinion makers. The director of any Hollywood movie is the boss of hundreds of people. And Oprah Winfrey, for instance, is one of the 500 richest individuals in the United States.

Senior politicians depend on corporations for the money for their campaigns.[10] More importantly, they often come from the ruling class or hope to join it. When their elected days are done, they typically join large law firms or corporations, and often sit on boards of directors. The striking thing is not how much politicians depend on campaign contributions and lobbyists, but how little their favours cost. Quite typically, a $5,000 or $10,000 contribution can win the ear of a congressional representative or governor. The reason is that most of them instinctively side with business. They look to contributors and lobbyists to tell them which businesses to support. But they already think business is a good thing, and in the interests of all Americans. They feel themselves to be part of the ruling class. Fundamentally, it's not that they're bought by one business, it's that most of them are loyal to business as a whole.

All these people in corporations, the media and politics are bosses day to day. They tell other people what to do. Their income comes from a mixture of salaries, stock options, bonds, royalties, property and shares. So they identify with money. But the key thing is that they have power over other people's lives. They identify with the ruling class because ruling is what they do.

Among the ruling class there are also the people with inherited wealth.[11] Some of them sit on boards, some are senior managers, some do public service and the thicker among them lead lives of leisure.

All these members of the ruling class argue among themselves about the important political issues of the day. Sometimes they disagree bitterly with each other, particularly when they face an intractable problem, like Vietnam in the 1960s or Iraq today. Often their interests diverge. Oil companies will want one thing and banks another. But a consensus usually emerges among them, which is then expressed by the federal government, the television anchors, the supreme court, the *Wall Street Journal*, the *New York Times*, the *Washington Post*, *Newsweek* and *Time* magazine. When almost all of them agree, you know the ruling class have come to a consensus about a particular political or economic issue. When they disagree, you know the ruling class are arguing among themselves.

There are, of course, conspiracies. The president's cabinet meets in secret, as do the joint chiefs of staff in the Pentagon.

So do the boards of corporations and banks, and the senior editorial teams in the media. Most of the conversations that create elite opinion happen in secret.

This creates a problem in interpreting the motivations of the rich and powerful. Sometimes individuals from the ruling class are open about their motivations. But the rich live in a democracy. Their public speech and writing has to be acceptable to the majority. They cannot say directly, for instance, that it would be a good thing to go to war for oil. Or that it would be politically useful to employ police and prisons to terrify black people. There are even limits to how clearly they can think about such things even in private, because gossip, after-dinner speeches, memos and emails have a way of leaking. It is best, and safest, to speak in code. Once you start speaking in code regularly, you begin to think in code too. This means that usually there is no 'smoking memo' that tells you directly about the motives of the ruling class.

From time to time things do become public, like the *Project for a New American Century* written by Bush's advisers before he became president.[12] Yet even when there is such evidence, it usually only tells you that some members of the ruling class were arguing about something. It doesn't tell you, for instance, why most ruling class opinion in the US switched from liberal views on prison in 1975 to support for mass incarceration by 1985. Nor does it tell you why most of the ruling class were against war on Iraq in 2000 and supported it in 2002.

So how can we guess the motives of a whole ruling class? The best method is the same one we use in our personal lives. There, too, motives are murky. But the best guide to an individual's motivation is that they intended the consequences of their action. This is not always a reliable guide. People make mistakes. But it's a better guide than asking people what their motives were.

So it is with the rich and powerful. The best guide to their collective intentions is to assume that they intended the result of their actions. Even when they didn't, we still know when they are able to live with the results. Let me give you an example of what I mean. In the 1970s, I was a union steward for porters and cleaners in a London hospital. We were paid weekly. Every Friday I went up to the finance office with a string of union members whose overtime and night-working supplements had been calculated incorrectly. The people in the finance office were all educated and the men wore ties. Many of the porters and cleaners had little education and were uncomfortable with maths, yet none of them ever made a mistake on their pay.

My brother Peter was a computer programmer for a factory in Sussex. I asked him one day why the people in my finance department seemed to be making honest mistakes, but all their mistakes cheated the workers. Pete said it was simple. All computer programmes have mistakes. If you write a programme that sometimes overpays the workers, the management will make you change it. If you write one that sometimes underpays the workers, the management can live with it.

I think ruling class intentions are like that. They talk things over, and then they try a policy. If important parts of the ruling class don't like the consequences, they find out soon enough. They talk to other people, and the policy changes. But if policy suits most of them, they leave it in place, even when it causes hardship for workers. So, as a rough rule of thumb, our rulers intend the consequences of their actions.

The middle class

The working class – the people who have to work and do what they're told – are about 80 per cent of Americans. The ruling class is small. The very top, the people from the biggest corporations and the highest ranks of government, number perhaps 50,000 people and their families. That's less than one tenth of one per cent of Americans. These are the nationally powerful people. You can also define the ruling class more widely, to include all the senior executives and directors of corporations that employ more than 500 people. These people still number less than half a million. Including all their families, that's less than one per cent of all Americans.

But there are a lot of people between the one per cent in the ruling class and the 80 per cent in the working class. They are usually called the middle class. The label is confusing, because it is used in so many different ways by different people. But I can't think of a better label than middle class that doesn't sound weird. The people I mean are the managers, professionals and small business owners. These are the people in between.

Let's take managers first. At the top, senior managers shade into the ruling class. At the bottom, a foreman in a car plant has pretty much the same life experience as a worker on the line, and is likely to marry a working-class person. In the middle, managers do the daily ruling for the ruling class. But they don't make the decisions. So they tend to resent both those above them and those below them.

Then there are the people who own small businesses. Again, at the top they shade into the ruling class. At the bottom is a self-employed plumber with his own van and a nephew who sometimes helps him. Both he and his nephew are likely to marry working-class women. Sometimes that self-employed plumber sympathises with other businessmen, and sometimes with other workers. The woman who runs her own grocery store and employs 20 people is also likely to hate big business – the supermarkets are driving her out of business. Yet she also supports them because she is a boss, trying to control workers day to day.

There is also an army of professionals – doctors, lawyers, accountants, professors and the like. Some of these effectively run their own business, are consultants in elite worlds of government and business or simply specialise in diseases of the rich. Other professionals increasingly find themselves in the ranks of white-collar workers.

Despite the hierarchical language often used to rank people by social status, the lines between the classes are not fixed. These are not labels, but relationships based on relative power. People can be ruling in some ways and ruled in others. The question is which is more important in their lives. So a senior manager has to do what he's told. But he spends most of his life telling other people what to do, and his whole place in the world depends on everyone following orders. A nurse in charge of a ward gives orders, but she spends much of her life making beds and comforting patients like the other nurses. She's more likely to side with the people below her.

You can argue that some working class people are middle class, and you can argue about how big the ruling class is. In every generation some people move up into the ruling class, like Bill Clinton. Some fall out. Professional parents often live in terror of their children moving down a class.

Because they are in the middle, both rulers and ruled, middle class people can take either side in major social controversies. As a general rule, when there is a confident mass movement from below, middle class people are attracted to it. That happened to many middle class Americans in the 1960s and is beginning to happen again. But when the ruling class is confident, middle class people tend to identify with ruling class values. That happened under Reagan and Thatcher in the 1980s. Because middle class people lead such contradictory lives, individual character and family background also make a difference in their personal and political views.

Talking about class

Up to now I have been talking about class in terms of power. Looked at this way, it doesn't matter what your lifestyle is or who you think you are. If you have no money, work night shift in a pizza place and spend your afternoons reading French philosophy, you're working class.

But it does make a difference how people themselves think about class. If most working-class people are proud to be workers, national politics changes. Different Americans think about class in different ways. And they think in terms of both status hierarchies and relationships of power.

The richest tenth of people in America tend to rely on a model of thirds: one-third comfortable, one-third working people and one-third poor. They ignore the ruling class and overestimate the numbers of both the comfortable and the poor. Thus they reduce the working class to a minority of society. When the richest tenth are liberal in their politics, they usually think of themselves as helping the poor minority rather than siding with the working class majority.

The working class 80 per cent of Americans usually think of society somewhat differently. The words 'working class' are seldom used in the media or public discourse. When they are, they mean 'really, really poor.' The usual public division is between upper, middle and lower classes. Asked which of these they belong to, most Americans say 'middle class'. After all, who wants to be lower class?

When Democrats or union leaders talk about the working class, they say 'the middle class', or 'ordinary Americans' or 'regular Americans'. This does not mean the same thing as when British or French people say 'we are all middle class now'. And it doesn't mean working class people are like the middle class. It means middle class is being used as a euphemism for working class.

However, Americans do still have some idea of a working class. A poll in 1996 asked them if they were upper class, middle class or working class. In answer, 53 per cent said working class, 45 per cent said middle class and 2 per cent didn't know.[13] No one said they were upper class. And many of the 45 per cent who responded that they were middle class simply meant that they were not poor.

Working-class Americans rarely, if ever, use the words 'ruling class.' In the 1930s communists and socialists used to speak in those terms. McCarthyism, the red scare of the 1950s, drove that way of talking underground. Working-class people are, however, aware that they live in a system they do not control. So they have ways of talking about that system. But those ways are ambiguous, because they avoid confrontation.

One common way of talking about the ruling class is to talk about *they*:

'*They* want to get us bogged down in another foreign war.' '*They* never let you speak to a person any more when you call up to complain, it's always a machine.' '*They're* moving all the jobs down to Mexico.' '*They've* gone and changed the rules on Medicare.'

Everyone knows who *they* are. *They* are the people I call the ruling class. But if you ask somebody, 'Who do you mean by *they?*', that person usually retreats, and mumbles something. And *they* is almost never used in this sense in written, published work. If you try to use it that way, an editor or a teacher immediately says to you: 'Who do you mean by *they?*' Then you change the sentence.

There is another weakness in the idea *they*. The opposite is not 'we'. In Latin America or Europe, many working-class people speak in terms of us and them, the working class and the rich. In the US, people have a clear enough vision of 'them'. But they don't have much of a sense of an 'us' who will stand by each other.

Again, working-class Americans talk about the middle class, but they know a nurse on the night shift is not the same as a Wall Street lawyer. Americans do have a word for the kind of middle-class person who will reliably side with the ruling class – 'yuppie' (young urban professional). The word yuppie is no longer necessarily attached to the young, but is increasingly used for people of all ages.

To summarise, America, like the rest of the world, is divided between a ruling class who want to restore profits and a working class they want to screw. Ordinary Americans understand that class system in their guts. They have to live in it, after all. But they have more difficulty talking about it directly than Europeans and Latin Americans do. The phrase 'ruling class' is taboo, and the phrase 'working class' is stigmatised. Americans can indicate with a '*they*' who the oppressors are, but cannot be more explicit.

The next chapter is about the strengths and weaknesses of movements for equality in America.

3 | The Opposition

With the election of Ronald Reagan in 1980, the ruling class went on the offensive. They wanted to drive up profits by cutting taxes, the welfare state and wages. To do that, they had to campaign against the whole idea of equality. So they had to take on the legacies of the 1930s and 1960s – the New Deal welfare state, the unions, civil rights, women's liberation, gay liberation and the anti-war movement.

To show what the corporations were up against when they tried to restore profits, this chapter gives some idea of the strength and feeling of the opposition movements of the 1930s and 60s. I also want, however, to analyse the weaknesses of those movements. To explain what is wrong with America, I have to explain what's been done to Americans in the last 30 years. To understand that, you have to know why Reagan was able to attack the old movements, and why they had such difficulty fighting back.

To simplify the argument in this chapter: Americans could build great mass movements, just like anyone else. But the union movement of the 1930s lost its radical wing in the red scare of the 1950s. The movements of the 1960s then changed a whole generation, but the unions were weak and the socialists barely present. So the radicals of the 1960s went into separatist identity politics, blacks fighting for blacks, women for women and so on. That led them to defeat. By the time Reagan was elected, the opposition of the 1960s had run into sand and the unions were left on their own.

The unions

The story of modern American unions begins with the Great Depression in 1929. That hit America harder than Europe, and a third of American men were unemployed. President Hoover, a Republican, believed in restraining government spending and did nothing. Democrat Franklin Roosevelt defeated Hoover in the 1932 presidential race. Roosevelt promised a 'New Deal'. The government stimulated the economy with increased public spending and public works. The idea was that increased jobs and government contracts would give people more money in their pockets, so they'd spend it and business would start making more goods. That would mean more people had jobs and more to spend – a virtuous circle. It didn't work that well and the American economy didn't really recover until World War II came along. But Americans felt that at least Roosevelt cared and was trying. The New Deal approach of stimulating the economy with public spending is now usually called 'Keynesianism' after John Maynard Keynes, the British economist who provided the economic theory to justify it.

Under Roosevelt, a Democratic congress also passed laws that made it far easier for unions to organise. And Roosevelt introduced 'Social Security', a national pension for all. These measures earned the Democrats the support of the unions and a majority of blue-collar voters for the next 50 years.

When Roosevelt took office, less than 20 per cent of American workers were in unions. The big factories and steel plants were non-union. Anyone who tried to organise a union lost their job and was often badly beaten. In response to the new laws of the 1930s, the more militant unions founded the Congress of Industrial Organizations (the CIO).[1] With mass unemployment, the employers could use scabs to break any strike. The new CIO had an answer.

In the winter of 1936, strikers at a General Motors auto plant in Flint, Michigan, barricaded themselves into the factory. In the streets outside their wives and girlfriends stood at the head of a large crowd of Flint residents. The police arrived in force. The women defeated them in hand to hand fighting and the police ran. The following year, 1937, there were over 200 such 'sit-down' strikes. Union membership doubled. By 1941 the unions had won recognition and negotiating rights in all the major industries. This was a revolt from below.

During World War II the US government banned strikes, but insisted that corporations negotiate with unions. When the war ended, there were strikes in the winter of 1945–46 in many industries. [2] At the time, it was the largest strike-wave in human history. The specific demands varied from one strike to another, but in all of them the underlying question was whether the unions would remain a power at work. The unions won.

The corporations were rattled. In the years that followed, the corporations replied with a complex strategy designed to win over the union leaders, while weakening rank and file organisation in the factories. [3]

The first part of that strategy was to keep the union leaders on board. They were able to win decent contracts for their members. The management no longer challenged the right of unions to negotiate. The long boom made pay deals possible that almost doubled the real wages of American workers between 1945 and 1960. Most factory workers had worked every Saturday and never had a holiday. Now they had weekends, sick pay and two weeks' holiday a year.

In return, the corporations insisted on binding three-year contract deals with the unions. These contracts reduced the power of the rank and file and activists in the factories. They covered not only pay, but also working conditions in every factory in the corporation. If the workers didn't like what the company did, they could enter a grievance and the union would represent them. But the contract forbade all local or national strikes for three years. If workers did walk out, it was called a 'wildcat' strike.

In 1947, the corporations persuaded Congress to pass the 'Taft-Hartley' Act. It made union solidarity illegal. Workers could not honour other people's picket lines, refuse to work on things made by scabs or strike in support of workers at another company. The law said union leaders had to do everything they possibly could to break wildcat strikes. If they didn't, the courts would fine the union large sums. Many union leaders had been prepared to be beaten by company thugs, defy the law and go to prison. They were not prepared to face fines that would ruin the union machine.

The union organising of the 1930s had been built on a willingness to break the law and fight the police. Strikes over local issues had kept union 'locals' (branches) strong. With Taft-Hartley, the balance of power shifted in the unions, making the leaders stronger and the members weaker. At the same time, the employers and the federal government launched a national campaign against communists.[4]

Anti-communism and the Cold War

The crusade against communism linked domestic and international politics. At the start of World War II the US was one of several great powers in the world, along with Britain, France, Germany, Japan and the Soviet Union. At the end of the war, in 1945, the only great powers left were the US and the Soviet Union. At summit meetings the two powers divided the world into two 'spheres of influence'. In effect, these were empires. The Soviet Union got the territory it occupied at the end of the war: Eastern Europe, East Germany, Mongolia and North Korea. In 1949 a Communist revolution added China to the list.

The United States became the dominant power in the rest of the world. It was also the largest industrial power, responsible for over half of global industrial production in 1945. After 1945 the old French, British and Dutch empires began to lose control of their colonies in Africa and Asia to independence movements. The US tried to move in as the new imperial power. The model was the way the US had run Latin America and the Caribbean for more than a century, by making close alliances with Latin American ruling classes. When necessary, the US encouraged coups or sent in the Marines. The US ruling class aimed to follow the same strategy in the ex-colonial countries, and also in Greece, Turkey, Spain and Portugal.

In Northern Europe – West Germany, France, Britain, the Low Countries and Scandinavia – the US ruling class formed close alliances with the national ruling classes. The cement of this alliance was opposition to the Soviet Union.

The Soviet empire was no better than the American. The Soviet Union had been born in an attempted working-class revolution. By 1945, nothing survived of that but some statues and a perverted use of socialist language. The Soviet Union and its allies were dictatorships of varying degrees of brutality. Workers had no power at all, could not have public meetings, were shot when they tried to demonstrate and were not allowed to strike. Like the US, the Soviet Union changed client regimes and sent in the tanks when they had to. After 1956, China split with the Soviet Union but remained the same kind of dictatorship.

In theory, the people owned the industries in the communist countries. In reality, the upper reaches of the bureaucracy – the communist ruling class – controlled industry. They too were driven by the imperatives of profit and accumulation. The Soviet Union and China were in constant military competition with each other and with the United States. If they did not squeeze their workers, they would not be able to invest in industry. And if they couldn't build industry, they would be helpless in modern war, a matter of tanks, planes, oil and nuclear weapons. The constant military pressure meant that communist state employers behaved to their workers just like General Motors. In fact, they were more brutal because they started from much poorer economies than the US and had to invest more to catch up. Discipline at work was backed by a network of secret police and prison camps. [5]

From 1946 to 1989 the world was divided between the communist sphere and the US-led 'free world'. The constant competition was called the Cold War, because the US and the Soviet Union, both with nuclear arsenals, did not fight each other. But there were a string of bloody proxy wars in the Third World, including Korea, Angola, Mozambique, Ethiopia, Cambodia, Laos, Yemen, Malaya and Vietnam, with perhaps 20 million dead.

The brutalities of the communist dictatorships were a gift to American propaganda, just as the US-backed dictators were to the communists. In both empires, the people most opposed to their own rulers usually idealised the rulers of the other side. They operated on the principle that 'my enemy's enemy is my friend', almost always a mistake in politics. So most opposition movements in Eastern Europe looked West to democracy and the free market, ignoring the accurate things their rulers said about that world. And in Western Europe, Africa, Asia and the Americas, the people who most seriously wanted social justice usually joined communist parties.

These communist parties in the 'West' had a split personality. Their leadership, in the end, always did what the Russian leaders told them. The Russian leaders had no intention of encouraging workers' revolution anywhere. It would be too much of a challenge to their power at home. But the rank and file of the communist parties joined because they wanted to fight for strong unions or land reform. That meant the communists were always a strong opposition, but almost always retreated whenever there was a possibility of taking power.

The business attack on unions in America began at the same time as the Cold War. The Cold War provided the American ruling class with an opportunity to combine foreign policy with taming the unions domestically. Many of the activists who built the unions in the 1930s had been communists.[6] They were now depicted as spies and tools of Russia. But the people who suffered were not spies. Overwhelmingly, they were communist union militants and shop stewards. Twenty thousand people lost their jobs, several hundred went to prison and two communists accused of spying were executed.

This crusade against communists is now called McCarthyism, after Republican senator Joe McCarthy. But he came late to the campaign. The earlier and crucial leaders included President Harry Truman, a Democrat; Representative Richard Nixon, a right-wing Republican; far-right racist FBI director J. Edgar Hoover; Ronald Reagan, then the liberal Democrat leader of the actors' union; Walt Disney, a far-right Hollywood producer; and Walter Reuther, the liberal Democrat leader of the strongest union, the United Auto

Workers. Moderate and liberal trade union leaders backed the red scare to consolidate their control of the unions. Both the AFL and the CIO passed rules that no communist could hold national or local union office.

The important issue, however, was not the 20,000 activists who lost their jobs. It was the effect on the other rank and file militants who knew them, but were too frightened to defend them. Like the ban on wildcat strikes, anti-communism weakened the militants and local organisation across the board. The red scare drove socialist and communist ideas out of public life in America and out of the unions. The moderate AFL unions and the radical CIO merged into one federation in the 1950s. In 1956, the Soviet Union's new premier, Nikita Khrushchev, delivered a speech that detailed the horrors of repression in the Stalin years and announced his government would be more gentle. The American communists had mostly stood by the party during the years of persecution. Now it seemed everything their own persecutors in the US had said was true. More than half the American communists left the party in one year.

The combined effect of the anti-union laws, the three-year contracts and the anti-communist crusade decisively weakened shop-floor militancy in the US. For the next 50 years, the union leaders would prevent wildcat strikes whenever they could. The unions of the 1930s had seen themselves as part of a general movement for social justice. Now the union leaders attached themselves to the Democratic Party, as very junior partners. As militancy declined during the 1960s and 70s, union membership slowly shrank as well. The less militant their members, the more the union leaders moved to the right and sometimes into outright corruption.

The 1950s were a time of general reaction. When opposition picked up again in the 1960s, there were effectively no communists or socialists able to raise their heads in the new movements. The unions did not revive in the way that the social movements did. The idea that working-class organisation was central to any progressive movement had gone. When the new movements for equality came along in the 1960s, they did not look to the unions.

Civil rights

The struggle for civil rights was the first and largest opposition
social movement of the 1960s. Race has always been central to
American society. Taking the land from the native people had
been justified by racism. Black slavery had been crucial to the
economy of the South. The Civil War, from 1861 to 1865, was
fought over slavery. The states of the South depended on slave
labour on the plantations. The states of the North were the
home of industry and free labour. This was a conflict between
different economic systems. The northern industrialists won.
But many of those who fought and died for the North were
ordinary white and black people who thought slavery and
racism an abomination.

After the Civil War, black people in the South were able to
organise politically, often alongside poor whites. Many black and
white 'populists' – supporters of workers, small farmers and
sharecroppers – were elected to office in the South. In 1877 the
northern industrialists and the southern ruling class combined
to end this. Over the next 30 years, the vote was systematically
denied to black people in much of the South. At the same time,
a system of racial segregation was introduced. It was much the
same as apartheid in South Africa. Black people were forced to
live in separate neighbourhoods and had to use separate schools,
colleges, hospitals, restaurants and public toilets, and separate
parts of buses, trains and cinemas. This segregation was backed
by state and local law. Laws also forbade marriage between black
and white. The secret Ku Klux Klan would hang any black man
suspected of sex with a white woman, or of general insolence.

The North was also racist, but different. Neighbourhoods
were largely segregated, but public services were not. As in the
South, blacks and whites shared workplaces, but blacks usually
got the lowest jobs. Federal government jobs were integrated,
although the armed forces remained segregated until after
World War II.

In 1945 African Americans were about an eighth of
Americans, the same proportion as today. After 1945, the new
movements in Africa and Asia began to worry the American

ruling class and inspire black America. These movements were winning independence from their old European rulers. They mobilised very large numbers of workers, peasants and middle-class city people. In all cases, these movements were led by middle-class professionals. What they wanted was the right to be a new ruling class in their own county, without racism, and be able to develop their own economies.

The US was trying to integrate these countries into its world economic empire. But the pervasive racism in America was a barrier to winning over the new ruling classes in Africa and Asia. Segregation in the American South was a particular problem. So in 1954 the US Supreme Court ruled that school segregation in the South violated the Constitution. Black people, both North and South, had been organising against segregation for generations. Now they saw their chance.

In 1960, four students from a local black college sat down at the lunch counter of the Woolworth's store in Greensboro, North Carolina, and each of them asked for a cup of coffee. The store refused to serve them. They stayed in their seats. The store closed.

That unleashed a wave of similar 'sit-ins' at cinemas, on buses, at swimming pools and in supermarkets across the South over the next two years.[7] The respectable leadership of the movement was in the hands of the black preachers of the Southern Christian Leadership Conference, led by Martin Luther King. Preachers, like undertakers, doctors and dentists, were employed by other black people, and wouldn't lose their jobs. The preachers were also trained public speakers and already leaders of their communities. The black churches were the only public spaces where the new movements could meet. And Martin Luther King, with his doctorate from Harvard, his personal courage, his eloquence and deep humanity, was a special sort of leader.

King and the other activists looked around the world for political inspiration. Because of the red scare of the 1950s, there were very few black socialists or communists in the movement, and those few kept their politics in the closet. What King and the others did see, however, were the national independence movements in Africa and Asia that had defeated

white racist colonialism. The leaders of these nationalist movements were professionals and middle-class people. Their nationalism had two sides. When they fought the colonialists, they
talked of social justice and mobilised workers, farmers and the
poor. But the leaders also wanted independent countries where
they could be part of a new, proud local ruling class. Once in
power, the Third World nationalists ran unequal societies and
gradually stopped talking about social justice.

This Third World nationalism would shape the politics of all
the American movements of the 1960s, including civil rights,
women's liberation, and gay liberation. In each case a crusade for
social justice built a movement of ordinary people. But rights and
power for the professionals and business people were always central. The American movements, and the Third World ones, were
thus able to win historically important victories for human
equality. Once they began winning, though, the gap between the
leaders and the led opened up. Another difference, of course, was
that women, black people or gays were unable to create their
own country inside the US. So the ideas of Third World nationalism changed in the US, and later became 'identity politics'.

Martin Luther King himself was particularly impressed by
the Indian independence movement led by Mahatma Gandhi.
Gandhi's movement was pacifist, relying on demonstrations and
civil disobedience.

King's movement was overwhelmingly urban, in cities like
Selma, Alabama, Albany, Georgia, Nashville, Tennessee and
Birmingham, Alabama. After the first sit-ins, civil rights leaders
turned to demonstrations for voting rights and equal employment opportunities. These were not token acts of civil disobedience by a committed few. They were marches by angry, fearful crowds. The organisers insisted on the crowds remaining
non-violent. For King, this was a matter of Christian principle.
For most people, it was a matter of tactics. The intention was
not to avoid violence. Everyone knew the police would be violent. The marchers were trying to provoke arrests and beatings.
They wanted to embarrass the local business class, who feared
a reputation as hard racists would prevent northern companies

bringing jobs to their town. At the same time, they would embarrass America in front of the world and force the federal government to intervene.

In Birmingham, Alabama, for instance, King was leading a campaign to integrate the stores. He faced a police chief, Bull O'Connor, who wouldn't budge. King told reporters, 'We intend to negotiate from strength.' [8] He sent hundreds of high school students to march into the police lines. Police dogs tore at them while high-pressure fire hoses threw them across the road and ripped the clothes from their backs. According to King's biographer, David Garrow:

Friday's clash made Saturday headlines across the country. Striking photographs of the snarling dogs and the high-pressure hoses appeared everywhere ... Reactions to such things were strong, and one group that visited President Kennedy Saturday morning stated that the Chief Executive had said the photos made him 'sick'. [9]

In the South white people were a small minority in the civil rights movement, often from church or union backgrounds. But white volunteers were important for keeping the black activists alive. If a black organiser died, no one would notice. When one black and two white activists were killed in Mississippi, it was front-page news.

The majority of white workers in the North thought that police dogs and the killing of organisers were wrong. But the movement had a particularly strong effect on black workers in the North. Many sat in front of their televisions and watched in angry tears as the police dogs attacked the children in Alabama. But the problems black workers faced in the North were different. They already had civil rights: the vote and integrated public spaces. Their main problems were poverty, police harassment and discrimination at work. The spirit of civil rights moved them. But because their circumstances were different, the way they fought back was different.

From 1963 on there were riots across many northern cities. The largest were in Detroit, the centre of the auto industry, and in Watts, since renamed South Central Los Angeles. These riots usually started in fury at yet another police beating or killing of a black teenager. Then people would loot and burn stores for two or three days. This was partly anger and partly poverty. In 1970 I asked a group of black college students from working-class homes what the point of rioting was. 'We got colour TVs,' they said. People also took a lot of food, liquor, shoes and children's clothes. The arrest sheets show that most rioters were holding down jobs. In each riot the police usually left the area for a day or two. Then the police, the National Guard and sometimes the army came back in and shot people until order was restored.[10]

The riots gave people a feeling of elation, of their own power. Then it was over. People didn't want to repeat the devastation, the fires, the dead and wounded. But other cities would follow their example. The riots put pressure on the police, the government and the business elite. The ruling class felt they were losing control of their cities and something had to be done. The response was President Johnson's 'War on Poverty' in 1965, a massive programme of job training, federal subsidies for welfare and nursery schools for the poor. The lasting achievements of this 'War' were Medicare and Medicaid – free health insurance for the elderly and the poor.

Under the impact of the northern riots, the southern civil rights movement began to splinter.[11] In the South the leaders of civil rights were black preachers and professionals. The marchers were working-class people, mostly young. Many of the activists were students from black colleges in the South, often from working-class homes but aspiring to join the professionals. As the experience of struggle gave them confidence, the activists became angrier and more radical. At the same time, non-violence was hard on the activists. In smaller southern towns, they were constantly afraid, listening for the sound of every car outside their houses, their shoulders hunched in fear of beatings. The success of the non-violence strategy depended on federal intervention. But Washington was always torn between the desire to look good in the eyes of the world and the fear of undermining the local power structure and police in the South. The Federal Bureau of Investigation, in particular, was supposed to intervene. But the FBI director was J. Edgar Hoover, an obsessive racist who saw Martin Luther King as the main threat to the American way of life.

The southern civil rights leaders constantly told the student activists not to go too far. It will alienate our friends, the white liberals, they argued. We'll get nothing. And the activists stopped listening. In their guts, the activists sided with northern rioters.

They began to reject the white volunteers who organised alongside them. This fitted with the political ideas then available to them. In the 1930s, many radical black Americans had moved to communism. The American Communist Party had started out overwhelmingly white, but they made a determined effort to recruit the most radical black activists. They did it by arguing with the black activists that the only way they could change the world was by uniting with white workers and by campaigning among white workers against racism. In the 1960s, there was no one to argue, as the communists had done, for a politics that was more radical than King's, but also emphasised black and white unity. Even the few communists who survived no longer had the confidence to argue this. Nor did the white volunteers in the movement, who also believed that nationalist politics was the radical alternative.

So when the student activists split with the preachers, they went for radical black nationalism. The white liberals in Washington had told the students not to go too far. The activists decided the problem was the whiteness, not the liberalism. They asked the white volunteers to leave, saying they would build their own organisations, separately. The slogan was 'Black Power'. The rhetoric was violent. The reality, however, was that armed resistance by a minority in the US was suicidal and everyone involved knew this.

King tried, with increasing difficulty, to hold a splintering movement together. He came to feel the only way to unite moderates and radicals was through a movement that united all poor people. As part of that, he came out against the Vietnam War in a fiery public speech in 1967. And in 1968 he went to Memphis, Tennessee, to show his solidarity with striking garbage collectors, almost all African Americans. He was shot dead on the balcony of his motel. No one knew who had done it. But African Americans felt it was the 'white power structure' in one form or another. African Americans honoured their pacifist prophet in the only way that now made sense to them. They rioted. Over a hundred cities burned.

Vietnam

As the civil rights movement split and the white activists were forced out, their black comrades told them to go organise white people. And suddenly there was something for experienced white activists to do. In January 1965 President Johnson began heavily bombing Vietnam and in the summer he sent 500,000 troops. The white civil rights activists began organising against the war.[12]

The Vietnam War was part of Cold War rivalry. Vietnam had been a French colony. In 1945 a communist-led peasant uprising began. They fought the French government for nine years for independence and to share out the land. By 1954 the communists had won. The final peace negotiations, however, were caught up in the deals between the US, the Soviet Union and China at the end of the Korean War. The result was that Vietnam was partitioned in two. North Vietnam was a communist dictatorship with a great deal of popular support, allied to Russia. South Vietnam was a private capitalist dictatorship with little popular support, allied to the United States.

The Vietnamese communists withdrew most of their local organisers and almost all of their guerilla troops and intellectuals from South Vietnam. Over the next five years the southern dictatorship imprisoned more than 90 per cent of the remaining communists, killing many in prison. The communist government in North Vietnam, obeying the Soviet Union, told them not to fight back. In 1959, the few surviving communists in the South disobeyed and launched a peasant uprising. The northern leaders, still nationalists in their hearts, now backed the southern communists. By late 1964 it was clear the communist-led rising would soon take power in the South. The southern leadership were mainly poor peasants – the intellectuals had gone north. As they took control in each rural area, the communists took the land from the landlords and gave it to poor peasants like themselves. That ensured them brave and enduring support.

The US government already had 20,000 troops in South Vietnam. Now they intervened with massive force. Vietnam itself didn't matter to Washington. The main export was rice. But American influence was under threat in many parts of the Third World. A radical guerilla group led by Fidel Castro and Che Guevara had taken power in Cuba in 1959 and then allied themselves to the Soviet Union. That had resonated across Latin America. Indonesia, close to Vietnam, had oil, and there a communist party with 3 million members was vying for power. If the US-backed regime in South Vietnam's capital of Saigon fell to an uprising of poor peasants led by communists, the oppressed across the Third World would take heart. And the local ruling classes might decide that an alliance with Washington was no guarantee of survival and look for deals elsewhere.

So Washington invaded South Vietnam to preserve its global influence and defend anti-communism at home. The red scare had cleaned out the unions and tamed the rank and file. If the American ruling class now admitted that successful communist movements didn't matter, they would lose much of the ideological high ground McCarthyism had gained them at home.

And the American ruling class thought they were going to win in Vietnam. But the nature of the American army meant it had a long logistical tail. Only 80,000 of the 500,000 Americans in Vietnam were combat troops. The 'Viet Cong' or 'National Liberation Front' had 250,000 full-time guerillas and more part-time farmers. The American troops in the field were heavily outnumbered. The only way they could win was to use their massive firepower. The Pentagon's strategy was attrition – kill so many Vietnamese that it broke the survivors. The main weapon was aerial bombing. In the next ten years the war would spread to the three neighbouring countries of 'Indo-China': Cambodia, Laos and North Vietnam. In all, 3 to 4 million people would die, most of them civilians. And most of the civilians would be killed by American bombs.

There was a ground war, too, also based on attrition. The key was the 'body count'. Each day, each American combat unit counted the number of people they'd killed. Battalion HQ added up the numbers, sent them to Saigon, where they were totalled and sent to Washington for the next morning. Marine Lieutenant Philip Caputo remembered:

> **General Westmoreland's strategy of attrition also had an effect on our behavior. Our mission was not to win terrain or seize positions, but simply to kill: to kill communists and to kill as many of them as possible. Stack 'em like cordwood. Victory was a high body-count, defeat a low kill-ratio, war a matter of arithmetic. The pressure on unit commanders to produce enemy corpses was intense.**[13]

Career officers knew promotion for the rest of their time in the army would depend on those numbers. The pressure to kill made some American soldiers cruel. But the major massacres, like that at My Lai, were all ordered by senior officers. This was not because the generals and politicians in Washington were personally cruel. It was because in the face of mass peasant support for the communists, it was the only way the generals could imagine winning the war.

The American troops were the children of blue-collar and routine white-collar workers. The children of the professional middle class got college or medical deferments to avoid conscription or joined the National Guard like George W. Bush. Some joined the Navy to avoid Vietnam, and a few of those, like 2004 Democratic presidential candidate John Kerry, ended up there. Others, like me, refused to go and became conscientious objectors. And some fled to Canada.

The cruelty of the war soon produced a mass peace movement in the US. The GIs were crucial here. When they came home, they didn't talk much. But their faces showed they'd been to a bad place. And they all said: I don't know much about the rights and wrongs in that country, but I do know the only people worth respect there are the enemy.

The anti-war movement wouldn't have been possible without civil rights. The activists who had been through the southern movement had learned how to organise, hold meetings, demonstrate, occupy and write a leaflet. They were ready to question federal government policy. The slur of communism had been thrown at the civil rights movement over and over, so it didn't work on the anti-war protestors. And the civil rights movement had broken the hold of McCarthyism on many ordinary Americans.

Doug Dowd had been a radical teacher at Berkeley all through the 1950s: 'Jesus Christ, you couldn't get anybody to say anything against the Korean War ... Everybody was scared shitless.' But when the Vietnam demonstrations started, Dowd said, 'it was as though spring had arrived after a very, very long fucking winter.'[14]

The first demonstrations in 1965 were small: 25,000 in Washington, 15,000 in San Francisco, and 50,000 in New York. But the organisers were ecstatic. They organised 'teach-ins' on the college campuses, taking the word from the black 'sit-ins'. The first one started at the University of Michigan in 1965 at six in the evening. Three thousand students showed up, and it finished at eight the next morning. There were over a hundred others that year. The first teach-in at the University of California at Berkeley lasted 36 hours and 30,000 people came.

By late 1967 the opinion polls showed a majority against the war. In November 1969 half a million people marched in Washington, the biggest demonstration in American history. In May 1970 the National Guard shot dead four student protestors in Ohio. Over 4 million students protested, and 536 colleges went on all-out strike.

The student movement largely ignored working-class people. But a small minority of pacifists and socialists set up coffee

houses outside a few military bases. This began a mass working class anti-war movement in the armed forces. [15] Rank and
file activists in uniform produced over 250 anti-war newspapers on different bases. Many of the soldiers, sailors and
marines who put them out went to prison or were sent to
Vietnam. The titles of some give the flavour of the movement:
the *Green Machine* at Fort Greeley, Alaska; *Custard's Last Stand*
at Fort Riley, Kansas; the *Ultimate Weapon* at Fort Dix, New
Jersey; *The Man Can't Win if You Grin* in Okinawa; the *Kill for
Peace* at Camp Drake, Japan; FTA (Fuck the Army) at Fort
Knox, Kentucky; *Duck Power* for the Navy, in San Diego;
Harass the Brass in Illinois; *All Hands Abandon Ship* in
Newport, Rhode Island; and the *Busted Puffin*, the newspaper
of the concerned officers' movement at an air base in
Keflavik, Iceland. [16]

The Vietnam Veterans Against the War became a part of every
major demonstration. [17] In 1971 they set up a camp on the Mall
in the centre of Washington. Over a thousand of them marched
to Congress to return their medals. The police guarded a fence
to stop them getting to their congressional representatives. One
by one, the veterans stepped forward and threw their medals
over the fence. Each one said something:

'My name is Peter Branagan. I got a purple heart and
I hope I get another one for fighting these mother-
fuckers.'

'I hope that time will forgive me for and my brothers for what we have done.'

'Second Battalion, First Marines – power to the
people.'

'My wife is divorcing me for returning these
medals. She wants me to keep them so my sons can
be proud of me. But three of my best friends died so
I could get that medal.'

Another man, pointing at the steps of Congress –
'we're not going to fight anymore, but if we have to
fight again it will be to take those steps.' [18]

John Kerry was one of the men who returned his medals that day.

The decisive impact of the peace movement, though, was among the American troops in Vietnam. They had no rank and file newspapers, no formal organisation and almost no demonstrations. But from 1968 on they began to kill their officers and sergeants when ordered out on patrol. They had a special word for it. 'Fragging' meant throwing a fragmentation grenade into the officer's tent. Many officers, however, were shot in the back while out on patrol. The point was to discipline any officer who tried to make them fight.

Lamont Steptoe was an officer with the 25th Infantry in 1969 and 1970. As he remembered it:

> **Generally there was a pattern. If you were fucking with the men, they would warn you. When you came back to your bunk, there would be a tear gas canister ... The next time there would be a booby, which when you tripped it would let you know it had been real. The third time it would be the real thing.**[19]

It is difficult to say exactly how many officers were killed. The Army tried several hundred soldiers for murder or attempted murder in camp, but many cases were hushed up and most of the officers probably died in the field. A thousand officers and sergeants killed is a low guess. As a result, first the Marines and then the Army stopped fighting. They had to be withdrawn from Vietnam. A combination of Vietnamese peasants, American students, GIs and Marines had broken the power of the American empire.

The fraggings traumatised a whole generation of Army officers. They include the men in charge of the Pentagon for the last 20 years, who never want to see a revolt like Vietnam again. Colin Powell, Bush's Secretary of State, served with the 46th Infantry in 1968. Tim O'Brien was an enlisted man in the same unit at the same time. The first sergeant in O'Brien's company was white. He refused to give black soldiers transfers to the rear. The black soldiers killed him on patrol. Then Alpha company got a new commanding officer. Colonel Daud liked combat assaults, scrambling out of helicopters into terrified villages. O'Brien wrote later:

> More combat assaults came in the next few days. We learned to hate Colonel Daud and his force of helicopters. When he was killed by sappers in a midnight raid, the news came over the radio. A lieutenant led us in a song, a catchy, happy, celebrating song: Dingdong, the wicked witch is dead. We sang in good harmony. It sounded like a choir.[20]

Powell and the Pentagon have dreaded a prolonged American occupation of anywhere ever since. The other enduring effect has been the 'Vietnam syndrome'. This is not an illness. It is the sensible refusal of working-class Americans for 30 years after Vietnam to allow their children to die for Washington's foreign policy. After 9/11, Bush and the whole ruling class hoped they had finally overcome this reluctance. The way Americans have rapidly turned against the occupation of Iraq shows the 'syndrome' is still there.

More movements

The civil rights movement came first and the anti-war movement years later. The American ruling class began to feel they were losing control of their country and the world. 1968 was the year of the Tet Offensive in Vietnam, when communist guerrillas took and held parts of the cities for weeks. It was a year of student strikes and demonstrations in Britain, Germany, Italy, Afghanistan, Pakistan and dozens of other countries. In France, student protests led to the largest general strike the world had ever seen. In the months and years that followed, ruling classes all over the world would face mass resistance – especially in Latin America.[21]

When attorney general John Mitchell watched anti-war demonstrators from his office window in 1969, he was reminded of the Russian revolution.[22] Robert McNamara had been chief executive of the Ford motor company and then the Secretary of Defense during the Vietnam War. In 1968 he became head of the World Bank. His first week there McNamara called a meeting of senior bank staffers. He was full of plans, convinced that if Washington and the bank did nothing about world poverty they would face many more Vietnams. His staffers sat, nervously listening to their frightened and aggressive new boss. The sky turned 'eerily dark' in mid-afternoon. As they left the meeting 'in shock', the bank staffers learned the darkness in the sky was smoke. The people of Washington were burning buildings in protest against the assassination of Martin Luther King.[23]

The movements were creating new movements. Women's liberation was founded in New York by white civil rights activists. Many had mothers who were communists in the 1930s. Within a year, millions of Americans considered themselves part of that movement. Within five years, hundreds of millions of women around the world identified with it.[24]

The political understanding of the women's movement built directly on civil rights. Women suffered 'sexism' – a new word – just as black people suffered racism. The way to fight back was pride, organisation and demonstrations. There were three central goals. One mirrored civil rights – equality of hiring in professional jobs. The second was equality in personal relationships. Here there was a new organising strategy. Women met in small consciousness-raising groups to talk about their lives. Suddenly all the things they had put up with over so many years made sense. My mother sat in front of the television a few years later, watching a feminist sing a song about women's resistance. As she sat there crying, her whole life fell into place, and she said 'fifty years, fifty years', over and over, and cried.

The third central demand was abortion. Abortion was illegal in every state, but it was like the draft. Working-class boys went to Vietnam and rich boys didn't. If a girl was rich or had slept with someone important she could find a doctor to do the operation. Ordinary women had illegal abortions. Sometimes the person doing it was kind and clean. Sometimes they weren't.

Many women, frightened and alone, did their own abortions. The journalist and historian Cynthia Gorney combed the medical journals of the 1960s and made a list of the things women had used. They included 'bleach, garden hose, curtain rod, coat hanger, clothes pin, knitting needle, pencil, vinegar, gramophone needle, bicycle pump and tube, and chopsticks.' Many of these were found in the uterine wall when women were admitted to hospital.[25]

In 1968 Robert Duemler was an obstetrician at a Catholic hospital full of nuns. One of the nurses was 'a big smart opinionated woman named Judith Widdicombe':

> Sometimes after deliveries Duemler and Widdicombe would lean against a wall in their scrubs and watch the commotion ... [Duemler] was older than she was, and it amused him to see Judy Widdicombe irritate the senior physicians by pointing out when and where she thought they had bungled their work. She was not deferential. She had no concept of deference ... [Sometimes after a birth] Widdicombe would say casually to Duemler, not looking at him, 'I bet she doesn't really want that kid.'
>
> Maybe not, Duemler would say. And they would talk about something else. But he understood that ... Widdicombe was signaling him. There was a code at work, and Duemler was not sure what it was.[26]

Within months, Widdicombe had recruited the doctor to her underground referral service, sending women to trusted illegal operators in Chicago and Mexico.

Women fought the issue through the courts and state legislatures as well. In April 1970 New York legalised abortion. Judy Widdicombe's group, not yet legal but no longer quite underground, started sending women to New York. The rich ones flew, the rest took the bus 1,500 miles each way.

Down in Dallas-Forth Worth a waitress named Norma McCovey went to see two young lawyers, Sarah Weddington and Linda Coffee. McCovey was a single mother, pregnant again. She had heard the lawyers were looking for a test case to challenge the Texas abortion law. There was nothing the case could do for McCovey, she'd have to take care of that herself. But she told the lawyers she was willing to be their plaintiff. They gave her a pseudonym, 'Jane Roe', like the anonymous American 'John Doe'. 'Roe' sued Henry Wade, the district attorney in Dallas.

Roe v. Wade went all the way to the Supreme Court. Sarah Weddington was 24 years old when she argued the case in front of the nine justices. Her father was a Methodist minister. She'd had an illegal abortion in Mexico when she was 19 and was now married to the man who had driven her across the border.

On 22 January 1973 the Supreme Court voted seven to two that as long as a woman and her doctor agreed, the state could not interfere with an abortion during the first three months of pregnancy. In a more complex ruling, they effectively allowed abortion during the rest of the pregnancy as well. Abortion was now legal in every state. The Dallas waitress had won.

It wasn't just abortion and it wasn't just women. Native Americans, still called 'Indians', organised the American Indian Movement. In South Texas, New Mexico, Arizona and California, Chicanos – Mexican Americans – started their own civil rights movement. The migrant farm workers in California, many of them Chicano, unionised.

In New York the police raided the Stonewall, a gay bar in Greenwich Village. [27] They'd done the same thing a thousand times before. This time one of the working-class Puerto Rican drag queens being loaded into the paddy wagon kicked a cop with his high heels. A riot started. With weeks there was a new organisation, the 'Gay Liberation Front'. The Stonewall riot would not have happened without the black riots. The new organisation would not have happened without women's liberation. And they took their name from the Vietnamese guerillas, the National Liberation Front.

The riot had started with gay men, but lesbians quickly joined the new movement. They too marched and leafleted.

The central tactic was tailored to the particular form of their oppression. Lesbians and gay men were forced to hide their sexuality in daily life, from fear of both shame and losing their jobs. In the movement they gave each other courage to 'come out' – to say proudly who they were.

Crisis

These new movements were all confident. Their victories were real and international. They stopped the Vietnam War. They broke the worst of racial segregation in America. The ideas of women's and gay liberation transformed the lives of hundreds of millions around the world. By 1975, though, the activists felt all their movements were running into sand. To understand why, we need to look at the weaknesses of the movements.

The first weakness was that they ignored unions and workers. In the anti-war movement, for instance, the opinion polls showed that the less education a person had, the more likely they were to oppose the war. This was not surprising. It was the children of the working class who were being sent to the war. But the student-led anti-war movement had the deep arrogance of the American professional class. We – I was one of them – simply assumed that workers were more right wing and less enlightened than us.

A firefighter's wife, whose son Ralph died in Vietnam, put it this way to an interviewer in 1970:

> I think my husband and I can't help but think that our son gave his life for nothing, nothing at all ... I told [my husband that the protesters] want the war to end, so no more Ralphs will die, but he says not, they never stop and think about Ralph and his kind of people, and I'm inclined to agree. They say they do, but I listen to them, I watch them; since Ralph died I listen and watch as carefully as I can. Their hearts are with other people, not their own American people, not the ordinary kind of person in this country. I know when someone is worrying about me and my

children, and when he says he is, but he's really somewhere else with his sympathy. Those people, a lot of
them are rich kids from the suburbs, the rich suburbs
... They don't come out here and talk to us.[28]

She was right. There were exceptions, of course. A small number of socialists and pacifists started the organising against the
war in the armed forces. The Vietnam Veterans Against the War
were largely working class. So were the soldiers who refused to
fight in Vietnam, most of the civil rights demonstrators and
almost all of the northern black rioters. And of course, so were
most of the women, gays and lesbians who identified with the
liberation movements. But the leadership of these movements
came from the professional middle classes. Crucially, their politics were one form or another of nationalism.

As the movements grew, the activists became more radical.
They began to understand the ugliness of the system they
faced, but they didn't have a name for it. In Europe and Latin
America the same sort of people looked to the unions and the
workers' movement. They had a tradition of socialism, they
were able to call the system they lived under capitalism, and
they could imagine an alternative. In the US, wounded by the
red scare of the 1950s, few activists thought that way. Instead,
radicals followed the example of the black movement and
looked to separate organisation. Gay men organised on their
own, and radical lesbians separately from them. Radical feminists cut themselves off from men. Some of the angriest students in the anti-war movement decided that white American
working class would never change the world. They should fight
for the oppressed of the Third World, and minorities in the US,
but not for all American workers.

The weakness of identity politics in the 1970s was perhaps
easiest to see in the civil rights movement, because it had been
the strongest movement. After King's murder, there was a general turn among radical activists to Black Power. They found,
however, that it didn't work. The stubborn fact was that African
Americans were an eighth of the population. National liberation

on the Third World model was not going to work. Black Americans could not found their own government in their own country. Armed revolt would have been drowned in blood. The Black Panther Party tried just exercising their constitutional right to bear arms, without using them. A concerted attack by the federal government left most of their leaders dead or in jail.

Black Power looked to the example of nationalist politics among people of colour in the colonial world. There nationalism had made sense. It had brought a variety of middle-class and upper-class nationalist parties into power. They had struggled in situations where they appealed to national and racial solidarity, and 99 per cent of the people were the same race. Moreover, once in power the nationalists in Asia and Africa had run societies that were almost as unequal as the United States. Nationalism was a recipe for middle and upper-class power.

In the United States, black people continued to be employed alongside whites. Every issue that affected black workers – contracts, welfare, pensions, discrimination, health care, police brutality – also affected white people. Without some alliance, black radicals could protest, but they could not win.

What happened to the black radicals in Detroit is one example. [29] Detroit was Motown – motor city. The auto industry dominated the city, and the United Auto Workers dominated opposition politics. There was a small, but living, tradition of Marxism and socialism. It was natural for the black radicals to organise workers. But they only went to black workers. They started at Dodge motors, with the Dodge Revolutionary Union Movement (DRUM). From there they moved on to build branches of black revolutionaries in other car plants. A wildcat strike revealed their fatal weakness. The DRUM agitators were able to get the majority of black workers out. But on principle, the DRUM pickets refused to give the white women workers leaflets and ask them to strike. Not surprisingly, the white women worked and the strike was broken. The more right-wing leadership of the United Auto Workers was able to move in on DRUM and break their base in the plants.

The same thing was happening in the student movement, the women's movement and the gay movement. Each was fighting for their own identity, their own sort of 'nationalism', in their own ghetto. Separate organisation did not work.

As the 1970s wore on, the black radicals came back into the 'white power structure'. Revolutionary separatism had failed them. Most blamed the revolution, not the separatism. Those who were politically talented, and the well educated, moved into the Democratic party, local politics and the professions. They took with them a more moderate, but still nationalist, form of identity politics. Others, like members of the Nation of Islam, hung onto the separatism, but didn't challenge the system. Throughout the 1980s and 1990s, blacks would fight for blacks, women for women, gays for gays and unions for unions. The division would cripple all of them. The black working people who had always formed the majority of the demonstrators and rioters were left behind.

By the late 1970s all the movements of the 60s had been decisively weakened. But, like the unions, they were still there. They had shaken the American ruling class and won real victories. By 1981 the corporations and the ruling class wanted to make the country far more unequal in order to restore profits. To do that, they had to attack the legacy of the old movements.

4 | Strikes and Taxes

Let me summarise the argument so far. From the middle of the 1960s onwards the rate of profit in industry in the rich countries began to fall. In 1973, this led to the first in a series of global recessions. After that, the world economy grew at a much slower rate than it had between 1945 and 1970, and there were high rates of unemployment in most countries. The corporations and the governments wanted to get the rate of profit back up. That meant deregulation, breaking the unions, privatisation, cutting taxes, reducing social spending and 'globalisation' – opening new markets for American profits.

The first big recession, in 1973, was a wake-up call for the American ruling class. During the rest of the 1970s, they weren't sure if their economic troubles would last. They tried to move society slowly to the right and argued among themselves about what to do. Then came the second global recession in 1980. That galvanised them. Something had to be done. They had to make America, and the world, more unequal. And 1980 was the year the Republican Ronald Reagan was elected president. He came into office in January 1981.

Reagan had the support of almost all the ruling class. His was the 'Teflon' presidency. No matter what he did wrong, or what out and out crimes senior administration figures committed, the media gave Reagan an easy ride. Like a Teflon pan, nothing stuck to him. There is some doubt as to how much Ronald Reagan himself led the government. But a widespread consensus among the rich and powerful was implemented by his whole administration. 'Reagan', here, is shorthand for that consensus.

'Reagan's' economic project, though, had to be part of a much broader right-wing campaign. If you want to make society more unequal, you have to make it more unequal in every way. This is because human beings are whole people. If I believe deeply in equality between women and men, between black and white, between gay and straight, then I am likely to believe in equality between rich and poor. It is true that we all have contradictory ideas in our heads. To a certain extent, we behave one way at work and another way at home. But if you want to stay sane, there are limits to these contradictions and to the splitting you do.

Relationships between men and women, parents and children, are the earliest and most intimate ties in our world. The inequalities there mould and shape our very bodies before we learn to speak. That is why the rich and the right defend 'family values' so strongly, because they are based on ideas of deep sexual inequality. It is also why the left and the poor are more likely to defend liberation. By the same token, if you think you're better than someone else because you're white and she's not, you're going to be more open to the idea that people who are richer and more beautiful than you also deserve more than you.

It works the other way round, too. When people fight for one kind of equality, that gives them the confidence to fight for another kind. A lesbian who comes out at the school where she teaches is more likely to vote for a strike over wages. The massive 15 February 2003 anti-war march around the world was followed by a demonstration of 300,000 in Berlin against cuts in the welfare state a year later.

In the same way, defeats in important struggles for equality resonate through a whole society. In 1982 a million and a quarter textile workers in Bombay, India, stayed out on strike for over a year before they lost. The unions and the left in India are only now recovering from the demoralisation of that defeat. The 1984–85 miners strike in Britain had the same effect.

The move to the right works in more insidious ways, too. In Britain, the left and the radicals were confident at work in the early 1970s. They'd won a lot of strikes and it felt like jobs grew on trees. After 1973 there was mass unemployment and unions were losing strikes. There's at least one right-wing loudmouth in every workplace in the world. In the 1960s he'd been quiet. Now he started talking, repeating what he'd read in right-wing newspapers. The radicals didn't have the heart to talk back. They were scared or tired or wanted promotion or didn't think it would make a difference anymore. So they did the crossword or tried to find someone to flirt with. Then the people in the middle, the ones who sort of agreed with the radicals but didn't feel very confident, figured that most people agreed with the loudmouth. And if that was what most people were thinking, probably it was better to move your own thinking a bit to the right.

What all this means is that if the 'Reagan revolution' wanted to change economic policy and break the unions, they had to discredit the legacy of the opposition movements of the 1930s and 1960s – particularly the unions, civil rights, the northern ghetto riots, the anti-war movement, women's liberation and gay liberation. No one part of their policy can be understood without all the other parts.

Reagan attacks the unions

Reagan came into office at a moment when the American ruling class had decided they had to break the unions to restore profits. And they thought the unions were weak enough that they could get away with it.

In 1981, the union leaders had been preventing wildcat strikes for 30 years. There was hardly any network of radicals or socialists in the unions. Some unions had become corrupt. Most had not, but there was a chasm between leaders and members. The result had been a slow but steady fall in union membership.

A 1978 Hollywood film, *Blue Collar*, expressed the confusion in the working class beautifully. In one scene, three auto workers, one white and two black, are sitting in a bar complaining about the union. They rail about corruption and badmouth the leaders of the local. A student from the nearby university sits down at their table and says something mildly critical about the union. They beat him up. It's their union.

In 1981 the unions still organised most of the main factories and industries. They still went on strike. They were still a major block to any attempt to restore profits. A few months after taking office, Reagan took on the unions by making an example of the Professional Association of Air Traffic Controllers.[1] PATCO was a small, democratic, feisty union. Just over 14,000 people, the great majority of the controllers, belonged. They were all federal government employees and most were smart, confident, physically coordinated and highly skilled.

The job, however, was extremely stressful. Each controller sat at a radar screen moving dozens of planes around at different levels. One mistake could kill hundreds of people. Controllers often worked for four hours without relief and were forced to do compulsory overtime. Most of them started at smaller airports, where the pace was manageable. With experience, after eight or ten years, they were compulsorily transferred to one of the larger, more hectic airports. They would spend the rest of their time on the job there, trapped.

They didn't want to leave the job, because they were mostly not well educated and there was no other way they could make the same money.

But the stress broke most people sooner or later. The great majority quit before they served the full 25 years that would earn them full pension rights. In the three years before 1980, 89 per cent of the controllers who took retirement did so on medical grounds before they had earned full benefits.

In 1980 Robert Poli was the newly elected firebrand leader of PATCO. A new contract was coming up and his members desperately wanted something done about the pace of work, compulsory overtime and pay. Poli's first strategy was political influence. He approached Ronald Reagan, then running for president. Reagan wrote Poli official letters promising to support the controllers. In return, PATCO endorsed Reagan.

Once elected president, Reagan reneged on his promise and did nothing. Poli was left to negotiate the best deal he could. His executive committee rejected it unanimously. When their decision was announced at a national union meeting in

Chicago, '500 local union presidents cheered wildly and chanted "Strike, strike, strike".' [2] The union members voted 13,495 to 616 to reject the deal.

They came out on Monday, 3 August 1981. The federal government had been preparing for the strike for months, from before Reagan became president. They had trained scabs at a secret facility in Oklahoma. Now the government cut the number of national flights in half and brought in the scabs, now called 'replacement workers'.

As the strike began, Reagan gave the controllers 48 hours to come back to work or lose their jobs. On Wednesday, the third day, the government sent letters to every striker at home. By Friday, 11,500 of the controllers had refused to go back to work.

The controllers could only win if other unions refused to cross their picket lines. AFL-CIO union federation leaders, meeting in Chicago as the strike started, personally went down together to join the picket line at O'Hare airport. But the union leaders didn't instruct their members to honour the picket lines. To do so would have exposed them to government fines, and the unions now obeyed the law without thinking about it. Meanwhile, the pilots flew the planes and the mechanics serviced them. A scab workforce and new hires gradually brought the service back to normal working over six years. The dismissed controllers were all blacklisted.

The strike was a massive object lesson for all the unions. The federal government had never fired a whole group of workers before. Reagan publicly took responsibility in a series of press statements. Moreover, everyone had assumed the controllers were in a very strong position. In firing them, Reagan was taking a considerable risk of a plane crash that would be blamed on him. Union leaders, and union members, said to each other that if Reagan could get away with firing the air traffic controllers, employers could get away with anything. The government had legitimated mass sackings and won a major battle against the union movement across America.

Plants began closing across the industrial Midwest. Union leaders, and members, were running scared. In 1980, the year

before the controllers' strike, 'not a single union contract nego-
tiation had ended in a pay freeze or cut. By 1982, 44 per cent
of new contracts conceded wage freezes or outright cuts.'[3]
These new 'giveback contracts' sometimes included negotiated
wage cuts of 20 per cent and usually sacrificed key working
conditions.

The long retreat

By the end of 1982, the recession was biting too deeply and lasting too long for industry. The Federal Reserve lowered interest
rates and Reagan began to stimulate the economy with
increased defence spending. The factory closures continued, but
at a slower rate. As profit rates fell, some factories went out of
business. There was less new investment. And the investment that
did happen bought new machines that made it possible for
fewer workers to produce more and put other people out of
work. The corporations didn't say that, however. In one factory
after another they said that if unions didn't accept worse conditions and low pay, the company would move the factory abroad.

In the years that followed there were a series of strikes where
employers followed Reagan's lead and dismissed whole work-
forces. During the 1980s these were mainly in relatively isolated places: meat packers in Austin, Minnesota, copper miners in
Arizona, paper workers in Maine. During the 1990s the strikes
began to move closer to big cities in the industrial heartland,
like Decatur, Illinois. They were not high profile strikes; there
was little national coverage in the media. But the union activists
watched them and lost heart. [4]

The unions were also losing members as the old plants
closed. Because unions either didn't fight, or worse, lost when
they fought, new people stopped joining unions. In 1955 over
a third of working Americans belonged to unions. In 1973 it
was down to 24 per cent. By 2000 it was 14 per cent and still
falling. The threat of moving jobs abroad was the key.

The important point was that both unions and workers
believed the threat, even though the company usually didn't
mean it. The economist Kate Bronfenbrenner studied companies

where unions had tried to organise in 1993–95. Half the companies, and 65 per cent of the manufacturing companies, had threatened to close the plant if workers voted for the union. She found that where the company threatened to move, the workers were less likely to vote for a union. Yet where the unions did win the vote, only 12 per cent of the companies moved.[5]

By 1992, when Democrat Bill Clinton was elected president, the unions were very weak. Clinton didn't need to attack the unions the way Reagan had. But the National Labor Relations Agency continued to favour the employer.

The journalist Stephen Franklin wrote a book about three long, grinding defeated strikes in Decatur, Illinois, in 1994–96. One strike was at the Firestone tire plant, owned by a Japanese corporation. The second was at the American owned Caterpillar tractor plant. The third was at Staley's, owned by the British firm of Tate and Lyle. In all three cases the management had welcomed the strike as a chance to break the union. Franklin spent years talking to strikers and the scab replacement workers for years, and tried to make sense of what they felt:

> Blue collar workers became more frightened and less sure of the world ahead. They felt vulnerable to foreign trade and to factories that seemed to desert them for nothing more than low wages ...
>
> Meanwhile their next-door neighbors had grown envious ... They did not work in the factories that still had good-paying jobs. They did not belong to unions that still guaranteed a decent salary ... They considered their [union] neighbors whiners when they talked about hard times. They looked at them, with all their benefits and protections, as pampered babies ...
>
> Some of the high-wage union workers in Decatur sensed the resentment that surrounded them. But most were surprised when they tried to make their case for public support and it was not there ... It was hard for them to deal with this resentment because they had nursed their own anger for years. Many still viewed

themselves as victims of a war they did not fully understand, the Vietnam War. They had gone to school, joined the military, and then returned home to no welcome ...

They were not the only ones who believed that America had slipped into a mysterious, inexplicable decline. There was a feeling shared broadly among Americans that something had gone wrong ... They were true believers, these factory workers ... They were nurtured by an incredibly enduring faith that as long as you worked hard you could get a job, a good job in a factory, and good pay, and, thank God, a good life too. And that made it all the harder for them to fathom what was taking place.[6]

Trade union lawyer Thomas Geoghegan put it this way in 1991:

'Organized labor.' Say those words, and your heart sinks. I am a labor lawyer, and my heart sinks. Dumb, stupid, organized labor, this is my cause ... I look at the other labor lawyers around town, none of us with much business, all of it shrinking faster and faster. One day I will wake up and the unions will be gone, completely gone ...

I know what I feel, what the other labor lawyers feel. Call up the client and say hysterically, 'Organize, organize.' Yet we, of all people, know it is impossible to organize ... And, of course, the clients know that too. They have tried it a million heartbreaking times ... Labor gives off an almost animal sense of weakness ...

I never mention [that I'm a labor lawyer] at parties. It sounds goonish even to me. My mother says, 'Just tell people you work for the poor. It makes it all simpler.' ...

[But unions are still] the damnedest un-American thing you ever saw ... Go to any union hall, any union rally, and listen to the speeches. It took me years to hear it, but there is a silence, a deafening Niagra [Falls] type silence, on the subject of individualism. No one is against it, but it never comes up. Is that America? ...

Individualism is for scabs. This country is set up for scabs ... Since the eighties, it has been insane to go on strike. Every strike ends in disaster. The members go out, roaring mad, like in the old days. Then they watch [the scabs] ... Our guys stand there, disbelieving, with picket signs on their shoulders, like batters looking at called third strikes. They stand there with their little buttons that say, in capital letters, 'SCAB HUNTER' under the barrel of a gun. But the buttons do not scare anyone. People breeze right over the line ...

Solidarity. Union. It is the love, the only love left in the country that dare not speak its name.[7]

The idea of solidarity had been lost. The unions had begun as a crusade for the working class. In the 1930s unions had organised unemployed workers to come fight the cops and shut down striking plants. They had argued that solidarity would bring equality in society. Many union activists still preserved those ideas. They said such things, sometimes, to each other in bars. But they were on the defensive.

Even in the boom of the late 1990s, unions still didn't recover and industrial wages didn't bounce back. Yet there were plenty of jobs around. Mainstream economists were surprised. They had treated as gospel the theory that unemployment was necessary to keep workers scared and therefore weak. The conventional wisdom even had a number for this – it required 6 per cent unemployment or more to keep workers afraid. For years government economists were careful and happy to keep unemployment above the magic 6 per cent. Then unemployment fell to 4 per cent in the late 1990s. Bob Woodward tells a story in his book about Alan Greenspan, the chair of the Federal Reserve (the Fed):

The old belief held that with such a low unemployment rate workers would have the upper hand and demand higher wages. Yet the data showed that wages weren't rising that much. It was one of the economic mysteries of the time. Greenspan hypothesized at one point to colleagues within the Fed about the 'traumatized worker' – someone who felt job insecurity in the economy and so was accepting smaller wage increases. He had talked with business leaders who said their workers were not agitating and were fearful that skills might not be marketable if they were forced to change jobs.[8]

Greenspan was the governments' chief central banker. He was relieved that workers were traumatised.

As industrial workers lost jobs and wages, new jobs did open up in service industries. The new Wal-Mart chain of superstores now employs more people than all the jobs lost in the auto corporations. But such McJobs had no union protection, often paid minimum wage and carried no health insurance.[9] They were often part time, so the employer could avoid paying various benefits. Men and women who had lost factory jobs found themselves working for half or a third of the wage they had made before.

There was some expansion of union numbers in government employment, where it was harder for employers to fire people, and in the expanding low-wage jobs in service industries. Hospital workers, janitors, supermarket workers, teachers and city employees joined unions and went on strike. [10] But it was an uphill battle.

The American working class was accumulating both helplessness and bitterness. This would surface, finally, in the explosive UPS strike in 1998 and the Seattle demonstrations by the unions in 1999. But that is to get ahead of our story. For the moment, the point is that the ruling class attacks on the unions in the 1980s and 90s worked. And they did not just weaken the unions. They weakened the whole idea of solidarity and equality. And they leached away at the way union workers thought of themselves.

Wages and profits

The result of 20 years of union busting and lost jobs, from Reagan to Clinton, was the most unequal society in the rich world.

In 1980, the year Reagan was elected, the chief executive of the average large corporation was paid 42 times as much as the average manual worker. By 1995, in the middle of Clinton's presidency, it was 141 times as much. Three years later, in 1998, the CEO got 419 times as much.[11] Seventy-nine per cent of Americans were making less than the average wage. That was because the top 20 per cent of Americans were making 48 per cent of the wages and salaries.

In the 22 years from 1973 to 1995, the bottom 60 per cent of Americans saw a fall in their real wages. The table below shows some of the figures.

(The wage figures are for hourly wages, but they include people paid monthly salaries. The figures have been adjusted for prices in 2001, so they give a comparison of real wages. The 20 per cent worker in the table is the person earning more than 20 per cent of the working population, but less than 80 per cent. The 50 per cent worker is the person earning more than 50 per cent and less than 50 per cent, and so on.)

Earning more than	1973	1995
20%	$7.61	$7.14
40%	$10.52	$10.04
50%	$12.06	$11.68
60%	$13.84	$13.83
80%	$18.37	$19.96[12]

The worker earning more than half the population saw a substantial fall in hourly wages. Those on the edge of the professional middle class, paid more than 80 per cent of the working population, saw their wages rise by $1.59 an hour over 22 years, or just 7 cents a year. That's a wage rise of less than 0.5 per cent a year.

Wages rose a bit more in the next six years, between 1995 and 2001. But still the person earning more than 80 per cent of all employed Americans saw an average percentage rise of less than 1 per cent a year for the 28 years between 1973 and 2001.

Here are the figures for the change in hourly wages from 1973 to 2001:

Earning more than	1973	2001	Raise per year
20%	$7.61	$8.07	$0.02
40%	$10.52	$11.03	$0.02
50%	$12.06	$12.87	$0.03
60%	$13.84	$15.06	$0.05
80%	$18.37	$21.71	$0.09[13]

During these 28 years, from the first recession in 1973 to 2001, real wages in the rest of the rich world were rising. They were not in the United States, Eastern Europe, parts of Latin America and most of Africa. At least until 1995, the American ruling class was getting its way. They were driving their wage costs down successfully, so as to compete with the rest of the rich world. In the boom of the late 1990s, wages recovered some. But even then they were hardly higher than 28 years before. During those same years, there was a massive rise in productivity, particularly in industry. Each worker was producing far more, but able to buy no more than before.

What these general figures conceal, however, is that working-class men were hit hardest. During the 16 years between 1979 and 1995 real wages fell not just for the man in the middle, but also for the man making more than 80 per cent of the population. Even when wages had recovered some by 2001, the man earning more than 60 per cent was only earning 7 cents an hour more than 22 years before. The man in the middle, and everyone below him, were still doing worse in the 2001 boom than in 1979.[14]

At the same time, women's wages were rising. But they weren't rising much, and most of the gains were going to well-paid women. For the 22 years from 1979 to 2001 the majority of women had a wage rise of less than 1 per cent a year. We will return to what was happening to women's wages in the chapter on family values. For the moment, the point is that women were catching up, very slowly, because men were standing still.

Taxes

The next part of this chapter is about how first Reagan and then Clinton tried to reverse the legacy of the New Deal by cutting taxes and public spending.

Government policy on the economy began to change under President Carter, a Democrat, during the recession of 1980. In America most people thought Keynesian government spending to stimulate the economy during a recession was a Democratic policy – 'tax and spend'. In fact it had been the standard response of both Democrats and Republicans in Washington to every recession, no matter how small, since 1946. When the first big recession hit in 1973, Republican president Gerald Ford had reacted with a tax cut and no reduction in government spending – the usual Keynesianism to get the economy moving again.

But when international recession hit again in 1980, Jimmy Carter was president. [15] He refused to stimulate the economy, arguing that it would encourage inflation. This was true. The more money people have in their pockets, the more prices are likely to rise. This doesn't hurt workers with cost of living allowances in their contracts. It doesn't hurt people on government benefits and pensions that increase in line with inflation. Inflation is really helpful to people who are buying houses on mortgages. Their house value goes up, but they only have to pay back the old price.

Inflation does hurt bankers. If I owe you $1,000 and prices and wages go up, then it's easier for me to pay back what I owe you. But the money I'm giving you is worth less in terms of what it will buy. So inflation is good for borrowers and bad for banks. Through much of the 1970s there was high inflation in America. Even with interest payments, the banks were getting back less in real terms than they were loaning out.

When recession hit, Carter sided with the banks. He agreed with the American government central bank, the Federal Reserve, that interest rates should be raised. At the same time, he agreed with the bankers that there should be no tax cuts and no increase in public spending.

The ruling class response to the falling rate of profit was kicking in. Public spending had to go down. This was a decisive shift in government policy. The Democrats had always been the party of spending. With no stimulation to the economy, unemployment rose during 1980 from 5.8 to 7.1 per cent. The Marxist economist Michael Meeropol puts it this way:

> The recession, though short, created great resonance for the rhetorical question asked by candidate Reagan on national television: 'Are you better off now than you were four years ago?' ... Enough people answered [no] that both Reagan and many conservative Republican senators were elected. This gave him outright control of the Senate and an ideological majority in the House [of Representatives] with which to put his programme into effect ...
>
> The negative reaction to the recession in 1980 proved that the public still expected (and even demanded) that the government would do something about high unemployment. Because Carter was perceived as having done nothing, he was voted out of office. When the congressional elections came in 1982, (two years later), the economy was once again in recession, an even deeper one. The voters took out their frustrations on Republican members of Congress despite strenuous campaigning by President Reagan. Only with the recovery of 1983–84 did the public begin to give President Reagan very high approval ratings and then reelect him in a landslide in 1984.[16]

In the early years of the Reagan administration, the tax laws were changed. The richest 1 per cent of people now paid less tax and the poorest 60 per cent paid more. More importantly, there was help for profits in manufacturing industry. Between 1965 and 1981 manufacturing corporations had paid an average of 46 per cent of their profits in tax – almost half. From 1981 to 1990, the Reagan years, they paid 28 per cent of their profits in tax: just over a quarter.[17] Another way of saying the same thing is that before Reagan industrial corporations kept 54 cents out of every dollar of declared profit. Under Reagan they kept 72 cents. For accounting reasons, the declared profit was only a part of the total 'gross profits' the companies were worried about. But the tax cut was welcome.[18]

Together with Federal Reserve, the Reagan administration intensified Carter's policy of raising interest rates, from 7.9 per cent in 1979 to 16.4 per cent in 1981. This was a very high-risk strategy for the ruling class. It meant every business and individual who owed money had to cut back on spending. There was little new investment. The economy nosedived. Factories closed all over the country. Unemployment hit 10 per cent. The effect, and the intended effect, was to weaken the unions by making members fear for their jobs.

However, the economic consequences of high interest rates were so severe that Reagan and the Federal Reserve reversed course. They cut interest rates and began to stimulate the economy with public spending. This wasn't social spending, but instead went on expansion of the military.

When the Reagan administration tried to cut spending on things workers needed they ran into a problem. In 1980 health and pensions accounted for over a third of the federal budget. Most of this went on social security and Medicare. The proportion was rising all the time. By 2000, health and pensions were 43 per cent of Clinton's last budget. Defence spending, by contrast, was 17 per cent. Interest on the national debt was 13 per cent.

The proportion of the budget spent on health and social security was rising because people were living longer. Moreover, old people make up a large percentage of sick people.

All over the world, the cost of health care as a proportion of the general income keeps rising. Doctors invent new treatments and we live longer. Patients who die are cheap. Patients who live are going to come back for more treatment. Health is the one industry where success means it's going to cost more.

Americans have only three major social programmes of the sort that social democrats have won in Europe. Two of them, pensions and Medicare, are paid for by the federal government. One, free public education through high school, is paid for by state and local government. All three of these are 'universal' programmes. There is no means test. Really poor people get them. So did ordinary working-class people and the affluent. When a benefit goes to everyone, they will unite to defend it.

In 1982 Reagan tried to push substantial cuts in pensions through Congress and failed. His own Republican allies in Congress told him that social security was the 'third rail' of American politics. Like the central rail on an electric train line, touch it and you're dead. [19] The same was true of Medicare for the elderly. Spending on primary and secondary education at all levels of government also remained at a steady 3.5 per cent of national income during the Reagan years. [20]

None of this prevented cuts in other programmes – welfare, transport, day care and so on. But the core public expenditures remained a problem for corporate profit.

Reagan won a second four-year term as president in 1984. In 1988 another Republican, George Bush the elder, the father of the current Bush, won the presidency. The economy went into recession the next year. Like Jimmy Carter, Bush was seen as doing nothing about the recession. The Democrat Bill Clinton ran on the economy in the 1992 presidential election and won.

Clinton was one of a group who called themselves the 'New Democrats'. Their idea was that Reagan had isolated the Democrats from a public opinion that was moving rightwards. So they would move the Democrats to the right. They would get rid of the tradition that the Democrats were the party of taxes and public spending, the party that was soft on crime and liberal on social issues. That way they would reclaim the voters who had gone Republican. The 'New Democrats' were the model copied by 'New Labour' in Britain.

But Clinton had not been elected on quite the same conservative platform as the Republicans. The people who voted for him expected something of the old Democrats. They wanted more social equality. And they expected the old New Deal/Keynesian policy – spend money to create jobs and stimulate the economy.

The corporations, Wall Street and the right moved to put pressure on the Clinton administration. Under Reagan and Bush, the corporations had tolerated 'deficit spending' – the government borrowing money to spend more without raising taxes. Under the Republicans that money went on arms and the military, and it stimulated business. Under the Democrats there was a threat that spending would go on social programmes for working people. So the corporations and the media began shouting about 'balancing the budget'. The radical economist Michael Meeropol explains:

> We often read and hear rhetoric such as the following: 'Just as every American sits at the kitchen table and balances his or her budget, just as every small business must balance its budget, Congress must begin balancing the nation's budget – now.' This statement is from the Republican Contract with America, but nowhere in the document do the authors bother to explain why it is necessary for the government to balance the budget.
>
> They don't explain because there is no serious economic argument ... to support the assertions of politicians and journalists that government deficit spending is always bad for the economy. However, there is no question that many economists and business leaders believe that government spends too much money on unnecessary projects and/or undeserving people. Seen in this light, balancing the budget is a means to an end. The end is not to stop running deficits, but to

reduce government spending. [Milton Friedman, the father of neo-conservative economics] stated this point explicitly: 'I would rather have a federal government expenditure of $400 billion dollars with a $100 billion deficit than a federal government expenditure of $700 billion completely balanced.' [21]

During the 20th century, no government in North America, South America or Western Europe had balanced a national budget. They all borrowed money by selling government bonds.

Clinton kicked and screamed a little against ruling-class pressure to cut social spending. [22] On 7 January 1993, after he was elected but before he was actually president, Clinton had a meeting with his main economic advisers. They were mainstream economists, bankers and Wall Street stock and bond traders. Clinton's advisers told him he had to cut spending, reduce the deficit and cut interest rates. If he didn't, the Republican Alan Greenspan at the head of the Federal Reserve bank would be unhappy. So would the bond traders on Wall Street. If Greenspan and the bond traders didn't think Clinton's policies would help the economy, Greenspan would talk down business confidence and the traders wouldn't buy bonds. Those two threats, in turn, would return the country to recession. 'You mean to tell me that the success of the programme and my re-election hinges on the Federal Reserve Board and a bunch of fucking bond traders?' Clinton asked.

Later in the meeting, his vice-president Al Gore spoke strongly for a plan to cut spending and pay off the national debt. He reminded Clinton of Roosevelt's daring in 1933. 'Roosevelt was trying to help people,' Clinton said. 'Here we help the bond market, and we hurt the people who voted us in.' [23]

Clinton was not an innocent about the relationship between business and politics in America. He had served four two-year terms as governor of Arkansas. His wife Hillary was a corporate lawyer. All his political life he had relied on campaign money from business. Crucially, he had appointed these very advisers from Wall Street, business and mainstream economics. He wanted and expected to do what business wanted. But he was thrown by how much they were asking of him. Clinton had hoped to find a balance between the business world and the people who voted for him. But he would soon be forced to choose.

In Clinton's first State of the Union address to Congress, right after his inauguration, he suggested taxing the rich. The Dow-Jones index of industrial stocks fell. It was a message – business was unhappy.

Clinton sent Robert Rubin and Alice Rivlin to talk to business leaders. Rubin, Clinton's leading economic adviser, had been a senior executive on Wall Street. Rivlin, an economist, was Deputy Director of the Office of Management and Budget. They had a private dinner with the chief executive officers (CEOs) of 'some of the nation's largest corporations, including American Express, NJR Nabisco' and CBS. According to Bob Woodward:

> The support of business leaders was essential to confidence, the delicate foundation underlying all business decisions.
>
> The executives were in a rage, at times a quiet slow burn and at other times openly hostile. Rubin and Rivlin faltered. Rubin looked exhausted ... The executives took issue especially with Clinton's attack on the wealthy [in his speech], some claiming that they were personally offended. Many had started with little and worked their way to reach the top ... The taxes, along with the class-warfare implications in Clinton's rhetoric, would erode business confidence. 'When do you think I'll make a decision to expand, make big equipment purchases, and hire new people?' one executive announced sarcastically.
>
> The next morning, Rubin went to the Oval Office to report to Clinton on the dinner. 'They beat the hell out of us', Rubin said. 'Mr. President, you're being seen as anti-business. You're seen as punishing the

rich.' ... Particular criticism, Rubin said, had been lev-
eled at the president's line 'We're all in this together,'
when it seemed to them the wealthy were being sin-
gled out ...

Rubin said ... if businesspeople felt the administration didn't believe in the capitalist system, business
wouldn't expand and hire, thus hurting the economy.
Anything that made the economy worse had to be
bad for the president politically ...

Clinton appreciated Rubin's argument, and in his
public statements he began scaling back, and even cutting out altogether, his rhetoric about taxing the rich.[24]

Soon the new White House staff were asking each other every
day: Are the bond traders happy? It was a joke but also serious.
Of course, it was not just the bond traders the Clinton administration were trying to please. They were trying to please the bond
traders, the stock market, the banks and the chief executive
officers of the corporations. They started to look everywhere
they could for cuts to both defence and social programmes.

Social security was still the big one. To cut social security, the
administration would need the support of Congress, which had
to pass all provisions for public spending. Vice-president Gore
had long experience in Congress. He went to Clinton and said
maybe they could do something about the cost of the auto-
matic Cost of Living Allowance (COLA) that increased social
security pensions in line with inflation:

Gore told Clinton that he wanted to confidentially
sound out some moderate Republican deficit hawks
in Congress about quietly exploring a bipartisan
agreement on a Social Security COLA freeze. Clinton
gave his approval, and Gore said he would do it in his
own name to preserve Clinton's deniability on such a
touchy political subject. Gore spoke with four
Republicans in the Senate and several in the House.
He had rarely received such point-blank refusals. He

reported to Clinton that not one would even discuss it. The new administration and the Democrats in Congress were going to have to make cuts on their own. Gore noted that these were the Republicans who pounded hardest on the federal deficit, but since he had promised to keep his exploratory conversations with the Republicans in confidence, he was prevented from going public with their hypocrisy.[25]

There was probably another reason Gore kept quiet. He would have been pilloried if the public learned he had been trying to freeze pensions. Social security was still the third rail of American politics. It seemed to the people in Clinton's administration that everyone in business they talked to was urging them to stand firm on 'entitlements'. This was the code word for pensions, unemployment compensation, Medicare for the elderly and benefits for veterans. All of these, by law, were increased in line with inflation, and everyone was 'entitled' to them. The cost would just keep going up unless the law was changed. Entitlements, in short, meant the things people needed badly and felt they ought to have. The Washington consensus was that they were bad. But they were also hard to cut.

During the next eight years of his presidency, Clinton consistently tried to hold down public spending. He was lucky, in that he entered office at the end of one recession and left office at the beginning of the next. So during his time incomes and stock prices went up, and that meant tax revenues rose too. By 1998, in a booming economy, he was able to balance the budget. Cuts in military spending after the collapse of the Soviet Union and the end of the Cold War were crucial to this.

The most important effect of the curbs on public spending was on health. In 1992 Clinton's most important campaign promise had been a national health scheme that would provide treatment for all Americans. He didn't keep the promise.

When Clinton came to power there were 37 million Americans without health insurance.[26] These were working people and their children. People on welfare got Medicaid. The retired got Medicare. People with unions, government workers and the better paid got health coverage as part of their employment. People in McJobs did not. Part-timers for big corporations didn't either, which is one reason there were suddenly so many part-time jobs.

People without health insurance could not go to a family doctor. In any city there was usually at least one emergency room in a public hospital they could go to and receive free charity treatment. In New York City, the wait in that emergency room was typically eight hours, but could be much longer. Waiting took up so much time it was difficult for anyone with a chronic illness or a sick child to keep a steady job.

In the early 1990s, people in work with health insurance were also finding that their health insurance was paying less and less of the cost. There were more and more provisions for 'co-payment', where you paid half or more of the cost and the insurance paid the rest.

More importantly, from the late 1980s on, employers began to switch their health cover to new 'health management organizations' (HMOs). These rationed health care. You could only use a doctor approved by the HMO. That doctor could only prescribe treatment the HMO authorised. Doctors who fought too hard to get their patients approved for extra treatment were dropped by the HMO. By the late 1990s, everyone had a horror story about some friend or relative denied treatment by an HMO.

All these holes in the healthcare net meant that in opinion polls from the early 1990s on, very large majorities of Americans support a national system of health insurance that makes sure everyone is treated. That's why Clinton promised it in his campaign. Once in office, though, he bowed to the bond traders and the CEOs.

There were two possible ways the Clinton administration could fund health insurance for everyone. One way was to give the insurance companies more money so they could cover everyone. This would mean expanding the federal budget, not cutting it. The CEOs wouldn't like that, so Clinton couldn't do it.

The other way was to go round the insurance companies. The government could simply take the money out of people's wages every month and pay for their health care direct. This would save all the money that was going to the insurance companies for paperwork and profits. But the insurance companies and the CEOs told Clinton he couldn't do that. It would cost the insurance companies profits. So Clinton didn't do that either.

Throughout the process Bill Clinton and his point person for health, Hillary Clinton, kept saying they didn't have a detailed plan for health reform. They needed a commission to find a plan. This was very odd. Every country in Western Europe had a health insurance system. They could have copied one of those. They have one in Canada too. It's not perfect, but Canadians wouldn't give it up for the world. The Clintons could have copied it, word for word. It's in English, and someone could have popped across the border and asked for a copy. But the Clintons didn't. And the whole of the American press behaved as if it made sense that the Clintons had to invent health insurance from nothing. They were reinventing the wheel.

In the end, the Clintons decided that in order to balance the budget there would be no health insurance. When Clinton came into office there were 37 million people without health insurance. When he left there were 43 million.

Clinton was not chasing votes here. If he'd given Americans guaranteed health care, they would have voted Democrat for 20 years. Instead, he was chasing CEOs. One of the hardest things to grasp about politicians is that votes are not as important to them as doing what business tells them to.

In 2000, Al Gore ran against George W. Bush for president. Gore won a small majority of the vote, but lost the election by a ruling in the Supreme Court. One reason Gore had such a small majority was that many Americans found him wooden; somehow he seemed unable to relate to ordinary people. They couldn't quite put their finger on it, but what they were seeing was the deep insincerity of the man who had secretly tried to freeze social security.

Once George W. Bush was elected in 2000, the mainstream business wisdom on balanced budgets changed. When Clinton the Democrat was in office, CEOs and Alan Greenspan of the Federal Reserve had insisted on a balanced budget. The point, as I have argued above, was not really a balanced budget. It was a means to hold down government social spending. Now that Bush the Republican was in office, suddenly big deficits in government spending were just fine. This was because business trusted Bush to keep social spending down. His deficits would be produced by cutting taxes for the rich and corporations. That sort of deficit was alright.

The Democrats, meanwhile, had lost their brains by 2001. For 50 years after the New Deal, they had supported government spending on the needs of ordinary people. After eight years of Clinton, they were no longer the party of 'tax and spend'. So they didn't attack Bush for his cuts in social spending. They attacked him for not balancing the budget.

The main thrust of Clinton's economic policy, though, was global. During his administration the US pushed through the new North American Free Trade Agreement and the World Trade Organization. Under Clinton, the US went for a full-scale policy of 'globalisation' – restoring American profits by doing to the world what they were already doing to American workers. Chapter Seven is devoted to this very important topic. For the moment I'll stay in the US.

As I argued at the beginning of the chapter, the ruling class had to do far more than break the unions and cut taxes. They needed to make people more unequal throughout American society. The next chapter is about the attack on African Americans.

5 | Race and Prison

The Reagan administration moved first against the unions, months after coming into office. They were also determined to deal with the legacy of the movements of the 1960s. The most powerful of these was the civil rights movement of African Americans. The ruling class reply to that movement from 1981 onward was the 'War on Drugs' and mass imprisonment. In 1980 there were 300,000 adult Americans in federal and state prisons and local jails. By 2001, there were 2 million adults behind bars, and another 700,000 in youth detention centres. The general population had increased by less than 4 per cent.[1]

This level of imprisonment was quite new. Nothing like it had ever been done in America. Other countries had imprisoned a similar proportion of their population for brief periods. The USSR under Stalin did that, so did Germany under the Nazis and Rwanda after the genocide. But these were political prisoners. No country other than the US had ever criminalised so many people, nor maintained such high levels of imprisonment for so long. All the American media and mainstream politicians treated this unique event as if it were normal. The intended consequence of imprisonment on this scale was to break the hearts, courage and families of working-class African Americans.

The ruling class and the Reagan backlash sought to stamp out any idea of equality. Civil rights and racial equality had been mass movements. The memory of those struggles legitimated demonstrations, occupations and riots. The ruling class had felt themselves losing control of the great cities. They wanted to reassert order. However, they could not attack African

Americans head on. Their movement had been too big, and support for racial equality among white people was too strong. So the ruling class looked for a sideways line of attack. They found it in 'law and order.'

Law and order had long been right wing code for racism. Richard Nixon was the Republican candidate for president in 1968. His close adviser H. R. Haldeman wrote in his diary, '[Nixon] emphasized that you have to face the fact that the whole problem is really the blacks. The key is to devise a system that recognizes this while appearing not to.'[2]

Nixon found two closely related ways. One was 'law and order'. As Nixon wrote in a letter to former president Eisenhower in 1968, 'I have found great response to this [law and order] theme in all parts of the country, including areas like New Hampshire where there is virtually no race problem and relatively little crime.'[3]

The other was drugs. In a 1968 campaign speech at Disneyland in front of the fake Matterhorn, Nixon said, 'As I look out on the problems of this country, I see one that stands out particularly. The problem of narcotics – the modern curse of youth, just like the plagues and epidemics of former years. And they are decimating a generation of Americans.'[4]

In office Nixon made small stabs at law and order. It was still not the time for a full-scale assault. But the idea had been planted.

The persecution of drug users developed slowly after the inauguration of Reagan in 1981. It quickened with the passage of a new crime bill in 1984. No senator or representative voted against it. Moments like this, when the entire ruling class combines to support a policy, are key turning points in America. Liberal senator Edward Kennedy hailed the bills as 'the most far-reaching law enforcement reform in our history'.[5]

The bill tightened up penalties and focused on drugs. The focus on drugs had several advantages for the backlash. The 1960s had seen both black and white opposition movements. The black movement had been associated with the riots in the northern ghettoes. Law and order was a reply to that. The white movement had been closely associated with drug use, particularly marijuana. This was obvious among students and hippies, but just as strong among working-class white soldiers. Anti-war GIs in Vietnam decorated their helmets with both peace symbols and paintings of marijuana leaves, just like the young people back home. The catch-all War on Drugs of the 1980s conflated marijuana, LSD, heroin, cocaine and crack into one thing: drugs. And it conflated the white long-haired hippie with the angry young black man in the inner city.

There was also a jurisdictional reason for the focus on drugs. The federal government wanted to get tough on crime. But almost all crime, and all violent crime, is the constitutional preserve of the individual states. Almost all arrests are done by state, county and city police. So federal law was changed to allow confiscation of the assets of people tried for drug offences in federal court. Cash-strapped police departments started supplying all the drug offenders the federal prisons could handle. In return, the local police were allowed to keep up to 90 per cent of the assets of those they arrested. This money could go to the police department budget. Under this law the arrested person did not have to be convicted in order to lose their house, car and bank account.

Another reason the War on Drugs appealed to the ruling class was that it had a resonance with ordinary people. This was not because they didn't take drugs. It was because someone they loved did, or might. Marijuana basically does no harm. Cocaine is not always addictive. But addiction to heroin and cocaine is destructive, in the same way that alcoholism is. The wife or child of an addict comes to hate the drug or the smell of alcohol. Buried behind that feeling is a hatred for someone they also love. Most parents, too, worry that their children will go down that road and get lost. There are few pains stronger than seeing that happen to your child. The threat can make a parent very afraid.

But it was that War, not the drugs, that was creating the worst problems. In some times and places, heroin users get the drug legally on prescription – as in Britain before 1970 and in the

Netherlands today. Then they can work and lead normal lives. The same should be true with cocaine. But the illegality drives up the price. That drives some users to crime, wrecks household budgets and means people steal from each other within the family. The illegality also means the drug itself is dangerous. Shared syringes spread septic infection, hepatitis and HIV. The unpredictable strength of less adulterated drugs leads to fatal overdoses. And illegality creates a world of chaos among users.

What users need is treatment, maintenance, and a steady income. The War on Drugs made that impossible, and created a fear and chaos that in turn made users and their families more defensive.

Closely related to the war on drugs was the fight against 'violent crime'. For the next 18 years American television and newspapers would relentlessly link black people and violence. By 2001, the filmmaker Michael Moore could put it this way:

> When I turn on the news each night, what do I see again and again? Black men alleged to be killing, raping, mugging, stabbing, gangbanging, looting, rioting, selling drugs, pimping, ho-ing, having too many babies, dropping babies from tenement windows, fatherless, motherless, Godless, penniless. The suspect is described as a black male ... the suspect is described as a black male ... THE SUSPECT IS DESCRIBED AS A BLACK MALE.' No matter what city I am in, the news is always the same, the suspect is always the same unidentified black male. I'm in Atlanta tonight, and I swear the police sketch of the black male suspect on TV looks just like the black male suspect on the news last night in Denver and the night before in LA. In every sketch he is frowning, and he's wearing the same knit cap! Is it possible that it's the same black guy committing every crime in America? ...
>
> Despite the fact that most crimes are committed by whites, ... ask any white person who they fear might break into their home or harm them on the street, and

if they're honest, they'll admit that the person they have in mind doesn't look much like them. The imaginary criminal in their heads looks like Mookie or Hakim or Kareem, not like little freckle-faced Jimmy.[6]

The new federal law of 1984 set an example for the states, which began to tighten their own drug laws. Two years later, in 1986, a popular African American basketball player, Len Bias, died suddenly after using the new drug crack cocaine. According to writer Christian Parenti:

That July all three major TV networks broadcast 74 evening news segments about drugs, more than half of them about crack. Likewise, the *New York Times* boosted its drug war coverage from 43 stories in the second half of 1985 to 220 in the second half of 1986. *Newsweek* and *Time* dutifully jumped in line, the latter running three cover stories on crack in as many months. Both called crack the biggest story since Vietnam/Watergate and 'the issue of the year.'[7]

Another drug bill passed Congress with only 18 votes against. It included new minimum sentences for 29 offences. The most important was a minimum of five years for possession of five grams of crack cocaine, the amount a user needed for a day. Parole was abolished for drug offenders in federal prisons. Again, the states rapidly copied the bill.

The president's wife, Nancy Reagan, called for a 'national crusade' against drugs and a 'new intolerance'. Again and again, she appeared on television in front of school audiences with her simple slogan: 'Just say no'. Her husband made it clear that the 60s were over: 'Drug users can no longer excuse themselves by blaming society. As individuals, they are responsible. The rest of us must be clear that we will no longer tolerate drug abuse by anyone.'[8]

Academic surveys showed, year after year, that white Americans took drugs as often as black.[9] But black people were far more likely to be arrested, more likely to be convicted if arrested and to received longer average sentences. The penalty for five grams of crack cocaine, seen as a black drug, was five years. The penalty for five grams of ordinary cocaine, seen as a drug for affluent whites, was often a fine.

Since the 1980s, many commentators have assumed that politicians were promoting the War on Drugs to get votes. This was certainly true of particular politicians. But it was only true after a media feeding frenzy. In 1977, four Americans in ten supported prosecuting marijuana users. By 1985 it was still only five out of ten. A year later, in September 1986, with the great fear on, it was two out of three. Again, it took until the summer of 1985 before any Americans talking to pollsters included drugs on their 'most important problem list'. Six per cent did so. In late 1986, only a year and half later, it was 19 per cent.[10]

But every opinion poll throughout these years said that people were far more concerned about jobs and health care. In these were the areas the politicians did nothing, despite the electoral gains to be made. Every opinion poll after 1986 also said a majority of Americans supported long sentences for violent crime, but thought that treatment for drug users was better than prison.

In 1988 Reagan was constitutionally required to retire after eight years in office. George Bush the elder, another Republican, replaced him. Four years later Bill Clinton, a Democrat, beat Bush to become president. During his eight years in office, Clinton backed further tough crime bills. In 1970, under Nixon, there were 200,000 adults behind bars. In 1980, the year Reagan was elected, there were 300,000. When Clinton won in 1992, there were 1,290,000. When he left office in 2001, it was just under 2,000,000. It is now just over two million.[11] As with union policy, the history of imprisonment can be written quite independently of which party is in the White House.

By 2002 there were another 700,000 young people in 'correctional facilities, such as detention centers, training schools, ranches, camps and farms.'[12] The average age of entry for boys is 16, and for girls 15. These 700,000 kids in prison are almost never mentioned, even in books and articles hostile to prison. It's too hard to think about children suffering on that scale. Nor do the supporters of law and order mention the children much. Their numbers are never included in the figures for the total in prison or detention. Include them, and you get close to 3 million Americans behind bars.

The number of prisoners was increasing because there were more arrests. More importantly, sentences were longer. A whole series of federal and state laws increased minimum sentences for many offences. Parole was shortened or abolished for many others. Judges, too, increased their discretionary sentences.

Under Clinton, the federal government passed a 'three strikes and you're out' law, which ordered minimum sentences of 25 years to life when someone was convicted of a third felony of any kind. Many states copied this. In California, for instance, truck driver Russell Benson was sentenced to 25 years for stealing a carton – ten packs – of cigarettes. In Florida, a homeless man 'with a string of petty offenses behind him' was sentenced to 40 years for stealing 22 rolls of toilet paper.[13]

The case of Billy Ochoa highlights the new enthusiasm for long sentences. Ochoa was arrested in California in 1994. He had defrauded the state of a total of $2,100 by signing on for welfare benefits under different names. Ochoa was a long-term heroin and crack user, with convictions for theft and drug use. His lawyer thought Ochoa was doomed under the state's new Three Strikes law. The prosecutor, Tamia Hope, offered a deal. In return for a guilty plea, she would prosecute only one of the welfare frauds, under one name. Ochoa would get the minimum Three Strikes sentence of 25 years to life. Ochoa was 51. He wouldn't get out of prison until he was 76. Against his lawyer's advice, he turned down the deal and went to a jury trial.

Judge Alan Buckner sentenced Ochoa to 326 years to life, saying, 'This man is above the law. He is out for himself and doesn't really care. And he ran foul of the fact that our society doesn't look with favor on folks who rip off welfare.'[14] At 326 years for $2,100, that's a year in prison for each $6.44. More realistically, estimating Ochoa would be in prison for 25 years

before he died, that's a year for each $84. There was no possi-
bility of parole under the Three Strikes law.

Two months after Ochoa was sentenced, the District
Attorneys' Association of Los Angeles held their monthly
meeting:

> Close to three hundred lawyers were present. Each
> month, the association honors one of their own. That
> month, the board of directors had decided to declare
> Tamia Hope their D. A. of the month. The president,
> John Perlstein, rose from his seat to present the ...
> award. 'The defendant got three hundred and twenty-
> six years to life,' Perlstein told his audience. And at
> that point, Hope recalled with pride three years later,
> 'they all broke out in applause. To me it reflected peo-
> ple really just don't like welfare fraud anymore,
> thumbing your nose at the system. It was nice to get
> the applause; nice to feel the support of my col-
> leagues.'[15]

Who went to prison

To summarise the argument so far, the War on Drugs, along
with law and order, increased imprisonment tenfold. Nothing
like this had happened before in any country in the world. The
whole American ruling class backed it. The effect was an attack
on the memory of both the black and white opposition movements in the 1960s.

There was a more important concrete effect on people's lives.
Two million or more might be in jail at any one time. Prison,
however, affected many more lives. By 2004 many millions had
been to prison at some time in the past 20 years. In addition to
these, there were the mothers, daughters, fathers, sons and lovers
of the prisoners. The lives of several tens of millions of
Americans were blighted by the imprisonment of a loved one.

Many more white men were going to jail than before. And
imprisonment hit men who had not finished high school, black
and white, particularly hard. Imprisonment was both racial and

class injustice. Consider the following percentages of black and white men who went to jail. Notice that black men are more than seven times as likely to go jail as white men. Notice also that a man who didn't finish high school is about three times more likely to go to jail than a man who did:

White men	Age 22–30	And did not finish high school
1980	1%	3%
1999	2%	10%
Black men		
1980	6%	14%
1999	12%	42%[16]

What these figures mean is that in 1980 there were roughly 126,000 white prisoners. By 1999 there were roughly 660,000 white prisoners. During the 1990s prison wrecked the lives of millions of working class white men and their families.

Yet prison bore down much harder on black men and their neighbourhoods. It is not just the men in jail at any one time, but the percentage of men who have been to jail at some point in their lives. Here are the percentages of men aged 30 to 34 who had done time by 1999:

	Black men	White men
Did not finish high school	52%	13%
High school diploma	24%	4%
Attended some college	9%	1%[17]

We can see both race and class at work again. A black man who didn't finish high school is six times more likely to jail than a black man with some college. A white high school dropout is 13 times more likely to go jail than a white man with some college. A white high school dropout is more likely to go to jail than a black man with some college. Of white men who went to college, one in a hundred went to prison. Of black men who left high school, one in two went to prison.

These statistics conceal national variation. In many of the big city black working-class neighbourhoods, a large majority of men have been to prison at one point or another. They, or their families, are scarred by prison. So is their whole community. Even outside these neighbourhoods, almost all African Americans have a relative who has been to jail.

Millions of white men and their families have seen their lives wrecked. Black people have seen whole communities wrecked. To see why, we have to look at what prison does to people.

Life inside

American prisons were never pleasant places. In the 1980s the federal and state governments wanted a massive increase in prison numbers. At the same time, the ruling class was desperate to hold down public spending. So new prisons were built, but nothing like enough. Overcrowded prisons are harder to control. Too few new guards were hired. The pressure to restore profits turned prisons into pressure cookers.

Some radical writers have argued that the explosion in prison numbers was driven by a desire to make profits for the companies that ran privatised prisons and exploited prison labour. But less than 5 per cent of inmates worked on corporation contracts like making toys and providing call centres. Prisons, public and private, were expensive for all the other corporations in America. General Motors and Citibank didn't want to spend any more than they had to on funding the profits of private prisons. The corporations supported imprisonment because they thought it was socially and politically necessary. But they did not want to give away money.

Prisons had always been run by the carrot and the stick. The carrot was parole. The stick was solitary confinement and transfer to a more brutal prison. Now new laws eliminated parole for many offences, particularly for prisoners on long sentences. And there were many more long-term inmates. Once upon a time, a man on five to ten years would follow orders because he could be out in three with good behaviour. Now some of the angriest men were serving life without possibility of parole. Others were at the start of ten and 25-year sentences.

With less prospect of parole, solitary had to be used more often. That posed the question of how to threaten men who were already in solitary and wouldn't get parole. This led to degrees of solitary punishment – for instance, two levels in California and three in Texas. New blocks and whole prisons were built for long-term prisoners on nearly permanent extra punishment. In the good part of these blocks, men were locked in their cells for 23 hours a day and had showers twice a week.

At the same time, the guards had to leave more and more control of daily life in the hands of prisoners. In the smaller states, without big cities, the controlling prisoners were bullies trusted by the guards. In the prisons that served great cities, in California, Illinois and New York, the controllers were special prison gangs. These prison gangs were different from the gangs on the outside, and were divided by race. The California prison system, for instance, had two Hispanic gangs, one black gang and one white – the far right Aryan Nation. The guards in California's medium and maximum-security prisons segregated prisoners by gang, which mean segregating them by race.

There were feedback loops in all these processes. As guards lost control to prison bullies, prisoners became more afraid. They also had to be ready to fight at a moment's notice or succumb forever to bullying. That made the prisons more violent. As more prisoners were punished, the guards had to find harder punishments. The experience of these punishments drove men to violence and madness.

Throughout the American prison system, solitary was renamed 'administrative segregation'. Both prisoners and guards called it 'ad seg'. In California by 2001, many prisoners in ad seg now 'routinely self-mutilate as an expression of impotent rage at their confinement, slashing at veins and arteries until the spurting blood has covered the walls of their cells in a spectacular mosaic of slime.'[18]

Joseph Hallinan, another journalist, describes ad seg in Texas: 'Many of the inmates are mentally disturbed. Some are called "frequent fliers" because they attempt suicide so much. Others are called "chunkers" because they pelt the guards with their feces.' Throwing shit is common on all American ad segs. This is because they can take weapons, clothes and personal possessions from you, but they can't take away your shit. Many prisoners mix their shit and urine into a consistency that makes it easy to throw and likely to stick. They throw it at guards, but more often at another prisoner with whom they are feuding.

In 1999, a federal judge ruled that the Texas ad seg units were 'virtual incubators of psychosis'. Dr Craig Haney, a penal psychologist, testified in court that 'many of the inmates he tried to speak with were incoherent, 'often babbling and shrieking'. Others appeared to be full of fury and anger, and were, in some instances, banging their heads on the wall and screaming.'[19]

Hallinan asked trainee Corrections Officers (COs) in Texas why they wanted to work in such places:

One of the trainees is a sullen, burly man named Donald Rinks. He, too, was drawn to prison by the benefits of the job. Rinks had previously worked as a construction worker, living in a motor home with his wife, who is blind. At fifty-four, he is old for a trainee, past the age when many COs retire. I ask him why he wants to be a guard.

'Well,' he says, 'my wife and I have been married twenty-eight years and lived nineteen years in a trailer.' He looks me dead in the eye.

After ten years, he will be eligible to receive medical coverage after retirement, a benefit so precious, he says, that he is willing to spend his days among killers and thieves. 'Be fifty-four and try to go out and buy health insurance.'[20]

The other trainees said the same thing: the steady paycheck. Across America, rural areas and small towns competed for new prisons to replace the jobs lost when the factory closed or the military base closed down. Increasingly, small-town white men controlled big-city black men far from home. But whether the guards were white or black, the job could change them, just as it changed the prisoners.

The journalist Daniel Bergner spent months in 1996 and 97 talking to inmates at Angola, the toughest prison in Louisiana. He learned about the guards:

Forces seemed to conspire against the better impulses of the employees. Their pay was low, with a scale that began around $15,000 a year, and awarded captains, who'd put in years of service, about $30,000. At night they were locked alone inside dormitories with sixty-four convicts. The guards were unarmed and, in most cases, didn't even have a walkie-talkie, just a signal box that would bring help guaranteed within three minutes. As a means of containing disturbances, the doors were bolted from the inside. The 'key guards' were instructed not to free a colleague until backup was present.

Combined with this vulnerability was a kind of authority few people could have anywhere else. The lowliest guard could tell a great number of men what to do ...

Since I had first arrived at Angola four months ago, two cellblock guards, in separate incidents at separate camps, had been arrested for forcing inmates to perform blowjobs repeatedly through the bars. Both had eventually been bit – the convicts knew that damage to the guard's penis was generally the only way they would be believed. In other, similar cases, inmates had held the semen in their mouths, spit it into the cellophane of a cigarette wrapper, folded the wrapper tightly, and mailed it to a lawyer with their plea for help.[21]

The Angola guards, like others across the country, worked in fear, as the prisoners lived in fear. The guards had to maintain an average level of brutality to protect themselves and control the prisoners. That meant the harsher than average guards could be very cruel. This was particularly the case in maximum-security and ad-seg units, where control was most fragile.

In California in the 1990s, corrections officers at Corcoran prison organised fights between members of rival gangs in the tiny isolation exercise yards. A few guards watched for fun and videotaped the fights for the other guards. When the fight became dangerous, the watching guards intervened, first with wooden bullets and then with high impact explosives. Over a period of several years, the guards killed seven men this way. In nearby Pelican Bay prison, corrections officers held down an insane man in ad seg who had covered his body in shit. The officers put him in 'a tub of scalding water, and held [him] down in it until the skin had boiled off his legs.'[22]

We know about these things because someone was prosecuted or disciplined. This does not mean that most guards did such things. It does mean that the cruelty of the prison system, not the personalities of the guards, created a space where some men wanted to be cruel and others tolerated cruelty. Because the guards, like the prisoners, were afraid, all the time. For the guards, cruelty could protect them, so they backed up each other's brutality. For the prisoners, violence could protect some of them from each other. But most were just too vulnerable.

Central to the fear in prison was rape. When asked in academic surveys if they've been raped, between 14 and 23 per cent of released prisoners say yes. These figures must be a considerable underestimate. I have worked as a counsellor with both men and women in Britain who have been raped. One thing I learned was that most people have a great deal of difficulty in saying they have been raped. I don't think American prisoners would be different. And an academic survey is not the best way of finding things people don't want to talk about.

If we accept the survey figures, between 280,000 and 460,000 men in prison at the moment have been raped. A more realistic estimate of 30 to 40 per cent gives 600,000 to 800,000 men. Of course, given turnover, the number raped in the last 20 years will run into millions.

This does not include the 700,000 children, mostly boys, in juvenile facilities. All penal experts agree that rates of rape are much higher there. This adds another 300,000 to 400,000 boys to the victims of male rape behind bars. Again, there are millions more men back in the civilian population who were raped as teenagers. For many prisoners, rape was not a one-off event. Often it was repeated by others, or the rapist forced the victim to become his permanent lover.

Prison broke people. Most prisoners got out sooner or later. What many of them took with them was fear, humiliation, a hair trigger reaction to any threat and a difficulty with sexual love. One of the ways to make sure you didn't get raped was to be so tough that you were other people's problem. Jack Henry Abbot wrote in his book *In the Belly of the Beast*:

> I was told by the pigs who transported me to prison that I was being sent there to be reduced to a punk, to be shorn of my manhood. They felt I would be less arrogant once I had been turned into a cocksucker ... Before I was twenty-one years old I had killed one of the prisoners and wounded another. I never did get out of prison. I never was a punk.[23]

More common are the feelings Dwight Edgar Abbott writes about in *I Cried, You Didn't Listen*:

> Dad was quite correct in believing that he was no longer looking at the well-behaved, polite loving son he had raised. What he saw was a walking time-bomb, ready to explode. It took the county of Los Angeles about four months to construct me, behind the walls surrounding that munitions-manufacturing plant they call juvenile hall.[24]

The inability of the guards to control the prisoners allowed an epidemic of rape. The fear of rape made prisoners violent. The violence made it harder for the guards to control. In some places guards punished prisoners by putting them in a cell with a known rapist. It was another feedback mechanism, raising the pressure. The more rape, the more violence, the more cruelty, the more violence, the more cruelty was needed. At the root of all these mechanisms was the increase in prison numbers.

These were the known, and intended, results of law and order. Mass rape was almost never discussed in public policy forums. But everyone knew it was happening. It's become a cliché in thrillers and cop shows. There's a scene where the police are trying to get a suspect to turn informer. They say to him, 'we're sending you up to the state pen. And there we've got a big black man in the shower. You bend over for the soap –'

The cop in the scene smiles. The suspect breaks. The audience knows what they're talking about.

Mass rape was part of the punishment. It was part of what prison was supposed to do to people. This was happening in a country where, throughout the 1980s and 90s, there was a national debate about the rape of women and a moral panic about child abuse. Yet the authorities were creating a system that raped millions of boys. They were doing it on purpose.

By the 1990s, the normal experience in a medium-security prison was that most prisoners were afraid from the moment they woke up until the moment they went to sleep. Then, sooner or later, most of them went back to their families, who were ashamed of them. To explain why, I now have to turn to the way Democrats and black leaders responded to mass imprisonment.

The politicians

Democratic politicians and African American leaders went along with mass imprisonment. This may seem surprising and needs explanation.

I'll start with the Democrats. In 1988 Reagan retired. George Bush senior was the Republican candidate for president. Michael Dukakis, the governor of Massachusetts, was the Democratic challenger.

Willy Horton, an African-American prisoner in Massachusetts, had been released on a temporary furlough, a halfway step to parole. Horton ran away to Maryland. He broke into the home of a middle-class white couple in the suburbs, tied up the man and raped the woman. It was the crime that comfortable white people fear most, and that hardly ever happens.

Bush's campaign ran the same TV ad again and again. It stressed that Massachusetts had released a violent rapist and implied Dukakis was soft on crime. The ad showed Horton's face, looking very black and quite insane.

Dukakis didn't know how to fight back. Remember, every Democrat had voted for the federal crime bill in 1984, and all but 18 people in Congress had voted for the 1986 bill. The only way Dukakis could have struck back successfully was to call George Bush a racist. To do that and make sense, he would have had to challenge the morality of the whole law-and-order crusade head on. No one in the American ruling class was doing that. Instead, Dukakis sputtered on television. His campaign faltered and never recovered. He lost.

Four years later, the Democratic challenger Bill Clinton was determined not to lose in the same way. Clinton was governor of Arkansas, where a black man, Ricky Rector, was to be executed for the murder of a policeman.

In the liberal years at the end of the 1960s the Supreme Court had banned capital punishment, arguing that the constitution forbade cruel and unusual punishment. In 1976, as the backlash began, the Supreme Court reversed itself and legalised the death penalty again. For many years the number of executions climbed slowly, from two nationally in 1982 to 23 in 1990 and 14 in 1991. All of these were in the socially conservative southern states – like Clinton's Arkansas.

Clinton was under some pressure to pardon Ricky Rector. Rector had suffered brain damage after the murder and no longer really understood what was happening to him. But Clinton wanted to underline his toughness. In the middle of the first, and most important, primary campaign in New Hampshire, Clinton returned to Arkansas and publicly refused clemency for Rector. According to the *Washington Post*, Rector:

> ... carefully put aside the slice of pecan pie that came with his last meal. Rector always liked to eat his dessert just before bedtime, and he apparently expected to return to his cell for his pie after he had received the lethal injection ... Just hours before he died, Rector told [his lawyer]: 'I'm going to vote for Clinton in the fall.'[25]

Clinton won the election in November 1992.

Before Rector's execution, the few executions each year were confined to the South. After Clinton stamped capital punishment with liberal approval, the number of executions increased markedly and spread to the North, Midwest, West and California.

The leaders of black America also allowed mass imprisonment to happen. They now had jobs that made them part of the system. The civil rights movement had fought, above all, to win equality in politics, education and public service jobs. They had not won that equality. But they did win a place at the bottom of the top table. In 2001, 20 per cent of white men and 10 per cent of white women were making over $26.10 an hour. So were 8 per cent of black men and 5 per cent of black women.[26]

To put it another way, one black man in 12 and one black woman in 20 were making $47,000 a year or better. They were the new African American elite. With the victory of civil rights, they had jobs in the armed forces, colleges, politics, the law and the police. Nowhere were they represented in proportion to the numbers of black people. But they were doing well. They had joined the system as administrators. They were often mayors or senior police officers in the inner city, judges in night court, social work managers and senior parole officers. They had an economic stake in the system.

Condoleezza Rice, Colin Powell and Oprah Winfrey are all in different ways the product of this new elite. They are unrepresentative, in that all three are now part of the ruling class and Winfrey is one of the richest people in America. But they represent the ideals the new black middle class was striving for.

At the same time, this new black middle class were differentiating themselves from black workers, the 92 per cent earning less than $47,000 a year. Just as life was improving for the professionals, it was getting tougher for the people below them. This was not just prison. After 1973, unemployment increased, and that bore heavily on black people – especially young men. Cuts in social programmes hit hard. The professionals' lives were coming together as other people saw theirs fly apart. And most of the professionals were only too aware that a few false steps, a few actions the employers couldn't tolerate, and they could find themselves back in the ghetto.

In the 1960s, black leaders like Martin Luther King spoke in a modified version of a black working-class accent. Now most of the new black professionals speak in the accents of TV anchormen and women. Their accent expresses their new class loyalties. They are also saying, as loudly as possible, I am different from the ghetto people.

The politicians and other leaders of the black community were the living expression of this new black professional class. Without exception, they backed the War on Drugs. In 1988, for instance, the Rev Jesse Jackson was the only black candidate for the Democratic nomination for president. Jackson had been there on the porch of the motel in Memphis when Martin Luther King was shot. He was a veteran of the movement. Now, at every campaign rally, the Reverend asked people to come down front and testify that they would give up drugs. Jackson was blaming the drugs, not the illegality of the drugs. This was the common approach among even the most radical black politicians.

Of course, Jackson was not as punitive as Bush. He has always been against the death penalty, supporting life without parole as the alternative. And he has consistently supported black victims of police brutality. But neither Jackson, nor any other African American politicians, mobilised against mass imprisonment.

Black and white families

Given that climate, the families of prisoners were deeply ashamed. The anthropologist Donald Braman did field research in the 1990s with the families of men imprisoned from the city of Washington – officially the District of Columbia. DC is over-whelmingly black and working class. A large majority of the families in DC had someone in prison or jail. Yet, Braman says, 'there is little public resistance to any part of the criminal justice system, and little outcry over the levels of incarceration.' Instead, 'most of the participants in this study told no one outside of the immediate family about their relative's incarceration.'[27]

Braman gives the example of 'Robert' and his wife 'Louisa'. Robert started using crack, and left Louisa and their son. He stole to feed his habit and went to prison. Robert gave up drugs inside, came out and reunited with his wife and child. They lived together for three years, going to church every Sunday, both working, saving to buy a house. Louisa was happy and grateful to God. They both knew, however, that there was still an outstanding warrant for robbery on Robert's record that the system had somehow missed. One day a traffic cop pulled Robert over, ran his details through the computer and found the old warrant. Robert went back to prison. Because Louisa had been so proud of him, she was now even more ashamed:

> **She began to avoid friends and family, not wanting to talk about Robert's incarceration, and lying to them when she did.**
>
> **'You isolate yourself because, you know, even though the other person don't know what you're going through, you really don't want to open up and talk to them about it. You don't want them knowing your business. Or it's a certain amount of respect you want to have. I just don't like the idea of people knowing that he's incarcerated ... So I live a lie.'**

> Her old friendships have suffered, and she has held
> back from making new friends ... Concerned for her
> husband's reputation when he returns, she said, she
> hides his incarceration so that 'when they look at him,
> they won't slap all these labels on him.'[28]

Louisa is well aware that most of the people she knows think
that if you have one criminal in the family, you will find others.
This is not just an idea from the media or the ruling class. The
people close to her believe it. So she tells her sisters that Robert
is in prison for a serious traffic violation, not for armed robbery.
They slowly realise she is lying, because no one would stay
inside that long for a traffic violation. But they don't press her.

Louisa also lies to the people in her church, the one place she
would usually go to give and receive comfort. The majority of
the people in her church group, and the city, are doing the same
thing. The majority of people in DC have a loved one in prison,
awaiting trial or on parole. Almost all of them keep it as quiet as
they can. In doing so, they ratchet up each other's shame.

The people who lie about their loved ones are mostly poor.
In the absence of a proper welfare system, they depend on those
relatives when anything goes wrong − for babysitting, loans, a
place to stay for a few weeks, a hot meal for the kids. As they
break family ties through shame, they lose that safety net.

Prison manufactures many kinds of loneliness. The majority
of both men and women in prison are parents who were in
regular touch with their children before they went inside. They
desperately want visitors. But the new prisons are in rural areas
far away. Californian prisons are mostly in the north of the state
− 16 hours from LA, where most prisoners come from. Upstate
New York is eight hours from the city. It costs one adult and a
little child at least $200 for the trip, meals and a motel
overnight.

The majority of prisoners have no visitors at all, from one
year to the next.

Prisoners can still talk to their children and lovers by making
collect calls (reverse charges) from pay phones in prison. The

state leases the contract to a phone company that charges special, high, prison rates. Because the prison is far away, the calls are long distance. Low-income families typically find themselves paying a fifth or a quarter of their income on calls from prison. Most families are unable to bring themselves to refuse calls from a husband or child. Within a few months many families have their phones cut off for unpaid bills. To avoid this, other families simply block incoming calls from the prison. Quite often one family member, a mother or grandmother, will agree to be the only one to take calls and pass on messages. Arguments about who pays for those calls can tear families apart.

Where fathers have been emotionally close to their children, prison leads, in one story after another, to trouble for the child. They quit trying at school, quit going to school and retreat into themselves.

Many conservative writers blame the troubles of working-class people on the lack of good role models. These children have a role model. But the man they love has been taken away. They can't talk to friends at school. Children tell, and then other children taunt. For these lonely children no one, not their mother, not their church, not their teacher or the television, ever tells them how to handle their pain with dignity.

In some ways, but only in some ways, it is worse for the families outside and the white men inside. Black prisoners do not have to be ashamed in front of other prisoners. They share an understanding of why they are in prison – racism. Robert, Louisa's husband, wrote a letter of political analysis to Donald Braman. It said in part:

Even though an annual study at the University of Michigan confirms that an overwhelming majority of drug users, abusers and sellers in America are white, even though the 1992 National Household Survey on Drug Abuse revealed that 8.7 million whites used drugs in one month versus 1.6 million blacks, the drug problem, which is an American problem, has

been conveniently depicted as a black problem. The
war on drugs is essentially a war on black men,
America's favorite bogeyman.[29]

Robert's views are widely shared by other black men in prison.
Families, unable to talk, do not develop such nourishing understandings. And the many millions of white convicts and their
families have had no comfort at all. Prison is a class catastrophe
as much as a racial one. But no one says this. White prisoners
disappear, even in much radical talk. However, watch the film
of any performance where Johnny Cash sings *Folsom Prison
Blues*. See the men, stomping their feet, howling with joy that
someone is shouting the truth.

Then, sooner or later, almost all men and women get out of
prison. People who have been afraid every day for years now
have to live on the outside. They have built a brutal, tough exte-
rior to protect themselves. This, and often the pain of rape,
makes it hard for people to love and be loved again.

The effect of prison has been to destroy the lives of millions
of individuals, marriages and families. Because the justice system has concentrated its fire on black men who didn't finish
high school, prison has broken the spirit of whole inner-city
neighbourhoods. This is what it was intended to do. The people who were at the core of the resistance of the 1960s now
cannot defend themselves. Where once there was struggle, now
there is a hole.

But there is a boiling rage that's hardly ever seen. It surfaced
in a riot against the Los Angeles Police Department (LAPD) in
1991.

The War on Drugs and the craze for imprisonment went
with an expansion of police powers and numbers, and a change
in policing styles. Almost all urban police departments had
SWAT teams modelled on the military. Throbbing police helicopters with powerful spotlights hovered overhead at night. The
police became more and more the enemy in many neighbourhoods, particularly black and Hispanic ones. The police knew
that, and like the prison guards had to become more brutal on

a regular basis in order to keep control.

In 1991 officers from the LAPD stopped Rodney King, an African-American driver, and beat him very badly for no particular reason. A passer-by caught the whole incident on amateur video. It played over and over again on American TV stations. The authorities were forced to prosecute the police involved, but an all white jury acquitted them. Black Los Angeles exploded.

The police had stopped black drivers millions of times before. I'm not exaggerating. Millions of drivers, many millions of times. There had been hundreds of thousands of beatings and years and years of prison. But this time it was on video and there was still no justice.

The rioters started from South Central LA, once called Watts, home of the 1965 riot. As in 65, they began burning and looting. The police withdrew. But this riot was different from every one that had gone before. It was a class riot. The authorities that the rioters faced were fronted by rich African Americans: 'The mayor, Tom Bradley, the incoming police chief, Willie Williams, and the chairman of the US Joint Chiefs of Staff, General Colin Powell, on whose orders federal troops were used to quell the rising were all black.'[30]

And for the first time in American history, Hispanics and white people joined a black riot. As the African-American rioters moved north to the shopping malls in Hispanic neighbourhoods, local Hispanic working people joined in, because they had the same experience of prison, police, work and poverty. As the riot moved northwards, people became more confident. They moved into mixed neighbourhoods. By the time the riot reached Hollywood, young white men on skateboards were looting. Of the first 5,000 people arrested, 52 per cent were Hispanic, 38 per cent were black and 10 per cent were white.[31]

There were no political theorists directing those crowds, no one saying that class was more important than race. It just seemed, after a generation of experience, to make sense.

Outside of LA something quite new also happened. In the 1960s there had been no public demonstrations of solidarity with any riot. Now there were demonstrations in dozens of cities, and the crowds were both black and white. They were showing their anger at the Rodney King verdict, but they were also open about their solidarity with the rioters. My father, then a 66-year-old white professor of economics at the University of Tennessee, marched through the streets of Knoxville with some of his graduate students on the first demonstration of his life. The marchers, black and white, like all the other demonstrators across the country, chanted the slogan of the rioters: 'No Justice, No Peace.' It meant if you will not give us justice, we will give you war. Feelings had shifted.

Then the riot was over. No politician of any standing, black or white, stepped forward to speak for the rioters. The feelings went back underground. Those feelings are still there, far more bitter after 13 more years of escalating injustice. No one speaks for those feelings. But they're there.

One last point needs to be made about the relationship between what happened to the unions and what happened to black people. In the 1960s the black riots and the white anti-war movement had happened in parallel. People had felt solidarity. Black and white soldiers had both refused to fight in Vietnam. The ruling class had seen the links between both movements. For them it meant they were losing control. But the movements had not fused.

Twenty years on, unions and African Americans were under parallel attacks. Many union and non-union workers were also black and Hispanic. Many white workers went to prison too. The ruling class understood that both imprisonment and union busting were important. Some in the ruling class understood this consciously, and some unconsciously. But all of them really understood that both were about restoring control.

Few of the defeated strikers or the prisoners said that their lives were under attack because the rich had to restore profits. But the loneliness, the feeling of a country and a world gone out of control, were the same. If a political movement arose that linked class persecution and racial injustice, there would be a firestorm of rage.

6 | Family Values

The backlash against civil rights went along with a backlash against women's liberation and gay liberation. In practice, this meant an attack on abortion, welfare and people with HIV. But it was presented as a defence of traditional 'family values'.

Conservatives felt that the traditional family was under threat. Women's rights were leading to sex before and outside marriage, and driving up divorce rates. Children were growing up without fathers. Gay men and lesbians, by their open existence, were undermining the old ways.

Leading the movement for family values were men with open right-wing politics, like the preacher Jerry Fallwell and President Ronald Reagan. For them, family values were part of hostility towards the whole 1960s. It is tempting to call them hypocrites. Southern fundamentalist TV preachers have been exposed as fornicators often enough. The Catholic bishops attacked condoms and abortion while shielding thousands of child-abusing priests. While Ronald Reagan was talking up family values, his wife was having an affair with Frank Sinatra. There is a picture in Kitty Kelly's biography of Nancy Reagan that shows Reagan looking at Nancy with Sinatra. The expression on Ronald Reagan's face is no different from what the rest of us feel in those situations.[1]

But to call them hypocrites would be to miss the point about conservative morality. Rich and powerful politicians have good reasons for spouting family values. First, a capitalist economy needs the unpaid labour of both women and men, but particularly women, looking after homes and children. If women weren't doing it as part of their family duties, the cost to capital of nursery schools and childcare would be enormous. So the politicians have to defend the family.

Second, the relations between lovers, and between parents and children, are the most intimate ones we know. We see inequality around us in our family from the moment we come shouting from the womb. We internalise inequality before we speak and live it in our sexual bodies every day of the rest of our lives. That makes inequality seem natural, biological, a basic way that human beings relate to each other. It prepares and reinforces all the other inequalities we encounter in society. Inequality is validated in the family where we learn to love and later look for love.

Third, the ruling class needs mass support, particularly in a democracy. It is hard to get that support for a campaign to drive down wages in order to increase profits. That's not a sure fire vote winner. So they turn to the places where ordinary people feel hurt or are unsure or compete with each other. They also look for ways of dividing us.

Individual ruling-class people may not put what I have just said into words. But they know it, deeply. That is why the ruling class almost always defend gender inequality. It is also why the left usually pushes for more equality. And it suggests how Ronald Reagan, the preachers and the bishops are forced into hypocrisy.

The problem for family values

So when Reagan came to power, he attacked the women's movement just as he attacked African Americans and unions. The ruling class as a whole, too, wanted to roll back the idea that women were equal. To do this, they used the idea of family values.

But they faced a serious dilemma. The corporations wanted women to leave the home and go to work. Among women of working age, 44 per cent worked for wages in 1973. By 2001 it was 58 per cent. The same thing was happening all over the world, but the US had the highest proportion of women working in any rich country.[2] By getting more women into work, the corporations could make bigger profits from the same families than before. This was a central part of their strategy for raising profits and they couldn't compromise.

From 1979 to 1995, as we have seen, most men's wages were falling. For working-class families, that meant that more women needed to go out to work. The combination of the new jobs and the women's movement gave women more control of their own money and a feeling of greater dignity. They also didn't need to stay with a man as badly as they used to. Divorce rates rose, and in the majority of cases it was the woman who left.

This contradiction between wanting women in the workforce and the social consequence of women's independence presented a problem for the defenders of family values. They had another one, too. Women's wages were catching up with men's. The real hourly wages of a woman making just more than 50 per cent of women increased between 1979 and 2001. But she was still earning less than a man making more than 50 per cent of men. Adjusting the numbers for what a dollar could buy in 2001:[3]

	1979	2001	22-year raise
50% woman	$9.38	$11.04	$1.66
50% man	$14.96	$14.60	$0.36 loss
difference	$5.58	$3.54	

The same pattern is repeated for the woman on the edge of professional work who is making more than 80 per cent of women, but less than the best paid 20 per cent.

	1979	2001	22-year raise
80% woman	$13.81	$18.89	$5.08
80% man	$21.01	$24.20	$3.36
difference		$7.20	$5.31

It's true too for the woman working close to senior management, and making more than 95 per cent of women and less than 5 per cent.

	1979	2001	22-year raise
95% woman	$20.32	$30.90	$10.38
95% man	$30.32	$40.98	$10.57
difference	$10.00	$10.08	

In 2001, women were still getting less than men at every level. But they were catching up. Even at the 95 per cent level, men got a raise of $10 from $30, and women got $10 from $20. Rich women were still doing better in percentage terms.

But the figures show that class made more difference than gender. The woman in the 95 percentile got a raise more than six times the woman in the middle. This was because the rich woman now had a management job. Between 1979 and 2001, both men and women with college educations were pulling away from the rest. For both sexes, the jobs that created this difference came from only three sectors: managers, sales including financial sales, and health professionals. Among richer working women, managers alone accounted for 68 per cent of the increased inequality. The rest was made up by women stockbrokers and women doctors.[4]

So more women were going out to work; they were getting management jobs and they were catching up with men. This meant they were feeling more confident in their daily lives. The corporations did want women to work and they were happy more families were adopting a dual income strategy. But they didn't want women's wages to rise or to make women more confident.

The backlash against working women

The ruling class were hostile to the legacy of the women's movement. But the ideas of that movement remained. Women were becoming stronger in their working lives. That provoked a massive campaign all through the 1980s to make women feel guilty about working. They couldn't be stopped, but they could be made to feel bad and weak.

This attack saturated the media. Susan Faludi's detailed it in her angry and comprehensive 1991 book: *Backlash: The Undeclared War Against American Women*.[5] Magazines and newspapers carried endless stories about the loneliness of career women, unable to have babies because they had waited too long. As Faludi demonstrates, all these stories were based on phony or nonexistent statistics. But it was not simply that some of the media took this line, sometimes. All of the popular media took this line, over and over.

In the 1980s real women were exiled from almost all TV shows and all Hollywood films. This was not a matter of chance or audience preference. The viewers loved the only strong women on TV, *Roseanne* and *Cagney and Lacey*. The TV executives hated them, kept trying to get rid of them and cancelled the shows while they were still popular.

In films the women were zeroes at best, like Princess Leah in *Star Wars*. Sometimes they were evil, as in the classic backlash movie *Fatal Attraction*. There a weak married man played by Michael Douglas has a one-night stand with an independent single woman played by Glenn Close. Afterwards he feels guilty and she stalks him.

The original ending to the film showed a depressed Close cutting her own throat. Test showings proved audiences didn't like that. A new ending was made. Close invades Douglas' home with a meat cleaver. Douglas drowns her in the bath. He hugs his wife and homemaker, a good woman who forgives him. Close, like any movie monster, explodes from the bath undead. Douglas' wife shoots her. Audiences liked that. Or some people in the audience did. Faludi writes:

> The theater in suburban San Jose, California, is stuffy and cramped, every seat taken, for this Monday night showing of Fatal Attraction in October 1987 ... [It] has played to a full house every night [for] six weeks. 'Punch the bitch's lights out! I'm not kidding,' a man up front implores Michael Douglas. Emboldened by the chorus, a man in the back row cuts to the point: 'Do it, Michael. Kill her already. Kill the bitch.'
>
> Outside in the theater's lobby, the teenage ushers sweep up candy wrappers and exchange quizzical glances as their elders' bellows trickle through the padded doors. 'I don't get it really,' says Sabrina Hughes, a high school student who works the Coke machine and finds the adults' behavior 'very weird. Sometimes I like to sneak into the theater in the last twenty minutes of the movie. All these men are

screaming, "Beat that bitch! Kill her off now!" The women, you never hear them say anything. They are all sitting there, just quiet.[6]

The men who made the movie knew what they were doing. Here's the director of *Fatal Attraction*, former British adman Adrian Lyne, on single women:

They are sort of compensating for not being men. It's sad, because it kind of doesn't work ... I see it with the executives within the studio area. The other day, I saw a woman producer who was really quite powerful; and she railroaded, walked all over this guy, who was far less successful and powerful than her. She just behaved as if this man wasn't there ... And it was much more disconcerting because it was a woman doing it. It was unfeminine, you know? ...

You hear feminists talk and the last ten, twenty years you hear women talking about fucking men rather than being fucked, to be crass about it. It's kind of unattractive, however liberated and emancipated it is. It kind of fights the whole wife role, the whole childbearing role. Sure you got your career and your success, but you are not fulfilled as a woman.

My wife has never worked. She's the least ambitious person I've ever met. She's a terrific wife. She hasn't the slightest interest in doing a career. She kind of lives with me, and it's a terrific feeling. I come home and she's there.[7]

Michael Douglas, the star of the film and a rich producer in his own right, echoed the director:

If you want to know, I'm really tired of feminists, sick of them. They've really dug themselves into their own grave. Any man would be a fool if he didn't agree with equal rights and equal pay but some women,

now, juggling with career, lover, children, [childbirth],
wifehood, have spread themselves too thin and are
very unhappy. It's time they looked at themselves
and stopped attacking men. Guys are going through
a terrible crisis right now because of women's unrea-
sonable demands.[8]

Douglas and Lyne knew what kind of movie they were making,
and why. They knew the feelings it would arouse, because they
had those feelings too. But notice their defensiveness too.
Douglas supports equal pay. Did Close get paid as much as him?
Don't be silly. But he has to say it. With Lyne and Douglas, as
with the men in the audience, there is a tone of deep resentment.
It's not quite like the backlash against black men and union
workers. These rich men don't think they're winning this one.

They weren't. When you read those quotes 20 years later, the
extreme sexism is unacceptable. But this should not blind us to
the women sitting silent in that cinema, or the tens of millions
of women who felt guilty and anxious at that time.

The defenders of family values needed to attack equality. So
they went for the soft spots, just as they had gone for drugs and
crime in attacking African Americans. On gender, they went for
groups of people who felt helpless and alone – women having
abortions, women on welfare and gay men with AIDS. I turn
now to the first two, and consider gay men in a later chapter.

Abortion

I worked as an abortion counsellor in London for nine years in
the 1980s. My employer was the Pregnancy Advisory Service,
a democratically run feminist cooperative. Their decision to
employ me, a man, was political. They thought women and
men ought to be able to live together on the planet and talk.
For me, the job was a chance to listen to women in a way I
never had before. What I learned is relevant here.

Having an abortion is usually not a simple matter. Abortion is
a physical experience. A woman lives it in her body, as she lives
sex or childbirth. What happens inside you, physically, has a special

power. Some of the women I listened to thought an abortion was killing, but they had to do it. Many didn't think that. But they didn't think it was nothing either. They mourned a possible child.

Those who felt most comfortable, by and large, were the married women with children already, whose husbands came to the clinic with them. For them it was a straightforward decision and they had the support of someone who loved them. But for many women abortion came at a moment of loneliness. Often they were in a relationship but when they got pregnant, the man said he wasn't staying forever. For some others, there was no steady relationship, and the pregnancy underlined how alone they were.

Almost all of us at PAS felt a particular tenderness for the women who thought abortion was murder but still came to us. One of the surprising things I learned, and all abortion workers know, is that women like that are just as likely to have an abortion as anyone else. This is because the forces that push women into abortion are not trivial. Such women just feel worse, and need more love.

The consequences of all these feelings cut two ways. The right to have an abortion, and to have one in dignity, matters a great deal to women who've been there. But there is a lot of shame, guilt or vulnerability. And there are women who do not forgive themselves for what they have done. These deep experiences lie beneath the surface of abortion politics.

In America, the most important victory for the women's liberation movement had come when the Supreme Court legalised abortion in *Roe v. Wade* in 1973. From that moment on, the 'Right to Life' movement in America started organising to reverse it. In the early years, almost all the activists in this movement were Catholics. As time went on, they were joined by evangelical Protestants. Both groups of activists were overwhelmingly white.[9]

The anti-abortion leadership, particularly the politicians and the Republican preachers, were committed right-wingers across the board. The local activists, though, weren't like that. Half of them were women. Like the men in the movement, most of these women made it clear they supported equal pay and women working. And they meant it.

They modelled their campaigns on the civil rights movement. The Right to Lifers put out leaflets, held marches and vigils, lobbied legislators, organised votes for pro-life politicians and took cases to court. They also picketed abortion clinics. As women went into the clinic, they passed through crowds of men and women begging them not to do it. Some in the crowd held high placards with a picture of a 12-week-old foetus, looking all too human. Others tried to shove leaflets bearing such pictures into the hands of women struggling through the crowds. In some places, the anti-abortion protestors sat down on the floor of the waiting room, and remained there, silent judges.

In the 1980s political activity was withering. But without intending to do so, the Right to Life campaigners kept local feminist movements alive.

The feminist side was the Woman's Right to Choose. Women, and some men, staffed the abortion clinics. To open a clinic in any state, and to keep it open, required mass mobilisation. In St Louis, Missouri, Fargo, North Dakota, and a hundred other cities, the women's movement fought for the clinics. That meant court battles, lobbying the city council and fighting over planning permission. It also meant that volunteers turned up every day to walk through the crowds with the women going into the clinic, holding hands, trying to give them courage. Almost all the women walked through the pickets. Like the women of their mother's generation, who had endured the knitting needles and the blood of botched back-street abortions, they really needed the operation.

Both sides knew that the key battle was over the Supreme Court. There were nine justices on the court. As one after another died or retired, the President would appoint a new one. During his 1980 election campaign, Ronald Reagan wrote to the National Right to Life Convention in Los Angeles: 'Never before has the cause you espouse been more important to the future of our country. The critical values you espouse are being increasingly accepted by our citizens as essential to re-establishing the moral strength of our nation.'[10]

Reagan won the election. As each of the judges who had voted for *Roe v. Wade* retired, Reagan appointed an anti-abortion judge. The liberals on the court decided they would die in harness if that's what it took to stop Reagan. By 1989 George Bush the elder was president. He appointed the crucial fifth anti-abortion justice. The court decided to hear a test case from Missouri. Both sides knew this was it.

The women's movement, the clinic workers and the clinic defenders mobilised for a national march on Washington, like Martin Luther King's and the anti-Vietnam marches. B. J. Isaacson-Smith had worked for years as a counsellor in a St Louis clinic. Now B. J. wrote a poem. It was published as a full-page ad in the city's *Post-Dispatch*, urging people to come with the clinic workers in buses to the march in Washington. It read in part:

Have you forgotten?
I recall shielding your shaking
body, guiding you and
your husband through the picket lines.
You broke our hearts.
You had just celebrated
your twelfth birthday when
you came to us. You clutched
your teddy bear, sucked
your thumb and cried out
for your mom who asked
you why you had gotten yourself
pregnant. You replied that you just wanted to be grown.
You're 20 today.
Where are you?

I pretend that I don't know you in the market,
at social gatherings and
on the street.
I told you I would.

I have no regrets.
But I'm angry.
I can't do this alone.

I'm not asking you to speak of your abortion, but
you need to speak out and you need to speak now.
Where are you?[11]

Judy Widdicombe, the nurse who founded the clinic, now lived
in Washington. She went to the march and looked for the banner of her clinic:

There were so many of them, Judy thought ... older
women and younger women together, Judy saw as she
elbowed, were these mothers and daughters marching
side by side? And men, really a remarkable number of
men, and teenagers ... and exuberant lesbians in crew
cuts and big shirts ...
[Judy saw the banner.] What moved her, what filled
Judy now with unspeakable relief, was the very ordi-
nariness of the banner and the women who carried it.
On this day, in this place, they were not big or special
at all. They were tiny. They were barely visible stitches
in a vast, amazing quilt. Already the rumours of the
crowd size had begun to pass from the front end back
... Judy worked her way over toward the base of a
broad statue, and climbed up for a look, steadying
herself beside others who had scrambled up already,
and as she straightened she could see for the first time
the full breadth and length and she said aloud, 'My
God,' knowing no one would hear her because the
shouting was too loud. She put one hand to her
mouth, and she began to cry. She had never seen so
many people in her life.[12]

The National Park Police estimated 300,000. The organisers
said 600,000. Two weeks later the Supreme Court heard oral
arguments on the Missouri test case. Ten weeks after that the
court delivered its judgment. The wording was complicated,
and each judge wrote an opinion. But the effect was to confirm
Roe v. Wade. Abortion stayed legal.

The justices had looked at those half a million women. They knew the right to abortion had been won because tens of thousands of women like Judy Widdicombe had organised illegal clinics and referral services in the 1960s and 70s. The size and spirit of that march meant that if the court made abortion illegal again, they would face a movement of resistance so large and determined it would humiliate the law. So the court did what the mass movement told it to.

Many women, including many marchers, thought that they had persuaded the judges, or that the court had changed. They didn't really understand the effect of an organised mass movement. The black movement had not organised over prison, and the comparison was stark.

There was one mass march organised to highlight the plight of black men. The Nation of Islam had recruited heavily in the prisons in the 1950s and 60s. One of their recruits was Malcolm X. Back then the Nation campaigned, with considerable success, to make prisons more humane places. In 1995 the Nation called a 'Million Man March' in Washington for black men only. Although a full million didn't come, many hundreds of thousands did. But this time the Nation and the marchers said nothing about prison. Instead, the Nation offered their own version of family values. The official line was that black men were coming together to apologise for the way they had behaved over the years, and rededicate themselves to taking care of their families and living respectably.

The men who marched were deeply moved by the experience. Had they marched about the million black men in prison, it would have transformed American politics. A demonstration of hundreds of thousands against prison, in the overwhelmingly black and working-class city of Washington, would have terrified the courts and the government in a way the Los Angeles riot could not. Organised mass demonstrations are more powerful than riots.

Housework and cleaning women

The 1989 abortion demonstration showed the strength of the women's movement. The fight over welfare revealed its weaknesses. Most people on welfare were women or their children.

But the feminist movement did almost nothing to defend them when their benefits were attacked. And once the right to an abortion was guaranteed in 1989 the women's movement largely stopped fighting for federal funding for abortions. The result was that working women could get their health insurance to pay for an abortion, but unemployed women on Medicare could not.

The problems were class differences. As in the African American movement, the leading feminists were becoming part of the system. This was not a matter of individuals getting older or selling out. It was because the women's movement of the 1970s, like the civil rights movement, had been led by professionals. Most of the women who supported feminism, like most of the civil rights marchers, were working class. But the leadership was not. And crucially, their understanding of what they were doing in both cases was 'nationalist'. They were getting more opportunities for middle-class blacks and women. Like the leaders of the independence struggles in the colonial countries, they saw equality as a matter of equality at the top.

While the movement was growing, that didn't present many problems. It was easy to fight for both equal opportunities at the top and equality for all. With the movements in retreat, the middle-class leaders had to make some choices. And as with black leaders, professional women were willing to settle for a small slice of the cake.

This changed feminism. Let me return to the statistics on wages and salaries at the start of the chapter. Women's wages were going up, but men were doing better than women at every level in 2001. However, class inequality was even more important than gender. Over 22 years a woman making more than 95 per cent of other woman had a raise more than six times bigger than the woman in the middle. And the richer woman was leaving the man in the middle behind:

	1979	2001	22-year raise
95% woman	$20.32	$30.90	$10.38
50% man	$14.96	$14.60	$0.36 loss
Difference	$5.36	$16.50	

Class matters more than gender. In 1979 the woman manager was earning a third more than the ordinary man. Now she's earning more than twice what he does.

The woman on the edge of the professionals, earning more than 80 per cent, has passed the man in the middle and is pulling away:

	1979	2001	22-year raise
80% woman	$13.81	$18.89	$5.08
50% man	$14.96	$14.60	$0.36 loss
Man gets	$1.17 more	$4.29 less	

These numbers make concrete the growing tension by the 1990s, on both sides, between professional women and working-class men. Many working-class men had increasingly confused feelings about feminism. Most of them were in favour of real equality for women. They wanted a decent life for their daughters and the family depended on the wife's wage. Yet feminism seemed to be passing these men by. They were being eclipsed by the increased benefits of a college education. Working-class men were losing out, their wives weren't getting much, and they felt professional women were pissing on them all.

At the same time, these figures help explain why many feminist professionals began to ignore working-class women, and some became more hostile to working-class men. The problem, they said, was men. Not so much men of our class, who aren't all that great, but they're sensitive, they're trying. The problem is fat, beer-drinking, white men. Homer Simpson is the enemy.

No one quite wrote this in books. But they said it. They didn't quite say working-class black men were the problem either. Instead they congratulated black feminists on their struggle against their 'triple oppression'. The unspoken subtext was often, 'their men beat them, you know'.

Several factors are important here. The successful women were making a lot more money. That tied them into the system. But they were still making less than the equivalent men. That didn't happen by chance, but through endless discrimination at work. They met the same sexism outside work and at home. So these women still needed to be feminists. But usually they were managing more women than men. They owed part of their wage rises to feminism, and even more to the generally increasing inequality in society. And day by day they were enforcing the system that exploited other women and men.

Like the black elite, some women too had a place at the bottom of the top table. They owed that place to the women's movement. Yet the existence of the table depended on keeping ordinary men and women in their place.

So feminism changed.[13] Barbara Ehrenreich was a 1960s feminist who never gave up. In 2002 she wrote:

> [In the 1970s] the radical new idea was that housework was not only a relationship between a woman and a dust bunny or an unmade bed; it also defined a relationship between human beings ... When, somewhere, a man dropped a sock with a calm expectation that his wife would retrieve it, it was a sock heard round the world ...
>
> Housework was not degrading because it was manual labor, as [early feminist Betty] Friedan had thought, but because it was embedded in degrading relationships and inevitably served to reinforce them. To make a mess another person has to deal with ... is to exert domination in one of its more silent and intimate forms ...
>
> [Then feminists got maids.] In 1999, somewhere between 14 and 18 per cent of [US] households employed outsiders to do their cleaning, and the numbers have been rising dramatically since ... Among my middle class, professional women friends and acquaintances, including some who made important contributions to the early feminist analysis of housework two and a half decades ago, the employment of a cleaning person is now nearly universal ... Strangely, or perhaps not so strangely at all, no one talks about the 'politics of housework' any more.
>
> Most Americans, more than 80 per cent, still clean their own homes, but the minority who do not

include a sizeable fraction of the nation's opinion makers and culture producers: professors, writers, editors [and] political figures ... In August 1999, the *New York Times* reported on the growing problem of dinner parties in upscale homes being disrupted by hostesses screaming at their help.[14]

This division between middle-class professional feminists and working-class women spelled trouble for women on welfare.

Welfare

When he got in, Ronald Reagan went for women on welfare just as he went for the unions, criminals, drug users, blacks and women who needed abortions. Indeed, his campaign against welfare recipients united all these themes.[15]

In a speech back in 1976, Reagan mentioned a black woman in Chicago who had 'eighty names, thirty addresses, twelve Social Security cards, and is collecting veteran's benefits on four non-existing deceased husbands. And she is collecting Social Security on her cards. She's got Medicaid, getting four stamps, and she is collecting welfare under each of her names.'[16]

Anyone who has ever signed on for welfare in just one name will appreciate the heroic amount of waiting-room time necessary to register under eighty names. The story was an obvious lie. The journalists present asked Reagan for the woman's name. He wouldn't give it. The journalists went to the South Side of Chicago and interviewed every welfare worker and claimant they could. They didn't find her.

When Reagan gained office in 1981, he also relentlessly attacked 'welfare queens'. These queens were black teenage mothers who had child after child in order to claim welfare. Reagan's 'favorite book [was] George Gilder's anti-welfare classic *Wealth and Poverty*'. Gilder's main argument comes across clearly in his 1995 testimony to a Congressional committee:

Essentially, welfare benefits are far better than low-wage, entry-level jobs. Welfare gives benefits far superior to entry-level jobs because they yield valuable leisure time for the recipient. Thus it usurps the male role as chief provider and undermines the foundation of families. His provider role is absolutely central to the family; if the state replaces the male provider, you don't have families. The welfare state cuckolds the man. That is why we have eighty per cent illegitimacy rates in the inner cities. The welfare state has been more destructive to black families than slavery ever was.[17]

It's all there – the worry about the lazy poor, the fear of black people who can't control their genitals, the suppressed envy, the little bit of pseudo-liberal concern after the racist remark.

The statistics are phony. In 1995, 76 per cent of 19-year-old black women had no children. Of the black teenage girls who did have children, three-quarters were working for a living. Sixty-six per cent of all black children were living with both parents. And there were more white people on welfare than black.[18] Which makes sense, because there are more poor white people than poor black people.

Such statistics were rarely repeated in the media. By the mid-1990s, after 20 years of attacks on welfare queens, most Americans believed that the federal government spent more on welfare than they did on defence.

This was far from the truth. Americans in need collect benefits in three ways. Some disabled people are able to claim under the social security programme that also pays pensions. Just under half of people who lose their jobs are able to claim unemployment pay for six to twelve months. The people who fall through these nets can ask for welfare. The cost is shared by the states and the federal government. In most states in the last 40 years, it has been very difficult for single people to claim welfare. Until it was abolished in 1995, Aid to Families with Dependent Children was the only hope for families with children. Paradoxically, this was only paid to single parents. Over the years, many millions of unemployed working-class men left home so their wives and children could qualify.

In addition, families on welfare, some low-paid people and those on unemployment benefit could qualify for food stamps. These could be exchanged at the supermarket for food. About 1 per cent of the combined federal and state budgets were spent on food stamps. Another 1 per cent was spent on welfare. Altogether, 2 per cent of the combined federal and state budgets were spent to help people in desperate need. In which case, we need to explain why Reagan, the right and the media cared so much.

One answer is that this was part of discrediting social spending as a whole. Medicaid – free medical care for people on welfare and the disabled – costs real money. So do education, social security pensions, social security for the disabled, and Medicare for the elderly. These were costs that had to be kept down to get profits back up. However, it was hard for the enemies of social spending to trash talk hospital treatment for poor children or free high school education. And social security was off limits. So the attack on welfare served to give all social spending a bad name.

It also paralleled the attack on African Americans. Women on welfare were depicted as the sisters and lovers of the men who were sent to prison. And it was an attack on the whole idea of sexual freedom and women's liberation. It was primarily an offensive on the level of ideas, but it was to have real consequences for the lives of millions, most of them women and their dependent children. That is why it was the women's movement should have felt rage about welfare cuts. But class differences prevented that.

The attack on welfare spending was also a way of splitting the working class. It was part of an old idea, a division between respectable 'middle class' workers and the 'undeserving poor'. Since the 1980s, the right and the mainstream media have been promoting the idea of an 'underclass' – as feckless, fatherless, criminal, poor and excluded form normal society. Many sociologists have taken this idea up, but it came in the first place from *Newsweek*, *Time* and the *New York Times*.[19] A kindly side to the theory treats the underclass as victims, and an ugly side fears them as the dangerous undeserving poor.

This idea cuts with the grain of a structure of feeling among American workers. They have long made a distinction between respectable, steady, regular working people and the others. But these two groups know each other. They're relatives.

A team of anthropologists led by Katherine Newman studied hamburger workers doing McJobs in Harlem in the 1990s. Being anthropologists, they wrote down family trees and asked people what their relatives did. Here's the answer for one restaurant worker, 'Kyesha Smith':

Smith's cousins and their spouses included a two drug dealers, two on public assistance, one in the military, a postal worker, a cook, a train cleaner and a college student. Her mother was on welfare and her father was a bus driver. Smith's aunts and uncles were a garage worker, a medical secretary, a veteran, a corrections officer, three truck drivers, a hair braider, a contractor, two in the military, one unemployed, a basketball player, one with a drug problem, one drug dealer and the vice-president of a bank.

Or take Latoya, a restaurant manager. The father of her first three children is in jail and so are five of her older brothers. Her current partner is a flooring contractor. His relatives include a social worker, a children's store worker, a construction contractor, plus one on disability and two on welfare. Latoya's aunts, uncles and cousins are the superintendent of a cable company, a housekeeper in a hospital, two home attendants, a construction worker, a truck driver, a maid, a fast food manager, someone who prepares tax forms, a fish market worker and one on disability.[20]

The divisions between respectable and 'underclass' run right through such families. Poor people need each other. They lose their jobs, their homes, or their kids get sick. They need to borrow money, leave the kids for a day, move in for a few weeks. The relatives who help out know they will need help one day too.

Only it's not that simple. You can let your sister's family move in for a few weeks. The apartment's small, it's summer, it's hot, and your sister and her husband scream at each other. Your kid wants their room back. Your sister keeps saying she's going to find a place and doesn't. Her husband can't stand it, goes out on the street and comes back drunk or worse. Soon you and your sister say cruel words to each other that will not be forgiven.

Or simply, you loan some money. And when you need it back, they say they haven't got it. Mutual help binds poor people together while poverty makes them hurt each other.

The relative who helps, the grandmother raising six grandchildren, knows she is a good person. But many young people growing up know they want to get out, to college and a clean steady job. That costs, in time and tuition and clean clothes and time keeping. To get those things for themselves, many people cut themselves off from their kin. They move out, refuse to share, and often join one of the religious congregations that encourages self-control, but not generosity.

They have to cut themselves off completely because the division between respectable and unrespectable doesn't just run down the middle of families. For many working people, it runs down the middle of their hearts and bodies. You can hear that listening to soul music or any country and western station. First there's a gospel song, begging for forgiveness. Next a love song celebrates fidelity. Then there's a somebody done somebody wrong song. Tammy Wynette sings *Stand By Your Man* one minute and *D.I.V.O.R.C.E.* the next. In the honky-tonk you grab a beer and dance to Loretta Lynn singing *Don't Come A-Drinkin*. There are good reasons to hold yourself in and try not to fall off the edge. But sometimes it's Friday night.

It's not just the poor 'underclass' these songs speak to, it's the whole of the working class. Even among the poorest, there are endless gradations of respectability and shame. The writer Adrian Nicole LeBlanc talks about Coco, a girl in a poor Hispanic neighbourhood in the Bronx:

> [Coco's new stepfather Richie] was intelligent; he read books; he registered Coco for her first library card, and he helped her with her homework. Ever since [her sister] Iris came out pregnant, Richie had been warning Coco to guard herself and aim for a better life.
>
> Exactly how she was supposed to do this was unclear, but Coco might have instinctively understood that success was less about climbing than about not

falling down. Since there were few real options for mobility, people in Coco's world measured improvements in microscopic increments of better-than-what-was-worse. These tangible gradations mattered more than the clichéd language of success that floated blandly out of everyone's mouth, like fugitive sentiments from a Hallmark [greeting] card. Girls were told to 'make something of themselves' as soon as the baby was old enough; boys were going to 'do right' and 'stay inside'; everyone was going back to school. But better-than was the true marker. Thick and fed was better than thin and hungry. Family fights indoors – even if everyone could hear them – were better than taking private business to the street. Heroin was bad, but crack was worse. A girl who had four kids by four boys was worse than a girl who had four by three. A boy who dealt drugs and helped his mom and kids was better than a boy who was greedy and spent the income on himself; the same went for girls and their welfare checks. Mothers who went clubbing and didn't yell at their kids the next tired day were better than mothers who did.[21]

The war on welfare queens stuck the knife in between what people were trying to be and what they could be. The knife shamed people. It shamed the whole idea of social provision. And it weakened the working class.

This mattered because the whole working class needed welfare. It's like a cheap inner city hotel. Two-thirds of the hotel rooms are occupied by long-term residents. A third of the rooms are taken by people passing through, staying for a few days or a week. So in any year, almost all of the people who stay in that hotel will be short-stay. Welfare is like that.

The really poor are a minority of the population, less than a fifth. But the people who have been poor at one point in their life, and needed welfare or unemployment benefit, are close to a majority of the population. Then add in their parents, husbands, wives and children. Add in the people on minimum wage who have to compete for jobs when women are forced off welfare. Most important of all, add in the people in work who are afraid of what will happen to them if they lose their jobs. The working class as a whole needs welfare. In Western European countries with a welfare state most workers understand this. They have welfare because unions and working class parties fought for it.

The campaign against welfare queens finally won when President Clinton signed the 1995 bill to, in the endlessly repeated phrase, 'end welfare as we know it'. It had been a long struggle – 14 years, since Reagan came to power. In those years real levels of benefit had been cut by a third. This was done inch by inch, year by year. The long campaign meant that by the mid-1990s the majority of Americans believed that welfare was the largest single item of government expenditure, bigger than the army, not the two per cent it actually was.

But the attack on welfare could not succeed until other battles had been won. The black and white poor had seen their leadership desert them as their lives were pulverised. They mounted no real resistance to the bill Clinton signed in 1995. The unions had been gutted over the years since 1975, and were left fighting only their own corner. The idea of a dangerous underclass, with all its racist connotations, held the field. The poor were ashamed. And the women's movement was now led by people who didn't see welfare as a feminist issue, even though women would be the victims, and even though the attack on welfare went along with an attack on sexual freedom.

Moreover, the 1995 welfare act could not have been passed in a recession or under a Republican. It was passed as the country was coming out of a recession, with more jobs opening up. Clinton at first resisted the bill and made a considerable show of reluctance in signing it. But he had been campaigning for full-scale welfare reform since 1992. And his approval of the bill meant that the black, feminist, and union leaders who supported the Democrats were unwilling to fight.

The act fixed a limit of two years on any one claim for welfare, and five years in a lifetime. In addition, people on welfare had to take whatever work was offered to them. In most cases, these were special welfare jobs previously done by regular workers who had been laid off. In New York City these new welfare workers did 22 hours a week. The starting rate was $1.80 an hour, a third of the minimum wage. Their total income, including all benefits and food stamps, was a maximum of $5,724 a year. Only 16 per cent of them went on to get permanent jobs.[22]

In the 1980s, family values ideologues had attacked abortion and women who worked outside the home. Now they were insisting that women with children had to leave them and go out to work. This fitted with the demands of the corporations and profit, not with any traditional idea of family.

Putting people into work didn't increase the number of available jobs. Many people on welfare welcomed the chance of a job, though. The catch came when they lost the job, and couldn't claim again. Or when they got sick. Forty-four per cent of households on welfare included someone with a disability. The jobs they got coming off welfare didn't pay health insurance and they lost their Medicaid as they came off welfare. So when a child got ill, they had to spend many hours, and often many days, waiting in the hospital emergency room. Nor would minimum-wage jobs pay enough for childcare. Many mothers in low-wage jobs had depended on someone on welfare – a sister, mother, or grandmother – to mind the children. Now there was no one.

The 1995 act allowed the states some leeway. Utah decided to cut off all benefits for life after 36 months on welfare. If a woman didn't get a job then, the state could take her children away and put them up for adoption. The state says they have taken 2,000 children in this way, but critics suspect the number is much higher. Researcher Rebecca Gordon writes:

[Utah] caseworkers inform Family and Child Services a month after a [welfare] family reaches its lifetime benefit limit. Within a month, Family and Child Services makes an unannounced visit to the family's home to determine its fitness as a place for children.

One respondent's weeping son was removed from her home with no investigation whatsoever, because at the moment the visitor from Child and Family Services arrived, she was tending his bloody nose. Another was told she didn't have enough canned goods in her pantry, not too surprising as her welfare benefits had been terminated. Her children were taken, too. Still another woman lost her children on laundry day. She'd had her kids throw their dirty clothes down to the foot of the stairs so she could bag it up and take it to the Laundromat. The FCS worker walked in, observed the pile of clothes and promptly removed the children from this 'unfit' home ... [One woman] managed to leave an abusive situation, only to lose her children because she 'allowed' them to see her being beaten up.[23]

The act was passed in 1995. By 2000, the number of people getting federal welfare benefits was less than half what it had been five years before. That's six million fewer people. But if you count in all the people who missed out on short-term claims, it's at least ten million and probably many more. While the welfare debate had targeted black and the inner city, more white people than black had missed out on benefits.[24]

Individual failures

In the last three chapters I have concentrated on the attacks on unions, African Americans and women. These were the three most important forms of the backlash. They were also attacks on groups of people. Now, I want to briefly treat some of the ways the emotional lives of individual Americans were also transformed.

Any serious system of control of people and ideas works across the board. In the years of the backlash, American public culture changed in many ways. All of these blamed the troubles people faced on the individual, not on social or economic inequality. This worked in two ways. First, personal failures happened because you didn't try hard enough. On another level, people failed because they were made that way, and inequality stemmed from biology.

For instance, until the 1980s there were two dominant models for the treatment of mental illness.[25] One model was the talking therapies. Madness was caused by suffering, and alleviated by listening and by insight. The other model was biological. In the biological model, each mental illness was a named disease caused by some physical flaw, often inherited. There was no blame. The individual, the family and society were all not responsible. Whatever was wrong could be treated, if not cured, by the appropriate drug.

By the late 1990s the biological model was dominant in the US. Almost all treatment in hospitals was with drugs. This was despite gaping scientific holes in the medical model. In 40 years of trying, the biological psychiatrists had not found a physical cause for any mental illness. Physical diseases have a 'differential diagnosis' – there are different features which establish the disease. By contrast, 'mental illnesses' are clusters of symptoms, which a person has some of, but there is no one sign of the disease.

Patients with physical illnesses have blood tests. Although biological psychiatrists insist mental illness is caused by a chemical imbalance in the blood, they never test the blood. By the same token, many physical conditions are now known to be inherited, and the genes for this are being discovered. In spite of the genetic revolution, no gene for any mental illness has yet been discovered.

No other dominant scientific model in the last hundred years has been so absolutely empty of predictive results. What drives the biological model, though, is drugs. Some drugs change people's moods, and for many people make life easier. The drugs often have painful, unpleasant, shameful or dangerous side effects, but for many they work. However, they also have the same calming effect on people without mental illness. This is quite different from aspirin, which only cures a headache if you have a headache. Also, the fact that a drug cures something does not tell you the cause. Aspirin gets rid headaches. But lack of aspirin is not the cause of headaches.

Two powerful corporate forces were behind the change to drug treatment rather than talking therapy. One was Big Pharma, the drug companies, whose role in AIDS I discuss in more detail in Chapter Nine. Psychiatric drugs were particularly important to Big Pharma because so many people took them for so many years. That made the market for psychiatric drugs much bigger than the market for short-term, acute physical illnesses.

The other corporations who pushed the biological model and drug treatment were the health insurance companies. Talking cures were enormously expensive. Even hospital stays with drugs were expensive. In the 1980s the insurance companies gradually cut out the talking cures. By the 1990s they were cutting hospital stays to a matter of two or three days wherever possible. Many mental hospitals were closed. The mentally troubled who came to the emergency room were turned away with kind words and a prescription. The rich continued going to therapists.

The shift to the biological model has been so complete that many liberal people reading what I have written will say, 'But of course bipolar disorder is biological. Doesn't he know that?'

I don't. I do know it involves great suffering, and drugs often help. Opium helps too, as it does for many kinds of sadness. That does not mean sadness is biological.

I'm not saying, either, that talking cures usually work. What I am saying is that in 1970 most liberal people in America thought mental illness had social causes. By 2000 most of them thought it was caused by biological illness. The psychiatrists came to agree, for if they did not the insurance companies would not authorise any treatment at all for their patients.

There were similar shifts in feeling about Attention Deficit Disorder in children. This had previously been known as 'naughty boys who can't sit still in class and are probably bored to death'. It was now obviously a biological disease caused by? At this point they began guessing – maybe food additives. In any case, attention deficit can be managed with very strong drugs. Many parents had known for generations that strong drugs will make naughty or unhappy children quiet. We were, however, reluctant to give them to our children. It is noticeable that in the middle of the War on Drugs, millions and millions more adults and children are being legally given mood-altering drugs.

The focus on biology also appeared in other contexts, including the growing numbers of Twelve Step programmes that sprang from Alcoholics Anonymous. The strength of AA, and it has changed many people's lives, comes from a community of drinkers and ex-drinkers who do not condescend, but offer equal fellowship. Yet with AA also came the idea that alcoholism is an individual, biological condition, for which, once again, there is no medical test. This ignored the long understood fact that people tend to drink heavily because they're unhappy.

Of course, one reason AA helped people was that it insisted the individual had to change. This is true of all compulsive suffering. It is also true that it's easier with a steady job, health insurance and a roof over your head.

Women's problems in relationships, too, are now blamed on biology, and natural differences between men and women. *Women Who Love Too Much* was an influential bestseller, as if what was wrong with the world was too much love. At its core is an argument that it's your fault if men treat you badly.[26] Similarly, a series of books argued that 'Women are from Venus', the goddess of love, and 'Men are from Mars', the old god of war. These are very old stereotypes indeed, and again the troubles people have in love were put down to their differences.[27]

In every American bookstore, there were sections for business success books and emotional self-help books. These two kinds of books were remarkably similar. They were the same size, same format, same number of pages and had similar bullet points. The business books taught how to compete. The emotional ones taught how to cope with the consequences of living with competitive, guarded people, or being one yourself. The self-help books usually suggested that if you pull yourself together emotionally, you too could succeed. Both sets of books were clearly directed at ordinary people, not the rich.

In a world without talking cures, these books were useful to many people. But almost all of them concentrate on how you can relate to other people to your best advantage. Very few suggest that consistent kindness and decency will make it more likely you will eventually find love. And that even if you don't, the world will be a better place for what you've done.

I am not saying that there are simple social solutions to the problems of distressed people. I worked as a counsellor for years. I am well aware that, in Freud's phrase, at best the achievement of therapy is to return desperate people to ordinary human suffering.

The emphasis on biology and individual failure did have a resonance with people. Most of the bad things that happen to Americans took a statistical form. Working-class people are more likely to be alcoholics, drug addicts, unemployed, go on welfare, die early, go to prison, kill themselves, smoke, get fat, get divorced, go crazy, rape someone, abuse their children and commit violent crimes. The more difficult your circumstances, the more likely you are to find yourself in one of these bad situations. All these things also happen to middle-class people and the rich, just not as often.

When any of these things happens to a person, they tend to blame themselves. Everyone knows that people in very similar situations may go down one particular road and others do not. Many people can see how they could so easily have ended in a disastrous place. Others can see how they got out. Explaining these differences in terms of the person, character, body, and the details of their loves and life experiences seems to make sense. But the statistical likelihood that these things will happen in your life has everything to do with your social circumstances.

In short, in the 1980s and 90s Americans were told to blame themselves, not society and not the rich. What that actually meant was that you should blame other people for the mess they made of their lives. Everyone knew it took individual courage to surmount your problems. This need for courage became the excuse for perpetuating the situation.

7 | Globalisation

Let's turn to a global perspective now. From 1980 on, the American ruling class was trying to solve the problem of falling industrial profits by squeezing Americans. At the same time, and just as important to them, they were trying to squeeze more profit from the workers around the world.

I use the word 'globalisation' to describe this strategy.[1] The word can cause confusion. When some writers refer to globalisation, they are suggesting that global economic integration is recent, and that governments and unionised workers have become unimportant. I don't agree.[2]

Global integration is old. A hundred years ago much of Africa and Asia was European colonial territory. The US has dominated Latin America for 150 years. It was only in about 1990 that international trade flows reached the peak of 1914. Mass European migration to the Americas and the African slave trade began five centuries ago.

Governments still matter. It is true that of the one hundred largest economies in the world, 51 are corporations and only 49 are countries. But the 23 largest economies are all countries. Turkey is number 23. The largest corporation, General Motors, is number 24. AT&T is smaller than the Czech Republic, Texaco is smaller than Algeria.[3]

Moreover, most of the major multinational corporations make the majority of their sales in their home country. The pattern of wars shows us that Texaco and Exxon would be helpless without the US. In other countries, too, corporations need national governments to push through the policies they want. When there is a riot against the IMF, the army arrives. Every time there's a strike, in every country in the world, the police turn up at the picket line.

There are now more industrial workers, and more union members, in the world than there were in 1970. Globally, wage-workers outnumber peasants. The majority of the world's population lives in urban areas. Among the predominantly urban and wageworking countries are Iraq, Iran, Turkey, Saudi Arabia, Egypt, South Africa, South Korea, plus all of Latin America and all of Europe.

In short, when I speak of globalisation, I don't mean an entirely new world. What I mean, instead, is a conscious attempt, led by the American ruling class, to restructure the world economy.

This policy has two sides. First, the US ruling class tries to increase the share of global income going to the corporations and reduce the share of working people. Second, they try to increase the share going to American corporations, as against other corporations.

The rich and powerful in France, China or Brazil like it when globalisation squeezes their own working people. But they dislike it when their own corporations are edged out by US pressure. However, the whole project of globalisation has been presented to the world as a package. American domination, the establishment thinkers argue, goes hand in hand with the domination of the market. In Margaret Thatcher's memorable phrase, 'there is no alternative'. This produces a deep ambivalence among the politicians and the rich in every country. One moment they support the American-led World Trade Organization. The next moment they criticise the American occupation of Iraq. The week after that, they are trying to raise the pension age in their own country and arranging a friendly meeting with the American president.

The bottom line for ruling classes in all the major countries, though, is that they face falling profits. This is not just an American problem. It affects Western Europe, Eastern Europe, Canada, Japan, Latin America and South Africa. It is not clear if it also affects China and India, but their ruling classes are now behaving as if it does. The rest of Africa is in such serious economic trouble the question is academic. So all the ruling classes grasp at American plans to restore profits.

Falling profits and open markets have accelerated competition. The company or the country that loses the race increasingly goes to the wall. Inequality has steadily increased since the world economy first went down in 1973. Every sort of inequality grows – between CEOs and workers in the US, between the rich and the workers in Brazil, between the US and Brazil, between Brazil and Bolivia. The logic of the system forces ruling classes everywhere to support inequality.

Since the fall of the Soviet Union in 1989 the US has been the world's only superpower, overwhelmingly dominant in military terms. However, the US rulers have had one great weakness. In 1945 the US accounted for more than half of the world's industrial production. By 2003 they accounted for about 21 per cent. In economic terms, the countries of the European Union are an equal force. The US has to worry that they might combine into a new superpower.

East Asia presents a slightly different picture. The Japanese and Chinese economies are both smaller than the American, and Japan has been stagnant since the early 1990s. But the Chinese economy is growing, and the American government worries that an economic alliance of China and Japan could create another superpower. So the US has been involved in a constant balancing act, emphasising their military might, while always looking over their shoulder.

The project of inequality and US domination did not spring full blown from the mind of an economist in 1973. It has steadily gathered pace for 30 years, with every victory for inequality encouraging the rich to think more confidently and creatively about further inequality. For the US, by the 1990s global inequality had restored between a quarter and a half of the profits lost. In the rest of the world, however, inequality had at best kept profits from falling further. The pressure does not let up.

The great majority of world trade is between the rich countries. Most international investment goes from one rich country to another, and the great majority of global profits are made there.

So restructuring the rich industrial countries matters most to the American government and transnational corporations.

However, the majority of people live in the poor countries of the world. There too profit follows its logic. And the consequences of economic failure are far worse for workers and farmers who have little to start with.

The ideal of globalisation

To understand the logic of globalisation, we have to see the process as a whole. A good way to do this is to consider a sort of ideal economic policy that guides American CEOs and shows how they would like to see the world go. In some countries, like New Zealand, Chile and Britain, most of this ideal has been achieved. In others, like France, Syria and Germany, some aspects of the package has been achieved, but key parts remain in the planning stage.

The globalisation project starts with tax and spending policy. Corporate taxes are cut. Sales taxes that bear hardest on the poor are raised. The national budget should be balanced. Social spending on health, education, housing, public transport, unemployment pay and welfare should be reduced. In the richer countries, the largest single government expense is usually pensions. The level of the pension should be lowered, and the age at which pensions start should be raised. In many poor countries the government subsidises the prices of basic foods, cooking oil, heating fuel, and fertiliser for farmers. These subsidies must be reduced and if possible eliminated.

Another part of the global project to raise profits is for the governments to charge for anything they still provide. That includes dentists, hospitals, midwives, universities, secondary schools, primary schools, libraries, swimming pools, cheap housing, driving on the roads, national parks, legal aid and museums. Ideally, these charges should be high enough to cover the cost of the system. This is often politically impossible. But lower charges will at least deter many people from sending the girl in the family to school or having a baby in hospital, and that will save the government money.

Then there is privatisation. Until the 1970s in many parts of Western Europe, Latin America and Asia the government owned some or all of the companies that controlled oil, gas, electricity, water, railways, buses, airlines, airports, mines, banks, the post, telephones, steel, shipbuilding, arms manufacture, prison, radio and television. In some countries the government also owned car factories and various other industries. In communist countries the government owned most industry. In the ideal project to raise profit, all these industries, in every country, must be turned into private companies and sold off on the stock market. This is typically done at a price well below their value, so banks and dealers can make a quick profit. The government also often pays off all the industry's debt before it is sold, so as not to hurt the profits of the new owners.

Some of these companies, like airlines, telephones and electricity, have always been profitable. Others, like the railways, have historically made a loss. In that case, the new private owners are promised a public subsidy to guarantee their profits.

The government makes money on these privatisations in the first year. After that, they lose the money that would have come in. But overall private profit in the whole system has risen.

Once an industry or service has been privatised, price increases are easier. If the local council puts your rent up, you can demonstrate outside the council meeting and vote your local councillors out. If a private railway company puts up fares, it is far more difficult to get at the CEO than a government minister. Cuts in jobs and wages are easier for a privatised company, too. The moment of privatisation can be the moment the union is broken.

Some services are politically very difficult to privatise completely. This is the case with hospitals, schools, police, the military, social work and tax collecting. The solution is to honeycomb the sector with subcontractors. For instance, some hospitals will be publicly owned and privately managed. Some will be charities. Some will be private. All three kinds compete with each other for contracts to provide parts of the service. All three drive down wages. At the same time, the government makes sure that the subcontractor's profit is effectively guaranteed.

To allow this sort of subcontracting, the public sector over-all is restructured to look like a private business. There must be purchasers, who put out contracts, and suppliers, who provide them. There is a whole array of checklists, targets and criteria. Meanwhile, the professionals who once ran the service are broken. The consultant doctors, matrons, professors, judges and generals may be conservative in their politics, but they have dedicated their lives to providing a service. The point now is not that service, but profit. The professionals will only get in the way. So, often before privatisation, the government brings in a new generation of managers whose value to the system is precisely that they do not understand the industry, and do not care.

Subcontracting is particularly important for the rate of profit. This is because profits have fallen hardest in manufacturing industry, where fixed investment is a very large and rising part of costs. In hospitals, schools and social work, fixed-capital investment is still small, and most of the cost comes from human labour, which can be squeezed. If the corporations in a country as a whole can take on a lot of this low fixed-investment work, the average rate of profit will increase, although at considerable cost to the workers.

From the point of view of the CEOs, subcontracting favours American companies. America has historically been the country where this sort of complex public-private mixture is most advanced. So American companies are well placed to put in bids. Privatisation and subcontracting also require a uniform bidding and target system across a whole industry. For that you need an enormous amount of centralised paperwork that seems pointless to the workers who have to fill it in. But standard targets and bids save money for the subcontractors, and they favour large multinational bidders over those from small local firms.

However, if American companies are to benefit, the whole national financial system has to be deregulated before privatisation. If American companies can't bid, they won't be part of the action. In the 1970s many countries had laws restricting foreign ownership of land or business. Some allowed foreigners only a part share, some of the restrictions applied only to certain industries, and some ruled foreigners out of certain sectors altogether. In the new global system, the rules that protect local capitalists have to go.

Another element in the new system was the abolition of currency control. Well into the 1980s many countries still had regulations about how much of their currency could be taken out of the country. The central bank often watched all transactions into and out of the currency, and sometimes put a small tax on them. Now American multinationals need to get their money in and out of the country quickly with no fuss. Indeed, the rich and corporations in many countries, like Japan, Britain and Mexico, are also now investing much of their money abroad, particularly in the United States. They too must be able to move their money without creating a stir.

Historically, socialist and nationalist regimes in many countries had taken over foreign companies, especially the most profitable. So American and multinational companies needed new rules to protect global investment. Now no privatisation by any government could be taken back into the public sector. Nor could there be any new nationalisation. The new rules provided protection against changes in the laws of individual countries. An international disputes procedure took precedence over national courts. If countries refused to join this international agreement, they could be locked out of world trade.

Again, until the 1970s many countries had supported local industries with high taxes on goods coming into the country. In the new globalisation that had to go, so that American, European and Japanese products could dominate world markets. American controls on imports and customs duties stayed, however, to protect American industry and agriculture. The rhetoric of globalisation celebrates 'free trade'. The practice protects American investment.

Health and safety regulations cost money. So do environmental controls. Ideally, these should be legally revised or eliminated. When that is politically impossible, there are two strategies pioneered by the Reagan administration and copied around the world. One is to appoint environment ministers and other regulators from the polluting industries, confident that they won't enforce the rules. The other is to cut the number of health and safety and environmental inspectors.

Finally, weakening the unions was central from 1980 on. Privatisation helped, because in many poor countries the public sector unions had always been the most powerful. In rich countries, private sector unions like the car workers had traditionally been powerful but mass unemployment and factory closures had already weakened them. By the 1980s, the public sector was the centre of union strength in most rich countries too.

Labour laws in each country were rewritten to make picketing harder and firing workers easier. Government and private employers were encouraged to hire on temporary and part-time contracts. Limits on working hours were ignored, as in the US, where 12-hour days spread through much of industry.

Set piece confrontations like the American air traffic controllers strike were important in several countries. In 1984 the British government provoked a strike by the miners, regarded by everyone as the strongest group of workers in the country. The miners were defeated after 13 months on strike. Their very tenacity convinced other workers that if the miners couldn't win, there was no point in fighting. In India, over a million textile workers in Bombay (now Mumbai) went on strike in 1981. Poor to begin with, they struggled on for 15 months before eating defeat. In the years after the strike, to increase the humiliation, most Bombay textile mills closed, just as most British mines closed after the miners strike. In both countries, the confidence of the labour movement had still not fully recovered 20 years later.[4]

In some countries where the unions had been particularly strong in the 1970s, the ruling class reacted with military coups, imprisonment and sometimes death squads that tamed the unions for a generation. This was the case in El Salvador, Chile, Poland, China, Turkey and Argentina. In other countries, the ruling class was not confident enough to go for confrontation. In some, like South Africa, Brazil and South Korea, the unions won important confrontations. In many poor countries unions were expanding even as they shrank in many rich countries. But everywhere workers were told over and over, there is no alternative. Buckle down or your job will move. Everywhere, high levels of unemployment encouraged fear. And everywhere, every day, the corporations and the governments tried to raise profits.

The 1980s, debt, the IMF and the World Bank

The US government and corporations implemented their strategy in the poor countries through the International Monetary Fund (IMF) and the World Bank. The IMF and the Bank were founded in 1944, but only became really important in the 1970s. They are international bodies, with representation from most of the countries of the world. However, like the UN, they are dominated by the United States. The IMF and the World Bank both have their headquarters in Washington, as the UN has in New York. This is not coincidence. The US controls the UN though a veto on the Security Council. Voting on the councils of the IMF and the World Bank is by the money each country contributes. The US has 17.5 per cent of the votes, and it takes only 15 per cent for a veto.

The IMF's job is to loan money to countries when their currency crashes or they cannot repay their debts. Since 1980 the IMF have loaned to most of the poor countries, but to no rich country since 1982.

Because it is harder to make profits since 1973, it is harder to repay loans. So companies and countries do what anyone in debt does – they borrow more. That puts them further in debt, and they have to borrow even more. The IMF has become important because debt has expanded steadily in all parts of the world.

This process is strongest not in the poor countries, but in the United States. The foreign debt of the American government and corporations is vastly greater than the foreign debt of any other country. So far, however, the US has held onto its position as the dominant economic power in the world. That means corporations and rich people around the world are prepared to lend money to the US and keep the debt rolling over. At that moment when the US ceases to be the dominant power, however, the dollar will also cease to be the dominant currency. Then the US debts will come due and the American economy collapse. This is a terrifying prospect not just for American corporations, but for all the other ruling classes in the world. The great fear is that the world is now so integrated that a financial crash in America would spread around the world.

This means that since 1980, every time a major corporation, bank or country seems unable to meet its debts, the American ruling class, and the ruling classes of the world, have been afraid that each particular failure to meet debts could easily radiate through the system. A crash in Mexico could lead to crashes in several New York banks, leading to crashes in American auto corporations, leading to crashes in European banks and the Japanese stock market, and so on. This is roughly what produced the Great Depression of the 1930s. But the overhang of debt in the world system is now much greater than it was in 1929. A crash would be far more catastrophic.

So the decline in profits leads to a rise in debt throughout the system. The decline also leads to an increase in lending and financial speculation. Precisely because the New York banks can't make much money lending to American industry, they lend to unreliable payers in the poor countries or put their money into currency and other speculation all over the world.

I am not arguing that the American economy is about to crash in a capitalist Armageddon. The expansion of debt has continued for 30 years, longer and deeper than anyone imagined it could. It may well continue for many more years. But the point is that the fear it could fall apart is always there for the ruling classes. So they both stoke their own debts and enforce debt in the poor countries.

Enforcing debt in the poor countries is what the IMF does. I will take the example of Latin America in the 1980s. Until the 1970s, most Latin American governments had tried to build independent national industries. They charged high custom duties ('tariffs') on industrial goods coming into the country, so local factories had a captive market. However, by the 1970s the rate of profit across the board in Latin American industry was falling. The protected economies were inefficient, charging much higher prices than the world market. In industry after industry, the cost of modern machines and integrated modern production was rising. That meant that even the national market of a big country like Mexico or Argentina was not big enough to justify investment to make industry competitive on a world scale.

The governments and ruling classes in Latin America decided they would have to stop protecting their local markets, and build bigger and more efficient industries directed at export. In return, they would have to allow cheap industrial goods from other countries in.

In the 1970s Latin American businesses and governments were able to borrow to expand their industries. The New York banks had to lend to somebody, anybody, and gambled that the Latin American industries would take off. In 1980 the US economy, the Latin American economies, and much of the world, went into recession.

Suddenly Latin American companies had trouble paying their debts. And because they weren't exporting enough, their currencies were in trouble. It worked like this. If Mexico doesn't sell many goods to the US, Mexican companies don't have many dollars. They still need to buy US goods. But New York banks don't need Mexican pesos. So too many pesos are trying to buy dollars. The dollar becomes worth more pesos. But Mexican companies borrowed from New York in dollars. Now their local income is in devalued pesos. They can't pay their New York debts.

Moreover, as the world went into recession in 1980, the American government was making banks raise the basic rate of interest in the States from 7 per cent to 16 per cent. Latin American companies, too, had to pay the new high rate of interest on any new loans. So they couldn't roll over their loans by taking out new loans. They couldn't pay, and their currencies began to crash.

At this point the International Monetary Fund stepped in. During 1982 and 1983 the IMF loaned money to 17 of the 22 countries in Latin America. By 1991 two more had borrowed, with only Colombia, Paraguay and the boycotted Cuba left out.[5] The rhetoric of IMF policy was that a 'structural adjustment policy' would restore profitability so the economy could recover. The practical consequences were permanent damage to the borrowing economies.

Most of the debt was owed by companies, but the IMF only loaned money to governments. So the IMF insisted the governments take over the debt of companies who could not pay. In doing this, they were protecting the American and European banks who had loaned the money.

The IMF would loan millions, and often billions, of dollars to each borrowing government. The loan was never as big as the debts, however. The banks were much bigger lenders than the IMF. But a loan from the IMF gave a country the stamp of approval from the United States Treasury, the banks and international capitalism. It made the country credit worthy.

There were, however, conditions. These conditions were set out in a letter from the borrowing government to the IMF. The IMF actually wrote the letter, and then sent a representative to the country to get the government to sign. The letter always contained very specific promises about government policy. So many civil service jobs would be cut, the subsidy on corn would be cut by so much, so many hospitals would be closed, the labour laws would be changed, the pension age would be raised and so on.

The IMF also insisted on raising interest rates and devaluing the local currency. Both these measures reduced the amount of money local people had in their pockets to buy imports. The IMF hoped that the country would then import fewer goods and have more dollars left over to pay their debts.

The consequence of all these 'structural adjustment policies' was to make most people poorer. That meant they spent less and there was less of a market in the country for goods. Just as Keynesian measures stimulated an American economy in recession, so the IMF measures de-stimulated the economy of the poor country.

It was obvious to everyone outside the IMF and the US Treasury that IMF measures didn't work. The borrowing countries and all the NGOs kept saying so. But this missed the point. The measures worked by taking money from working people to give to banks. It was the economics of the Sheriff of Nottingham, not Robin Hood. These measures hurt the possibility of development in the local economy. But after all, it was

The World Bank's 'mission' was to loan money for development projects. They maintained touchy-feely representatives in each country, and talked loudly about gender, environment and sustainability. However, their central tool was a Sectoral Adjustment Loan. This meant the borrowing country got the loan if they agreed to change part of their economic policy in detail.

From about 1987 on, the World Bank and the IMF backed each other up. If a country wanted an IMF loan, they had to agree to the Bank's conditions, and vice versa. And now the lenders had a much more detailed set of plans. All of them were devoted to getting profits back up.

They still wanted to cut public spending and devalue the currency. Now, though, privatisation was central. That went with deregulation, 'labour flexibility' and 'tax reform'. The World Bank also concentrated on restructuring health and education. They had a particular obsession with introducing school fees.

In health, the conventional wisdom in the early 1980s, backed by the UN's World Health Organization, was to extend primary care by local doctors in poor countries and rural areas. This would reach the neglected. When the World Bank intervened in health later in the decade, they reversed this, insisting that aid money and government spending favour the big hospitals in the cities. In many countries the poor couldn't get into these hospitals, even when they were theoretically free.

These policies hit Africa hardest. By the 1990s, new industrial investment had largely dried up there. Paying the interest on debt took up more and more of a government's budget, sometimes over half. Unemployment in most countries in the regions was running 20 to 50 per cent by the 1990s. Sub-Saharan Africa had 10 per cent of the world's population, but 40 per cent of the world's abjectly poor. Figures for the annual spending on health per person in 1990 include private spending:

US	$2,763
UK	$1,039
Zimbabwe	$42
Kenya	$16

Ghana	$14
Malawi	$11
Nigeria	$9
Uganda	$6
Mozambique	$5
Tanzania	$4[8]

Spending on health in the US was 460 times the rate in Uganda. Of course doctors and nurses were cheaper in Uganda. But these figures conceal all the Ugandans for whom health expenditure was zero.

Life expectancy fell, squeezed by health cuts, poverty, war and Aids. The really striking statistic, though, was the median age at death. If the median age is 20, it means that half the people who die are that age or younger, and half are that age or older. Throughout Africa there are many more children than old people, so many of the dead are children. Here is the median age of death in 1990 for a representative range of countries:

All industrial countries	75 years old
Zimbabwe	26 years old
Senegal	15 years old
Zambia	11 years old
Ivory Coast	10 years old
Ghana	7 years old
Tanzania	5 years old
Malawi	4 years old
Uganda	4 years old
Angola	3 years old
Mozambique	2 years old[9]

The big socialist parties in Latin America and the nationalist and socialist regimes in Africa mounted little opposition to globalisation. In most of Latin America the resentment burst out in what came to be called 'IMF riots'. In Caracas, Venezuela, for instance, the government doubled the petrol price overnight in 1989. James Ferguson takes up the story:

The Monday morning of 27 February 1989 started as usual for most of the hundreds of thousand of Venezuelans who live in the shanty towns encircling Caracas ... Making their way down the precipitous paths and stairways which wind between the hillside shacks, they headed for the nearest main road and the bus ...

As people flagged down buses, the drama began. Bus drivers angrily insisted that they had had to double fares over the weekend because [President] Perez had doubled the price of petrol. Students were told their discount cards were no longer valid. The first violence erupted at the Nuevo Circo bus station in the city center. Rocks and bricks were thrown, roadblocks went up, buses were set on fire.

Within hours Caracas was gripped by insurrection. People streamed down from the slums to help themselves to food, clothes, and anything else from the shops whose windows they smashed. Some police and troops tried to intervene. Others actively helped the looters ... Grateful slum dwellers passed soldiers presents through the smashed-in shop windows. People careered along the main streets of Caracas, pushing supermarket trolleys crammed with loot or dragging entire beef carcasses from butchers' shops. As news of the caracazo reached other towns in Venezuela, similar riots broke out.

Eventually, on Wednesday, a massive military presence retook control of Caracas. By then, many shops and entire streets were in ruins. The army arrested thousands of people as they swept through the shantytowns searching for stolen goods. In the course of the following week, perhaps 1,500 people died at the hands of the military, although the government admitted to only 287. Soldiers opened fire without warning in poor [neighbourhoods], people who appeared suddenly at windows were shot dead by nervous troops.[10]

The Caracas rioters were defeated, as they were in most of Latin America. They were a movement of fury from below, like the rioters in Los Angeles. But like the people in LA, there was no political voice speaking for them on the national stage. Here too the question is what had happened to the political opposition?

The old opposition

By 1989 there was the general support for globalisation among ruling classes and professional economists throughout the poor countries. Equally striking was the weakness of the established opposition in the poor countries, Europe and of course the US. Bill Clinton's roll over for the bond traders was not exceptional.

Let's start with Western Europe. With the exception of Thatcher's Britain, the cuts in the 1970s and 1980s were not on the same scale as in Latin America and Africa. But almost everywhere in Western Europe there was a marked increase in unemployment, a weakening of the unions and a slow attack on the welfare state. And everywhere the old socialist, communist and labour parties went along with this.

These parties had built the welfare states of Western Europe after World War II. During the years of the long boom they had steadily expanded social spending. They were the parties that wanted a better life for working-class people. Simultaneously, trade union membership expanded. In many countries, like Germany, there were regular national negotiations between the union leaders, the employers and the government. The leaders of these unions were loyal to one or another of the workers' parties – the socialists, labour or the communists. So were the majority of union members. Even the communists, many of whom had once been revolutionaries, came to accept the capitalist system.

Then, from 1973 on, came international recession and high unemployment. Suddenly, for no reason anyone could explain, the capitalist system wasn't working. The socialist politicians and the union leaders had always argued that the workers should get more of the cake. Then there had been enough cake to go round. Now there wasn't. Union members and voters were losing their jobs. Union leaders and politicians had a choice. They could junk the capitalist system. Or they could try to make capitalism work in their own country.

However, this didn't really appear to them as a choice. Revolution had become unthinkable. So the politicians had to make the economy work. They had to get profits back up in France, Britain, Germany, Italy and the rest. So they cut spending, deregulated and broke strikes like the elite in the US and everywhere else.

Usually the politicians of the left began doing this with a heavy heart. They were, above all else, confused, and felt helpless in a sea of economic troubles. The leaders of the unions were torn. They were under pressure from angry members to do something. But they personally supported the parties of the left. Tightening up the capitalist system was the only alternative they could see. And they felt that any big strikes against a socialist government could only strengthen the right.

The politicians and union leaders of the left behaved pretty much the same way out of office, too. Again, this was because they couldn't see an alternative, and they wanted to present themselves as the next government.

On one level, they were quite right. There was no way to fix the economy of any one country just by becoming the government. In an international system, it takes an international movement to change things. After the Seattle demonstrations in 1999, such a movement began to grow. But in 1980 almost everyone thought another world was impossible.

At first, the socialist parties were reluctant apostles of globalisation. But as the 1980s went on, the experience of doing globalisation changed the leaders of these parties. In life, people adjust their views and values to fit what they have to do. This obviously affected government ministers. Probably more important was the effect on local activists.

In the 1980s I lived in the London borough of Islington. At the start of the decade, our local left-wing Labour council was nationally known as 'Red Islington'. The elected local councillors, however, had to deal with a national government controlled by Margaret Thatcher's conservatives. That government consistently cut the money going to Islington and other councils. The council, in turn, was left with discretion to choose which local services to cut.

In 1980 they tried to close my local library. The librarians had a union. They mobilised readers, both adults and children, to invade a meeting of the council library committee. There were 90 of us. While my two-year-old Siobhan and her friends played noisily under the council table, I gave an impassioned speech telling the councillors to be ashamed of themselves. They were. You could see it on their faces. They voted to leave the library standing.

Ten years later, still under a Conservative government, the Labour councillors moved to close another local library. This time they were impervious to shame. In between, they had spent years cutting. They had faced two strikes by the council union. When I listened to councillors in private, it was clear they hated the council union with a personal bitterness. That came, I think, from guilt. These local councillors had not joined the Labour Party to make life worse for working people. But that's what they had done. In the process, they had become cynical, ready for Tony Blair and 'New Labour'.

A similar process was going on all over Europe and Latin America. It was affecting nationalist regimes in Africa and Asia too. Some of these regimes were led by men who had always wanted to get their own piece of the action. Others were led by people who had once believed that the struggle against colonialism was part and parcel of the struggle for social justice. By 1990 almost no one in Africa, outside South Africa, believed that. By 1995 the new rulers of South Africa had joined their continental brothers in administering globalisation.

The socialist and Third World nationalist parties were rotting from the top down. That hollowed them out at the base, as more and more local activists stopped going to meetings or left in disgust.

The growing inequality was particularly marked in many of the poor countries. Mexico and Brazil might be in economic trouble, but the top fifth of society were doing very nicely indeed. All you had to do was stand in New York's JFK airport and watch the professional families and the rich stand in line for the flight back to Caracas, surrounded by box after box of consumer goods. In every country in the world some people were enjoying the new inequality. And some of them were leading members and activists in the socialist parties.

The unions felt the pressure of the socialist parties moving right. Equally, they were suffering with privatisation and set piece defeats. As the local activists of the unions felt weaker, the national leaders began to argue that nothing could be really changed.

Then came 1989, and the fall of the Soviet Union and the communist governments of Eastern Europe. The brutality of these regimes became obvious to all when East German workers demolished the Berlin Wall with their bare hands. The people of these countries hated their rulers, and said so.

I agreed with them. But by 1992 I realised how much I had underestimated the place of the Soviet Union in the hearts of the left. The communist parties of the West, Latin America and the Middle East were obviously thrown into turmoil. But the faith in the Soviet Union went much deeper and further than that. Left-wing labour activists in Britain, rank and file socialists in France, and many others, now accepted that the fall of the Soviet Union proved there was no alternative. This was a political proposition you could only accept if, somewhere deep inside, you had once believed the Soviet model was an alternative.

This political confusion was to cost the left, and working people, dear in the next few years. The American project dominated the world of ideas now. And the American military was about to dominate the world. The next chapter deals with war, and then Chapter 9 returns to economic globalisation.

8 | War

American economic domination could not proceed without American military power. After 1945, the US applied to the rest of the world the method of control it had long used in Latin America. In normal times, this meant a partnership between American corporations and the local ruling class. Sometimes, this happened through an elected democracy. When opposition became too strong there was a military coup, supported by both the American embassy and the local ruling class. In some situations it was necessary to send in the American army to restore the local ruling class to power.

The American elite faced significant constraints, however. The US could not invade large countries like Brazil and China. In Western Europe, the US had arrived as an army and maintained large garrisons. But they were only able to do so because the threat of the Soviet Union persuaded European ruling classes to keep the Americans in place. Where possible, they avoided war in large industrial powers, and instead fought proxy wars in poor countries.

From 1975 on, the US ruling class faced a second constraint: the 'Vietnam syndrome'. Most Americans thought they had been lied to about the Vietnam War. The generals were afraid of a repeat of the revolt of the troops. So both ordinary Americans and the generals were deeply reluctant to become involved in another war. Since 1975 we have repeatedly seen the odd situation of civilians in the US State Department pressing for military intervention, while the Pentagon resists.

Liberal opinion among politicians and commentators in America constantly says this Vietnam syndrome exists because ordinary Americans don't want to die for their country. What stops them, it is said, is the prospect of body bags coming home. The real situation is more complicated. The American people have traditionally been reluctant to go to war. In 1916 they voted for the anti-war candidate Woodrow Wilson, who promptly took them into World War I. In 1940 Roosevelt ran for president promising not to join World War II, and then did so after Pearl Harbor. In 1952 Americans voted for General Eisenhower, who promised to end the war in Korea and actually did so. In 1964 they voted against Barry Goldwater, the pro-war candidate. But the winner, Lyndon Johnson, himself promptly began the Vietnam War. In 1968 Americans voted for Richard Nixon, who promised to end the Vietnam War and didn't. This is not a bellicose population

But Americans have fought bravely, and died, in many wars. What created the mass opposition to Vietnam was a widespread feeling that the war was cruel. An institute in Chicago continues to poll Americans on the issue. In 1998, 63 per cent still said the war was 'fundamentally wrong'.[1]

Since Vietnam, working Americans have passed on to their children and grandchildren a contradictory set of ideas. Patriotism is good, and we should support our country. What our country does in the world is probably right. If the Air Force is bombing somewhere, and no American pilots are killed, and we don't hear much about it, maybe we can back our country. But don't trust the politicians in Washington. And don't die for them.

For the politicians, the bombings of New York and Washington on 9/11 offered a cause Americans might be willing to die for. For a period, that seemed to work. The rising opposition to the occupation of Iraq among both ordinary Americans and serving troops, however, suggests the Vietnam syndrome is still there.

Since 1975 the US has been involved in a series of wars. Until 2001, many of these were proxy wars fought by someone else, as in Angola and Afghanistan. Or they were small set piece wars like Grenada and Somalia, where American troops were welcomed, and could appear as liberators or humanitarians. These were designed to rehabilitate the image of war for Americans.

The American ruling class has also pursued a steady policy of rewriting the history of the Vietnam War. This has centred on the image of the veteran. The overwhelming majority of veterans returned from Vietnam opposed to the war. They faced high levels of unemployment and uncertain futures. They felt ignored, forgotten and useless.

The ruling class played on this sense of loss. In 1980 they began to build a new version of what had happened to the veterans. The veterans, they said, had loved their country and their buddies. When they came home, they had been dishonoured. Protestors demonstrated against them and hippies spat on them. In this new version of history, the liberals hated their own country and their own soldiers. The Army had only lost because the politicians in Washington had been reluctant to really fight the war. So, the new history concluded, we should honour our forgotten brothers. And implicitly, but not said aloud, then we can go to war again.

Stories about spitting on veterans appeared in the newspapers. In seemingly liberal movies like *Coming Home* and *Forrest Gump*, protestors demonstrated against returning troops. In 1985 Jerry Lembcke, a college professor and a veteran himself, began investigating the stories.[2] When he went back to the papers of the time, including both the right-wing ones and the anti-war ones, he found not one single instance of demonstrations or spitting against returning troops. He did find protesters demonstrating against troops having to go to Vietnam.

The whole story was made up. It was part of a consistent attempt to contaminate the memory of the protests. To go to war abroad again, the American ruling class had to persuade people that the 60s were a troubled time of upheaval that tore the country apart, something not to be repeated. The lies about the anti-war movement were a part of discrediting the black movement and the women's movement. But the attacks on unions, black people and women were also part of getting America ready to go to war again.

The campaign to change the image of the veteran had some success, even among veterans. But still, in 2000, most veterans' favourite symbol of the war was still the Vietnam

Wall in Washington, one of the least triumphant, saddest and most decent of all the war memorials in the world.

The Vietnam syndrome left American power with a serious problem. They were trying to be a superpower without an army on the ground. Moreover, America was steadily losing economic dominance. Western Europe, Japan and China were gaining. In that situation, the assertion of American military dominance was key. Without troops, there were two solutions: hi-tech war and proxy war. And the US might also try out very small ground wars to see if the American people would warm to them.

Hi-tech war took advantage of the one area where the US was superior. When the US went to war, they used robot technology, satellites and computer-guided missiles that could terrify most enemies into submission. Sometimes, as in the Gulf War in 1991, that was enough. The weakness of hi-tech war arose when the bombs had to be followed by low-tech boots on the sand. Throughout the 1990s, both opponents and supporters of American power emphasised that the US spent more on the military than the next nine countries combined. That was true. But that was money. When it came to troops, several countries, including India and China had larger armies.

Another advantage of hi-tech war in the 1980s was that the Soviet regime tried to match the expenditure, and impoverished their economy. Under Reagan, the American military began their hugely expensive 'Star Wars' project.[3] Ostensibly, this was a programme for satellites in space that could stop an intercontinental missile attack on the US. Behind this, however, was a project to build laser-ray stations on satellites in space. These lasers could be used to target and vaporise buildings and people anywhere on earth. They would be the perfect weapon for attacking a training camp or village in Afghanistan, or a parliament in Paris. If the US became the only laser power in space, they would really rule the world.

After the Soviet Union collapsed in 1989, Star Wars was deemed too expensive. But it was revived by the Bush the younger in 2001. There is still no way to get fuel to a space station in order to power the lasers. The only solution is a nuclear reactor in space. The

American space shuttle has blown up before now. The idea of shooting a whole nuclear reactor into the air is worrying.

The 1970s and 1980s

The first problem after Vietnam was in Southern Africa. Portugal held two large colonies: Angola and Mozambique. For many years the Portuguese army had been fighting Marxist-led guerrillas in both countries. In 1975 the Portuguese army mutinied and brought down the dictatorship that ruled Portugal. The colonial war was over.

South Africa was just south of Angola and Mozambique. The defeat of white power in those colonies brought hope to black people living under apartheid. Demonstrations spread across South Africa, particularly among school children. Washington had several reasons to worry. Angola had oil. South Africa, with considerable foreign investment, was the largest industrial power in Africa. The new Angolan and Mozambique governments were declared Marxists. Nelson Mandela's African National Congress (ANC) was partly funded by the Soviet Union and included the South African Communist Party. The great fear in Washington was that the US might soon lose the whole of Southern Africa to Communism, right after losing Vietnam. With the encouragement of the American government, South Africa invaded Angola in alliance with UNITA, an Angolan right-wing movement. South Africa also funded the right-wing guerrilla force, RENAMO, in Mozambique.

As the South African troops and UNITA advanced north, the leaders of the Soviet Union did something that made Henry Kissinger, the American Secretary of State, furious.[4] The Russians sent Cuban troops into Angola to fight the South Africans. The military tide turned. Kissinger went to the Pentagon and demanded a plan for sending American troops to stop the Cubans. The generals at the Pentagon stalled. Part of the American army was black. Many of the Cuban troops were black. Many American soldiers spoke Spanish. They didn't like apartheid. It was not possible to know in what direction they would point their guns. The Pentagon generals didn't refuse to do what Kissinger ordered, they just didn't do it. The South African Army was eventually driven out of Angola. The US continued to support UNITA, however, and the proxy wars ground on for more than 20 years. No one has counted the cost in dead, wounded, maimed and raped, and in disease and HIV. It has been in the millions.

The next trouble spot was Nicaragua.[5] The US backed the dictator, Somoza. The opposition Sandinista guerrillas were not communists. All of their central leaders had been part of the Catholic youth movement. Their politics came from liberation theology, a new movement in the Catholic Church that combined Christian compassion and socialism.[6]

In 1979 the Nicaraguan people finally turned on Somoza. His regime had embezzled most of the aid money that flowed in after an earthquake. The resistance began rather like an IMF riot, but soon became a full-scale uprising in the working-class neighbourhoods of Managua and other cities. The Sandinistas put themselves at the head of the uprising. Somoza fled.

The Sandinistas were not allied to the Soviet Union, but they were radicals at the head of a workers' uprising. The US government, under Carter and then Reagan, wanted to crush them. The American people, and Congress, would not permit an invasion so soon after Vietnam. So the first task for Washington was to stop the Sandinista example spreading.

Neighbouring El Salvador had more people, and a much bigger working class.[7] A strike movement started in El Salvador almost immediately after Somoza was brought down in Nicaragua. Washington and the ruling class in El Salvador replied with military death squads. They killed thousands of peasant insurgents and trade-union activists. When a friend disappeared, people knew to go to the rubbish dumps outside the city to look for the body. Within months the movement in El Salvador lost momentum, though it took years before it was finally broken in the countryside.

Meanwhile, the Sandinistas in Nicaragua, afraid of American retaliation, did not back the rebels in El Salvador. Instead, they appealed to the dictatorship in Mexico to make peace with the Americans for them. But the US wasn't having it.

Once El Salvador was in hand, the Reagan administration organised the Contras (from the Spanish for counter-revolutionary). The Contras were mercenary guerrillas, funded and armed by Washington, and based in the countries surrounding Nicaragua. Many were veterans of Somoza's National Guard, but some were experienced right-wingers from other Latin American countries. They raided into Nicaragua, causing constant damage, but not substantially eroding support for the Sandinistas.

The CIA was in charge of the Contras, but had problems funding them. The US Congress, wary of another Vietnam, would not authorise money or arms. So the CIA took some of the money illegally from other budgets. The Contras were also encouraged to make money by flying cocaine from Bolivia and Colombia to Central America, and then on to the US. And some of the arms came from Israel, whose government does covert work for Washington.

When the cocaine smuggling by the CIA and the Contras was finally reported in the American media many years later, it caused an outcry.[8] Many African Americans felt it showed the CIA had deliberately introduced crack to wreck the ghettoes. In fact the CIA didn't care. They have a long record of supporting drug dealers in Laos, Vietnam, Central America, Afghanistan and Colombia. In all cases, it's because the CIA is running a covert operation on a limited budget and is in an alliance with right-wing crooks.

In any case, it wasn't really the Contras that broke the Sandinistas. The long war was expensive and sad. But the economic blockade organised by Washington wrecked the Nicaraguan economy. In an attempt to hold the economy together, the Sandinista government itself forbade strikes and broke them with police. As the poor became more desperate, they could see that their leaders were still living well. The Sandinistas held regular elections and in 1989 they lost to the right-wing opposition, who promised an end to the American boycott.[9] Washington had won. The boycott ended, but the Nicaraguan economy remains a disaster today.

The US was also involved in two other proxy wars. In December 1978 communist Vietnam invaded communist

Cambodia and deposed Pol Pot, the leader of the Khmer Rouge. Between 1975 and 1978, Pol Pot's government had murdered at least a 200,000 Cambodians and presided over a famine that killed many more. The Vietnamese army then remained in Cambodia for ten years. The US, under Carter and then Reagan, wanted both revenge for their defeat in Vietnam and to stop the spread of Soviet influence in Southeast Asia. So the CIA, in alliance with the Thai and Chinese governments, provided Pol Pot and the Khmer Rouge with sanctuary in Thai refugee camps, and arms, money and landmines to fight the Vietnamese. In 1987 the Vietnamese Army withdrew and Washington then dumped Pol Pot.

Afghanistan provided a better opportunity to harass the Soviet Union.[10] Until 1978 Afghanistan was ruled by a royal family and a military dictatorship. Popular politics was divided between right-wing Islamists and left-wing communists.[11] The communists won majority support among students, and probably among city people. But most Afghans lived in the countryside, where the communists were weak.

In 1978 a communist coup overthrew the regime. The Soviet Union had not authorised the coup, but the Afghan communists quickly allied themselves with Moscow. Their coup had the support of army officers, but not the conscript soldiers, mostly from farming families. The first acts of the new communist regime were utterly decent: they decreed a law to take land from the big landlords and give it to poor sharecroppers, and a law for women's equality. But the Islamists, with support from the local mullahs and landlords, soon launched an insurrection in the rural areas. By late 1979, 18 months after the communist coup, the Islamist uprising was close to taking power.

In December the Soviet tanks rolled into Kabul. The Russian rulers could not contemplate a victorious Islamist rising against a communist regime that bordered the oil-rich Muslim provinces of the Soviet Union. But the Russian invasion now turned a large majority of Afghans, including most city people and many former communist supporters, against the communists.[12] Russia soon had its own Vietnam. As in Vietnam, the only way to fight a mass guerrilla movement with popular support was with bombs, torture and helicopter gunships. All the figures for the dead are guesses, but between half a million and a million died, mostly civilians. Half the population of rural Afghanistan became refugees in Iran, Pakistan and in the Afghan cities.

Washington faced a dilemma in Afghanistan.[13] As we will see, they were involved in hot and cold wars with Islamists elsewhere in the Middle East. The Afghan fighters were a particularly right-wing and anti-feminist group, and many of them had deep suspicions of the Americans. Their senior leader, Hekmatyar, refused to shake Ronald Reagan's hand. Washington didn't want to be caught supporting an Islamist government. On the other hand, the chance to kill Russians and gain revenge for Vietnam appealed deeply to the CIA and the right. All through the Reagan years there was controversy in the administration, but the CIA and the right gradually won the argument. Together with Saudi Arabian and Pakistani intelligence, the US armed and funded the Islamist Afghans, the Mujahedin.

The Mujahedin could not have fought without outside support. But the Afghan rebels were not simply tools of the CIA. They had mass support inside the country. As in Vietnam, millions of Afghans were willing to risk death to rid the country of the Russian invaders.

As time would show, the Afghan Islamists and the US were only in temporary alliance. As elsewhere, the CIA was on the wrong side in the War on Drugs. The Afghan peasants, under attack from the air, their fields often mined, survived by growing opium for export to Europe and the US as heroin. Many Islamist leaders and Pakistani officers were soon involved in the opium trade.

Saudi Arabian intelligence provided a rich, brave young Saudi, Osama bin Laden, to help the Afghan resistance. Bin Laden was in charge of the volunteers who came from all over the Muslim world, but particularly from Arab countries, to fight alongside the Afghans. His organisation, called Al Qaida, worked closely with the CIA.

After eight years of war the Russians left, defeated, in 1987. Washington, not wishing to support an Islamist regime, withdrew support from the rebels. The leaders of the resistance parties promptly fell out among themselves. Intermittent civil war lasted seven more years, as ex-communist generals and Islamist leaders tried to divide the spoils. Afghans lost all faith in either communism or Islamist politics, though most remained apolitical Muslims. Bin Laden, equally disgusted, left Afghanistan and went home to Saudi Arabia. He had learned, among other things, not to trust the Americans.

Set-piece wars

Nicaragua, Angola and Afghanistan were proxy wars. But there were also two set-pieces in the Reagan–Bush years designed to accustom Americans to war.

The first was Grenada, a small Caribbean island.[14] In 1979 the New Jewel movement took power. They were a mixture of communists, 60s radicals and black power nationalists. New Jewel established friendly relations with Castro's Cuba, but made little change in the daily life of the island. Washington at first made noises, but didn't send troops. That alone was an indication of American weakness at the time.

In 1983 the leaders of the New Jewel movement fell out with each other. One faction took power and arrested Maurice Bishop, the popular leader of the movement. The people of the island replied with a general strike and marched on the prison to free him. The army opened fire, killing dozens, and then executed Bishop. The protesters were horrified. The people of Grenada had not thought of themselves as living in a place where that kind of thing happened. They didn't immediately know what to do.

The Reagan administration did. The US marines invaded. Many islanders welcomed them. Others, suspicious, still had no wish to support the New Jewel movement. Several hundred Cuban construction workers were prepared to fight for several hours, and some died. At least it could pass for a war. Unlike Vietnam, the Americans were welcome and none of them died. It was as good an advertisement for war as you could get.

Somewhat more serious was the American invasion of Panama in 1990.[15] The US needed to retain effective control of the strategic Panama Canal. Noriega, the Panamanian dictator, was making nationalist noises. And he was an important drug dealer, so an invasion of Panama could be part of the War on Drugs. The downside, for Washington, was that Noriega had also been a CIA contact, and was involved in the Contra drug-running to the US. He had links with George Bush the elder, at one time the director of the CIA and, in 1991, the president of the US. That made Noriega an embarrassment, but also a danger if he talked.

The US invasion met little resistance. To turn it into a real war for the television, the Air Force bombed working-class neighbourhoods of Panama City, killing several thousand civilians. When one mass grave was later exhumed, 130 bodies were found inside. The US Army soon captured Noriega, who was taken to a prison in Florida.

The Middle East

The wars we have discussed so far all more or less served their purpose for the US, although several million people died, and Afghanistan, Cambodia, Angola and Mozambique were laid waste. None of these wars, however, erased the memory of Vietnam. And in none of them was Washington able to use ground troops in a serious way. But then, they didn't have to. By contrast, the Middle East presented a far more serious challenge to American dominance.[16]

The Middle East matters because of oil. Oil is the most important fuel of industrial capitalism, and the one thing that almost every industrial country has to import. There are enormous amounts of money to be made. And there is power. Of the 40 largest corporations in the world in 1997, 16 were oil companies or car manufacturers.[17] Five countries in the centre of the Middle East – Saudi Arabia, Iraq, Iran, Kuwait and the United Arab Emirates – control 65 per cent of the known reserves of oil in the world.[18] The power that can cut off that oil, or raise the price to a level rich countries cannot afford, controls the world's industry.

Of these five countries, Saudi Arabia has much the largest reserves and Iran has much the largest population. Iraq, too, matters politically. The smaller oil-producing powers, Kuwait and the Emirates, depend on Saudi and American support to survive. The other Middle Eastern country that really matters is Egypt. Egypt has no oil, but like Iran, it has 60 million people. Egypt is also the traditional home of Arab nationalism and controls the Suez Canal, the main route for oil tankers to Europe.

Until World War II, most of the Middle East was dominated, or directly colonised, by France and Britain. By 1950 most of the region was ruled by kings backed by the old imperial powers. The popular reaction was Arab nationalism. In Egypt, the army officer Gamel Abdul Nasser defied Britain and France to nationalise the foreign owned Suez Canal. Similar nationalist regimes came to power in Algeria, Libya, Yemen, Syria, Iraq and Iran. These nationalist governments mostly took the land from the big landlords and gave it to the small peasants. They threatened, as well, to take over the British, French and American oil companies.

In the 1950s the US replaced France and Britain as the dominant power in the Middle East. Washington soon came to see Arab and Iranian nationalism as the main threat to their control of oil. This nationalism was secular, not Islamic. Of course most nationalists were Muslims in the same way most Americans are Christians. Socialists and communists both supported the nationalists. The communists were particularly strong in Iraq, where they led a successful uprising against the king in 1958. This point is important, because many people write about Middle Eastern politics as if Islam were always the most important thing. It may be now, in some places, but that is new. Fifty years ago it was the secular nationalists who held people's hearts. The Islamists have since become strong because of the failure of the nationalists and the communists.

Three things were central to this failure. First, the nationalists usually came to power in a coup with considerable popular support. But they ruled deeply unequal capitalist economies as a military dictatorship. They broke strikes and used the secret police to quell any opposition. As the years went by, ordinary people lost faith, just as they lost faith in corrupt ex-colonial governments in Asia and Africa.

Second, the communists were often the principled and decent opposition to the nationalists. Sometimes the communists had the support of the majority of workers, but they always followed the lead of the Soviet regime. The Soviets told them to support the nationalists against the Americans. In country after country, the communists passed up the chance to contest for power and were sent to the prisons of the very nationalists they were supporting.

Third, there was Israel.

Israel

Saudi Arabia, not Israel, is the most important country in the Middle East to Washington. The relationship between Israel and the United States is often misunderstood. Many claim that the US will always support Israel because of the Jewish vote and Jewish money in America. But the Jewish vote is small. Most American Jews vote Democrat. The Republicans also support Israel, without hope of the Jewish vote. Most people with money in America are not Jewish. If it becomes necessary to dump Israel for the central purposes of the American empire, Israel will be dumped. Every Israeli government since 1948, whether of the centre or the hard right, has known this.

Before World War II, Zionism, the campaign for a Jewish homeland in Palestine, had minority support among European Jews. Most of them voted socialist or communist. The Holocaust changed that. So did the refusal of Britain and the US on racist grounds to admit most of the Jewish refugees from the Nazis. After all that, it seemed to most European Jews that the Zionists were right – they couldn't trust anybody. Many went to Palestine.

Britain ceded independence to Palestine in 1948. The country was partitioned into a Jewish state, Israel, and an Arab state, Jordan. The Zionist militias wanted a larger share of the old state. They went to war and extended the boundaries through ethnic cleansing – massacring several thousand Palestinian Arabs, enough to persuade most of the rest to flee. The new state of Israel was supported by both the US and the Soviet Union. The neighbouring Arab states either avoided the 1948 war in Palestine or, like Jordan, did little fighting. One consequence of 1948 was several hundred thousand Palestinian refugees in the neighbouring Arab countries. Many have lived in refugee camps ever since.

When Nasser nationalised the Suez Canal in 1956, France, Britain and Israel invaded Egypt. The United States backed Egypt diplomatically and compelled the invaders to withdraw. At that point, in 1956, the US was still concerned with replacing France and Egypt as the dominant power. US support of Egypt and opposition to Israel was crucial in allowing that to happen.

But soon after 1956 Washington decided that the European powers were right – Arab nationalism was the main threat to control of the oil. In 1967 Israel attacked Egypt, Syria and Jordan, defeating the Arab armies in a war that lasted only six days. Nasser, and Arab nationalism, never recovered from the humiliation. From that point on, the US government strongly supported Israel. Before 1991 the US found it politically almost impossible to invade a Middle Eastern country. But Israel could punish America's enemies. Israel became, and has remained, the major recipient of American foreign aid. Today, aid and loans are so important that the withdrawal of American support would lead to the collapse of the Israeli economy.

Israel and the Arab lands went to war again in 1973. By the end, Israel occupied the West Bank of Jordan and the city of Gaza, previously in Egypt. That meant over a million Palestinian refugees were now back under Israeli control. For the next 36 years, to this day, these Palestinians have lived under a colonial occupation.

The long occupation made most ordinary Israelis brutal and racist. This was not because they started as bad people. Think of the conscript Israeli soldiers you see on television, being stoned by children. When children throw stones at a man, he has two choices. He can leave. Or he can stop the children. But the children outnumber him, because he is an occupier in their land. So the only way he can stop them is to shoot them. The choice he does not have is to stand and be stoned. Forty children with stones can bury three soldiers. So the soldier becomes a man who shoots children in order to occupy their land. To do that, he has to become a racist, and he has to hate those children. That's what's happened to Israel over the last 40 years. I am not arguing that Zionism didn't have a racist basis to begin with. Obviously the idea that land belongs to people of one race is racist, and so was the ethnic cleansing in 1948. But 50 years ago many Jewish Israelis accepted that racism because they thought they had to survive. That moral certainty has now been hollowed out, replaced by hate among many and confusion among even more.

Arab nationalism and Islamism

In 1967, the reason Israel mattered was that it broke the back of Arab nationalism.

During the 1960s and 70s every Middle Eastern oil state had nationalised the drilling and production of oil, taking over from French, British or US oil companies. The Arab nationalists had started this. But in their wake, the governments of conservative regimes in Iran and Saudi Arabia had done the same. The US had learned, uneasily, to live with this. The oil companies still controlled most of the refineries and all of the transport of oil and sale abroad.

Then, in 1973, at the end of that year's war with Israel, the Arab oil countries combined to restrict the supply of oil to the world in protest at US support for Israel. This coincided with the beginning of the first big post-war recession. The American media blamed the recession on the oil price. In fact, there had been oil price rises before without recessions, and there would be big recessions later without oil price rises. But there is no doubt Washington was worried. The government of Saudi Arabia was the key.

Saudi Arabia is the largest oil producer in the world and has been a close American ally since 1945. The Saudi royal government is also the most corrupt and widely despised regime in the Middle East. They agreed to resume oil supplies and Washington breathed freely. Since then Saudi Arabia has remained the ally the US must have.

For the last 30 years, most Middle Eastern governments have been in alliance with the US. Washington needs that alliance to control the oil. And Washington needs dictatorships. If the people of the Middle East controlled the oil, they would ration it,

save it and sell it for more. To keep the US government and corporations happy, the Middle Eastern dictatorships have to sell
the oil cheaply. To do that, they have to keep their own people
in line. So the US, dictatorship and oil are bound together. Any
opposition to dictatorship will find itself confronting the US.

This combination of US influence, local dictatorship and
economic inequality has created the space for Islamism.
Islamism is a political movement based on Islam. It is not the
religion itself, any more than Martin Luther King, or the Pope,
or right-wing fundamentalist Christian preachers have a
monopoly on Christianity. Nor is Islamism a traditional movement. It is a response to imperialism. The roots of Islamism go
back to the Muslim Brotherhood in Egypt in the 1930s, but it
only emerged as a serious political force in the 1970s.

There is not one form of Islamism, any more than there is one
form of socialism. Some Islamist movements, like that of Turkey,
are deeply parliamentary and constitutional. Some are terrorist
and elitist, like Bin Laden. Some are armed but part of mass
movements, like Hamas in Palestine and Hezbollah in Lebanon.
However, most Islamist parties since 1975 have had two things in
common. They are opposed to American imperialism. And they
talk of social justice. In this way they have filled the space previously occupied by nationalism and communism.[19]

The Islamist breakthrough was Iran in 1978.[20] Iran was ruled
by the Shah, a tyrant and American client. The Iranians began
demonstrating against the regime. They were shot down. Larger
crowds came back to demonstrate and mourn the dead. People
began to march in their white burial sheets, to show they were
not afraid. The workers in the oil fields went on strike against
the Shah, and so did bank workers.

At the climax, hundreds of thousand marched down one of the
wide boulevards of Tehran. The Shah sent the air force to bomb
and strafe the crowd. A friend of mine was there. He said the first
plane flew low over the long lines. People looked upward. He
held his breath. They waited, the plane loud just above their heads.
The plane banked upward. The next plane buzzed the crowd and
the next, and none of them fired. The crowd knew the Shah was

finished. Maoist revolutionaries rode motorcycles to the air force base. The airmen gave them guns. The Shah raced for the airport and left on an American air force jet.

Who took power was a different matter. There were three political forces in the revolution. One was an alliance of secular leftists and revolutionaries. The second were middle-class liberals who didn't know what to do. The third, and largest, were the Islamists. Their leader was Ayatollah Khomeini, a respected Muslim scholar. For several months there were power struggles at the top. Then the Islamists took the initiative with a stroke of genius. Islamist students occupied the American embassy. The students let the African Americans and women working in the embassy go free, on the grounds that they were both oppressed in the United States. But they kept the white men prisoner for almost a year.

People all over the Middle East enjoyed this massive humiliation for American power. After Vietnam, the US couldn't invade a country of 50 million people. After the 1973 oil price rise, they couldn't risk alienating the whole Middle East. In America, right-wingers had bumper stickers saying 'Nuke Iran'. The slogan underlined American impotence. No one had a bumper sticker saying 'Send Our Boys to Iran'. Working-class Americans weren't prepared to allow that. The embassy occupation confirmed Islamist power in Iran.

The Iranian revolution suddenly gave people across the Middle East an example of how to topple a dictator and defy American power. Islamist movements grew rapidly in Algeria, Lebanon, Syria, Egypt, Saudi Arabia, Morocco and Turkey. They quickly became the main opposition force, leaving communism, socialism and nationalism on the retreat.

For the next 20 years, Islamism would be the main challenge to US power. Washington began a campaign of anti-Muslim propaganda that continues today. Prejudice about Islam became the only publicly acceptable racism in the Western world. Read almost any Western newspaper or magazine article about 'fundamentalism' and Islam. Then substitute the world 'Jew' or 'black' for 'Muslim'. The racism will leap off the page at you.

The point of this campaign was to prepare Europeans and Americans for a war for oil.

The other US strategy was to attack the Islamists through proxy wars. In 1981 an alliance of the Islamists, the Palestinians and the left was winning a civil war in Lebanon.[21] So Israel invaded Lebanon and took the capital, Beirut. But they dared not hold it. American and French troops were sent in to secure the city. One Islamist suicide bomber, a rare thing in those days, drove a truck of explosives into a US base and killed 230 marines. (Two days later, the US invaded Grenada.) Within weeks, all American troops were withdrawn from Lebanon. Americans still wouldn't die for oil or Washington, and the Reagan administration knew it.

The US also encouraged the Iraqi dictator, Saddam Hussein, to attack Iran.[22] Saddam hoped to seize part of the Iranian oil-fields. The US hoped to crush the example of the Iranian revolution. A million people, mostly Iranians, died in trench warfare. The Iraqi army used poison gas against both the Iranian army and rebel Iraqi Kurds. The US government ignored it, and the US media barely mentioned it. The kingdoms of Saudi Arabia and Kuwait, both afraid of Islamists among their own people, bankrolled Iraq.

After seven years of killing, the Iranians were winning. They would soon drive into Iraq. At that point the US intervened. The Sixth Fleet was sent to the Gulf to tell the Iranians to go so far and no further. The Iranians ignored the warning. An American naval ship shot down a civilian Iranian airliner, killing all the more than 200 passengers on board. The American captain was not disciplined, and Bush did not apologise. The Iranians understood the US threat and made peace.

But Saddam Hussein was in trouble. He was a dictator who had lost a war. His government was in serious debt. Now that the war was over, Kuwait was refusing to pay the aid it had promised. Iraq had been claiming sovereignty over Kuwait ever since the British split that small country off from Iraq in 1920. Now Saddam Hussein's Iraqi army invaded Kuwait. It would give him a victory and persuade the Kuwaitis to pay up.

Saddam, who had been supported by the US for a decade, also thought Washington would allow him to do it.

The US couldn't do that. The Saudi government interpreted the invasion of Kuwait as a threat to their own rule. Long America's ally, Saddam was now the enemy. All his old crimes, the poison gas and the tortures, were dredged up. Suddenly, he was portrayed as the dictator he had been all along.

Since the fall of the Soviet Union, President Bush had been speaking about a 'New World Order'. Now he had a chance to demonstrate that order in practice. Bush assembled on the sands of Arabia a joint army of most of the relevant world powers in the world. Only Russia, Germany, Japan and China were missing. But many of the European powers, and most of the Arab ones, were there. For the first time in history, the US was leading the world into a war.

The buildup took months. The war took weeks. It was an astonishing display of military power. The bombing may not have been as precise as was claimed at the time. But the destruction was extensive. In a few days of bombing, more than 100,000 Iraqi soldiers and several thousand civilians died. The Iraqi army, conscripts who mostly hated Saddam, broke under the B-52s and fled. Many were buried alive by American bulldozers. Thousands were shot and burned alive as they fled down the Basra road from Kuwait to the border.

The US army stopped on the border. Colin Powell, chairman of the joint chiefs of staff, with his two tours of duty in Vietnam, dreaded a long occupation of Iraq.[23] So did President Bush, an oilman and former CIA director who knew the Middle East well. Very few Americans had died so far. As the elder Bush and his national security chief wrote in 1997:

Trying to eliminate Saddam, extending the ground war into an occupation of Iraq ... would have incurred incalculable human and political costs ... We would have been forced to occupy Baghdad, and, in effect, rule Iraq. The coalition would instantly have collapsed, the Arabs deserting it in anger and other

allies pulling out as well. Under those circumstances ... the United States could conceivably still be an occupying power in a bitterly hostile land.[24]

Well, yes. The other possible thing on Bush's mind was that both the Kurds in the north and the Shias in the south, led by Islamists, were ready to rise up. Indeed, they did so without an American invasion. American planes sheltered the Kurds. But the US left the Shias to Saddam's secret police.

Saddam's regime remained in place. But as with Nicaragua and Cambodia, the economic noose was tightened. The US pressed the UN into sanctions against Iraq, cutting off the sale of most of its oil and denying many essential goods, including medical supplies.[25] This had a particularly strong effect because the bombing had concentrated on destroying Iraq's water and sewage treatment plants. Now Iraq, one of the richer countries of the world, became one of the poorest. Without proper sanitation, malnourished children were particularly vulnerable to disease. Medical researchers from the Harvard School of Public Health and the UN calculated that, by 1999, 500,000 Iraqi children had died who would have lived without the UN sanctions. Other researchers put the number at a million, but that included adults. This was in a country of 20 million people. Between 1991 and 2003, every Iraqi must have walked behind a small coffin. For millions, the body in that coffin was their child, brother or sister. Twelve years of UN sanctions go far to explain Iraqi feelings toward the UN today. They also tell us why US troops were not welcome in 2003.

Osama Bin Laden had returned to Saudi Arabia, disgusted by the factionalism of the Afghan resistance. He initially supported the US response to Saddam Hussein's invasion of Kuwait. But the bombing of Iraq and the sanctions reminded him of what the Russians had done to the Afghans. After the war, the Saudi government welcomed a permanent American garrison. This outraged Bin Laden, because Saudi Arabia was supposed to be the custodian of the holy cities of Mecca and Medina. Bin

Laden concluded that not just the American ruling class, but all Americans, were the problem. He left Saudi Arabia.

During the 1991 Gulf War the US promised their Arab allies that Washington would force Israel to give the Palestinians an independent state, but this didn't happen. The Palestinians began another uprising. The Israel army met demonstrations and boys throwing stones with bullets and helicopters. Many Palestinians, enraged but helpless, turned to suicide bombing. An escalating war killed far more Palestinian civilians than Israelis. Most Arabs knew that without the massive American economic support, Israel would have been forced to make peace.

During the 1990s, the US embarked on three more set-piece wars, in Somalia, Haiti and Kosovo. Each was a 'humanitarian war', designed to rehabilitate military invasion and display American power to the world. The US intervened in Somalia right after the Gulf War.[26] After the fall of the Soviet Union, the people of Somalia had overthrown their dictator, Barre, long backed by the US. There was then a power vacuum, with several large clans competing for control of the fertile agricultural land and the capital, Mogadishu. The possibility of famine threatened, although people were not dying of hunger. The NGOS, the international charities, began to distribute food aid. The image of Africa in the West was as a continent of helpless famine, a bony hand stretched begging to the world.

The US sent in the marines. Some Somalis welcomed them, none resisted, and many hoped the US would bring peace. Internationally, and in the US, the invasion was sold as a humanitarian intervention. The marines would help the hungry Somali mother. Within a year the US forces had alienated almost everyone in Mogadishu, and brought no peace. Clinton was now president. The US decided to solve that problem by attacking the Somali leader with the most popular support, Aideed. The response was an uprising by the people of Mogadishu. A crowd of tens of thousands launched themselves against a unit of American special forces and killed eighteen, the crowd dragging their bodies through the streets. US troops were soon withdrawn. Clinton knew the American people were unwilling to let Americans die in a war where the local people clearly didn't want them.

The next invasion was Haiti, in 1994.[27] Here, as in Nicaragua, the enemy was liberation theology. Haiti had long been a military dictatorship. After 1989, though, as in Somalia, the old regime was overthrown. The newly elected president of Haiti, Aristide, was a former Jesuit priest who promised social justice to the poor. The military and the thugs of the old dictatorship took power. Aristide fled. As the economy crumbled, tens of thousands of Haitian refugees tried to reach the US in small boats. They were poor black peasants, on the bottom of the US ethnic hierarchy, and they were not welcome. The US made a deal with Aristide in exile. He would agree to implement globalisation, austerity and IMF plans in Haiti, and US troops would restore him to power. The invading US army were greeted by ecstatic, dancing crowds. Again, this could be marketed as a good war. The Pentagon's policy was to protect the Haitian military officers, police, thugs and torturers from those crowds. The rule of terror was to remain. The IMF policies were enforced and the US troops left.

The next intervention was in what had been Yugoslavia, a communist country, but neutral in the Cold War.[28] After 1989, there was an upsurge of democracy, and widespread strikes against IMF backed policies of globalisation. The old communist leaders reacted by repackaging themselves as elected nationalist leaders of the various ethnic groups. The old Yugoslav federation fell apart in a series of wars, with ethnic cleansing and night murders on all sides. The brutality of these wars polarized the population along ethnic lines. Resistance to globalisation was effectively ended.

The European Union, led by Germany, intervened in a particularly brutal war in the old province of Bosnia. This threatened American ambitions. The US had been the dominant power in Western Europe, and aspired to be the main power in the east as well. Then Kosovo gave Washington an opportunity. Kosovo was a largely Albanian-speaking province in the new country of Serbia. The Kosovo Albanians wanted independence. The US backed a guerrilla army of ethnic Albanians. Then Washington insisted they should be allowed to intervene as peacemaker, and effectively occupy both Serbia and Kosovo. The Serbian government was led by Slobadan Milosevic, a brutal nationalist, but an elected one. He rejected the American plan.

The US mustered a coalition of invasion forces along the Albanian border of Kosovo, and began bombing mostly civilian targets in both Kosovo and Serbia. The Pentagon insisted that no ground troops were used. The bombing wore down the Serbian people, who by this point had endured years of war, and they forced Milosevic to make peace. American-controlled UN troops took control of Kosovo. Like Bosnia, it remains a colony run by the UN to this day.

Kosovo too was sold as a humanitarian war, with the US going in to protect hundreds of thousands of Kosovan refugees from the Serbian army. The flaw in this picture was that there were no refugees until the American bombing started, and the Serbian army then reacted by forcing people out of their homes. The Kosovo war, though, served to cement the power of the new world order. The US, it seemed, had won a war in Europe by massive firepower. It also cemented the alliance between the US government and the charitable NGOs, who almost all first worked in the American run refugee camps and then went into Kosovo with the US army.

All of these wars were meant, like the Gulf War of 1991, to show the people of the world and competing powers like Germany, that resistance to Washington was futile. Throughout the 1990s, that military power served to reinforce US corporate power. The next chapter is about economic globalisation in the 1990s.

9 | The WTO and AIDS

After the fall of the Soviet Union and the Gulf War, the thrust of US international economic policy changed again in 1922. The US was now the sole superpower. There was no coherent set of opposing ideas. During the 1980s, debt, the IMF and the World Bank had disciplined Latin America and Africa. Now it was possible to think of dominating Western Europe, Eastern Europe, India, East Asia and China as well. That meant a turn to trade agreements – the North American Free Trade Agreement (NAFTA), the World Trade Organization (WTO) and the European Union (EU).

Of course, trade agreements were not the only way the world was being restructured in the 1990s.[1] The IMF and the World Bank did not go away. If anything, they extended their reach. The foreign debt of almost all poor countries increased. But it would be a mistake to think that the international agencies are the central driving force in restructuring the world. In fact, American corporations constantly deal directly with foreign governments and corporations. So do the US Treasury and the president's trade representative. At crucial times like the Mexican debt crisis in 1995, the American government steps in and takes over from the IMF and the WTO. The governments of Western Europe, too, moved to cut and privatise during the 1980s. The governments of Eastern Europe fell into line after 1989. So did the Indian and Chinese governments.

However, the new international trade agreements did mark a shift. Unlike the IMF and the World Bank, they were designed to control both rich and poor countries. The first one, the trial run, was the North American Free Trade Agreement (NAFTA).[2] This linked Canada, the US and Mexico. Negotiations started under President Bush the elder. The treaty was signed under Clinton, and came into force in 1994.

NAFTA was really about Mexico – the US and Canada already had a trade deal. In theory, NAFTA created free trade between the US and Mexico. In practice, both countries already had something very close to free trade. Mexican goods going to the US paid an average customs duty of 3.5 per cent, too little to make any difference, and US goods going to Mexico paid 10 per cent.[3]

In fact, NAFTA was about guaranteeing investment. A free trade agreement is very short. The text of the NAFTA treaty was over 3,000 pages long, and most of those pages were restrictions on what Mexico could do. The key provisions forbade the Mexican government to take over any companies without paying full compensation immediately. That compensation had to be paid in US dollars or another G7 currency, but never in pesos. It had to be as much as the company was worth before rumours of nationalisation. And the Mexican courts could not judge the legality of any move. That would be done by a foreign arbitrator in effect appointed by the US.

Mexico had a long, and proud, record of nationalising companies, especially oil. In 1993 Mexico had been ruled for 70 years by the dictatorship of the Party of the Institution-alised Revolution (PRI). Under the PRI much of industry was government owned. Peasants in many areas retained the collective ownership of the land they had won in the revolution 80 years before. The leaders of the PRI and the Mexican ruling class as a whole wanted to move towards democratic elections, mass privatisation and the end of collective ownership of the land. NAFTA would guarantee the economic side of those moves, preventing any democracy from changing the rules. It would protect both Mexican and US corporations.

For years American corporations had been threatening their workers, saying the company would move the jobs to Mexico. NAFTA would make that easier. The American union federation, the AFL-CIO, was bitterly opposed. Bill Clinton fudged the issue during the election race. Once elected, he swung hard behind NAFTA.

In practice, NAFTA hurt American workers, Mexican workers and Mexican farmers. Between 1994 and 1998 the American government certified 211,582 workers as eligible for aid because they had lost their jobs as a result of NAFTA.[4] There must have been more who weren't certified, and the aid didn't get them their jobs back.

As American jobs moved south, they replaced jobs in closing Mexican factories. Between 1993 and 2000, the number of industrial workers in Mexico fell by 0.3 per cent, three workers in a thousand. In the same period industrial productivity grew by 45 per cent, almost half.[5] Productive new machines had destroyed jobs in the US and now they were being moved south. From the corporations' point of view, this still helped profits, because Mexican wages were so much lower.

But Mexican workers were suffering in an economy dominated by the US. The Mexican currency crashed in 1982, and again in 1995, a year after NAFTA. Both times the American banks and the US Treasury insisted on devaluation, spending cuts, privatisation and wage reductions. The real buying power of the minimum wage has dropped 60 per cent since 1982 and 23 per cent since NAFTA was signed. 'Contractual' union wages have dropped more than 70 per cent since 1977 and 55 per cent since 1987. Manufacturing wages fell 25 per cent in the first two years of NAFTA. They went up some after that, but by 2002 industrial wages were still 12 per cent less than when NAFTA was signed.[6]

The superstore chain Wal-Mart, on the other hand, did well. By 2002, they had 520 giant stores in Mexico and sold $9 billion in goods a year. Wal-Mart's Mexican shelves were almost entirely devoid of locally-made goods. Even its bestselling popcorn brand was made from US rather than Mexican maize.'[7]

Maize, called corn in the US, is traditionally the main crop in Mexico. It's what tortillas are made from. In the US, maize is grown on large farms at a cost 40 per cent below that in Mexico, with large federal government subsidies. The yield in the US is four or five times higher per acre. Even without government subsidies, American crops, farmed on extensive good land with expensive machines and fertiliser, are more productive and cheaper than the crops of small farmers in the poor countries. With the added government subsidies, there is no competition. As one poor country after another was opened to American agricultural imports in the 1990s, the small farmers could not compete.

In August 1994, just over two years after NAFTA began, the price of maize in Mexico had fallen 48 per cent. By 1992 that was 58 per cent.[8] In other words, farmers were getting less than half what they were used to for their main crop. NAFTA now allowed them to sell what had previously been communal land. American agribusiness moved in. Mexican farmers took their lives in their hands and sneaked across the border to become illegal workers in the United States.

To cap it all, while the price of maize plummeted, the price of tortillas went up.

The WTO

The World Trade Organization (WTO) was NAFTA on a global scale. There had been international negotiations on trade for many years, in an organisation called the General Agreement on Tariffs and Trade (GATT). In 1995 the WTO replaced this, with a far more wide-reaching remit. It would be the linchpin for implementing the full plan for globalisation.

The leading figure was Mickey Kantor, Clinton's representative for international trade. As he said in 1999, 'I don't believe in free trade. There is no such thing. We want rules based trading systems, not free trade. Free trade is chaotic. I don't know anybody who wants free trade.'[9] And Kantor knew everyone in the world who was negotiating 'free trade' agreements.

The WTO, like NAFTA, was about protecting American industry and agriculture, opening up world markets and guaranteeing the investments of transnational companies. The US had a veto in the UN, the World Bank and the IMF. In the

WTO every country had a theoretical veto, because decisions were made by consensus. In practice, that meant that the US imposed its will and had a veto on anything it did not like.[10] In 1995, no government felt they could stand up to that.

Between 1995 and 2003 the provisions of the WTO tightened. Industry in the poor countries was opened up to competition, but the US continued to limit imports. American maize and wheat flooded the world market. The World Bank encouraged poor countries to stop growing maize, wheat and rice, and start growing high value luxury crops for export: coffee, tea, flowers, fruit and the like. The Bank's theory held that these countries could produce such goods cheaply, and earn dollars and euros. The flaw in this reasoning was that the Bank was encouraging every country to switch into coffee or flowers or whatever. That only increased the competition, and the price of almost all agricultural exports fell steadily.

It wasn't that the world had too little food and too many people. It was that the world had too much food, and so people all over the world went hungry. India, with a billion people, is a case in point.[11] During the 1980s the Indian ruling class resisted globalisation, and kept currency controls and nationalised industries. The result was a growth rate of 10 per cent a year during the 1980s, far better than the US at any point since 1945. The majority of this growth was coming from an expansion in Indian industry. But in the 1990s the Indian ruling class changed track and opened to the world market. Both the main political parties, Congress and the right-wing BJP, supported this policy, as did most of the Indian ruling class. As the Indian economy opened up to grain imports, the government was also cutting fertiliser subsidies and low-interest-rate loans to small farmers. Farmers had to pay more for fertiliser, had to borrow from gouging moneylenders and got less for their crops. Like Mexican farmers, they began to lose their land. By the late 1990s the Indian newspapers were reporting waves of suicides by small farmers in several states.

China, with 1.3 billion people, is another example. The Chinese government's economic strategy has three parts. First,

in the 1980s, they broke the agricultural collectives up into
family farms. The collectives had been a way of taxing peasants
heavily and production had been low. Now it shot up as families worked for themselves. For a few years the growth rate was
astonishing. That growth produced increasing inequality. Farms
in the fertile coastal regions did much better than those in the
dry interior. Some families did well. Others lost their land,
moved to the city and became day workers if they were lucky,
and beggars and prostitutes if they weren't. The collectives had
supplied health care and education to the villages. Now no one
supplied that.

In the cities and towns, government-run Chinese industry
had concentrated on supplying heavy goods for the domestic
market. The Cultural Revolution in the 1960s had been a time
of chaos and persecution across much of China. Industrial
workers took advantage of that upheaval to go on strike and win
shorter working hours, guaranteed jobs and better working conditions. They also had the 'iron rice bowl' – the promise of permanent jobs, with housing, health care and schools for their
children.[12]

By the 1990s the Chinese government wanted to take all
that away. They wanted to move to light industry for export,
particularly of cheap goods to the US – shoes, clothes, plastics,
electronics and the like. China's great selling point here was
very cheap workers, paid far less than people in Mexico,
Thailand or Indonesia. But those cheap workers were in new
factories. Many of these were still publicly owned, but by
provincial and local governments, rather than the state. Others
in 'special enterprise zones' along the coast were foreign
owned, at least in theory. In fact, many of the foreign owners
from Taiwan and Hong Kong were fronting for communist
bureaucrats from China itself.

These new workers had no iron rice bowl. In the zones,
they were mainly young women from rural areas. They lived in
dormitories attached to the factories, working morning,
afternoon and evening, their whole lives consumed by the
employer. The traditional industries were closing down. By

2000, the government announced that they had cut 20 million traditional industrial jobs in preparation for joining the WTO. They planned to cut another 20 million after joining. What had been done to the workers of Detroit and other American inner cities was now being done on a far vaster scale.

Many of the new low-wage factories in China made clothes and shoes. They were competing with similar factories in Mexico, Bangladesh, Vietnam, Indonesia and other poor countries. In one sense, these were Chinese or Indonesian goods being exported to Europe and the United States. However, much of the clothing and shoe market was controlled by American corporations. Increasingly, the US corporations had few factories of their own. Instead, they were marketing and coordinating bodies. But they were not simply buying products. They were in charge of design and controlled every step of the process. The US corporations would place orders for two or three months with different clothing factories, often in several different countries. Some US corporations, like Liz Claiborne, also put their own inspectors on the factory production line. These short-term contracts allowed corporations to play competing factories against each other. Any dip in the market would be borne by closures and lay offs in the supplying factory. It would be some other capitalist's problem.[13]

One result of these economic changes in China was a sharp fall in the number of girls born. In the 1980s the Chinese government had introduced a 'one-child' policy to limit population growth. This meant large fines and criminal prosecutions for people having more than one child, along with what were in effect forced abortions. The American right wing, vicious opponents of abortion at home, supported the Chinese regime, capitalists after their own heart.

In some rural areas, angry peasants were able to prevent the one child policy by force. But in the cities it held. The economic changes in China meant that if a family had only one child, he'd better be a boy. This was not a traditional sexism. It was because pensions and secure housing were disappearing. In their old age, parents would be dependent on their children. If that child was a girl, she was more likely to move out and go live with her husband and his parents. The new ultrasound technology spread across China in the 1990s, allowing parents to find out the sex of a foetus and abort the girls until they found a boy.

One cannot blame the parents, nor imagine what pregnant women and little girls must have felt. This atrocity, done to the bodies of hundreds of millions of pregnant women, provoked very little protest around the world. Many in the West, who would have been outraged had such a thing been done to them, felt that there were too many Chinese. Population control was more important than a woman's right to choose. The one-child policy depended on dictatorship. No people able to vote would tolerate it, anywhere in the world. The 1995 UN Conference on Women met in Beijing to celebrate feminism around the world. No one, unfortunately, tore the organisers limb from limb. There could be no stronger evidence of the rule of the right and the market in the 1990s.

The WTO agreements in large part extended the earlier policies of globalisation. The IMF and the World Bank continued on their merry way. Critical here was the East Asian currency crash of 1997. Thailand, Taiwan, South Korea, Singapore, Hong Kong, Indonesia and Malaysia had industrialised and grown quickly, while the rest of the world stagnated in the 1980s. Most of these countries had done so by ignoring the rules of globalisation. They had protected their industries with customs duties, government support, sometimes government ownership, and considerable investment from Japan. The 1997 crash grew out of currency speculation and a classic bubble in real estate. These combined with the opening of so many new computer and clothing factories that they couldn't sell their products, and prices fell. Moreover, the Japanese economy was in trouble, caught in falling profits, a mountain of debt, and its own burst real-estate bubble. As Japanese banks and corporations moved their money home, the East Asian currencies fell.

The IMF came to town with their letters of agreement. The result was the usual currency devaluation, cuts in public spending and increases in unemployment. Local corporations were going bust and the IMF insisted on widespread privatisation. Swift changes in the law allowed American corporations to buy failing and newly-privatised corporations. The most dynamic area of the world, once dominated by local and Japanese capital, now came under increasing American corporate control.

Of the East Asian countries, only Malaysia refused to cooperate with the IMF. The Malaysian government kept control of the movement of its currency. As a result, Malaysia was the least damaged of the East Asian economies. But Turkey went down with East Asia. Textiles and clothing were a large part of the Turkish economy. When the prices collapsed in East Asia, they collapsed in Turkey too, and the country was soon in the hands of the IMF.

The root of all these troubles, however, was not in currency speculation. It was the falling rate of profit coming home to roost in Japan and the new economies.

In Western Europe, the main force for globalisation was the European Union. Many ordinary Western Europeans supported the EU because they had not forgotten the horror competing nationalisms had visited on Europe in World War II. Many in Eastern Europe saw joining the EU as their ticket to the rich world. But what the EU did was to take budgetary control from elected governments and put it in the hands of a European central bank responsible to no one. The Maastricht treaty in 1992 set limits on the budget deficit of every country in the EU, thus forcing cuts in social spending.

So in Italy, for instance, a right-wing government under Silvio Berlusconi lost power after the unions organised a march of 3 million people in Rome in 1994 against cuts in the national pension. But the new government of the left parties pushed through deep cuts in social spending, explaining to their supporters and the unions that the EU left them no choice. The unsurprising result was that in 2001 Italians voted Berlusconi back into power. And he was soon trying to cut pensions again.

By 2002 most of the governments in the EU were trying to introduce similar pension cuts, along with changes in laws protecting job security. This was a coordinated move, justified by globalisation and the need to compete with the United States.

In Eastern Europe, the push combined privatisation along with deep cuts in the old welfare state. In response, the voters in many countries turned to the old communist parties, now made over into democratic socialist parties. These parties promised a return to the old days. Once in office, they too privatised and cut. In the old Russian empire, the former Soviet Union, life expectancy for men plummeted with mass unemployment, alcohol and a vanishing health service.

In 1998 the Russian government, too, found itself unable to meet its debts. The IMF demanded payment. But, unlike East Asia, the Russian government in effect refused to pay. The IMF and Washington were helpless. Russia was too important a part of the world market. The Russian government was announcing that they were major players in the world system. Like the American foreign debt, or the Japanese bank debt, their debt did not have to be paid. That protected the new rich in Russia.

As the 20th century drew to a close, the US and the transnational corporations seemed to dominate the world. I will use the example of AIDS to suggest the relationship between American poltics and global economics.

AIDS

AIDS is an appropriate example because it is a global epidemic. The disease was first discovered in Africa and the US around 1980. There is general agreement that HIV, the virus that causes AIDS, HIV, originally came from chimpanzees. The most convincing theory about how HIV came to infect humans, and the only one with any real evidence, is that it came when researchers from an American laboratory tested a new polio vaccine partly developed in chimps. They gave the vaccine to hundreds of women convicts in New Jersey and hundreds of thousands of people along the border between Congo and Tanzania. The evidence for this origin is not a scientific certainty, but probably strong enough to win a civil case in an American court for compensation by the US government.[14]

The medical and political response to AIDS in the United States was affected by both gay liberation and family values.[15]

Gay liberation had been an important part of the movements of the 1960s. It was particularly offensive to the right wing, and to Ronald Reagan. Hostility to gay men and lesbians was a necessary part of family values. These are ideas that depend on an assumption that men and women are completely different, and that the inequalities between them are natural and biological. The open and unashamed existence of homosexuals suggests the conventional views of gender differences and the family are false. So the oppression of gay men and lesbians has its roots in the family and the oppression of women.

In the US, AIDS was first discovered in gay men in 1981. At that time there were also cases among Haitians and both heterosexual and gay drug injectors. Drug addicts and Haitians, however, were people of even less importance than gay men. Their condition was at first ignored.

Probably the greatest achievement of the gay liberation of the 1970s was that it made an open response to AIDS possible in 1981. Think for a moment what the epidemic would have been like if almost all the gay men with AIDS had still been in the closet. The disease would have spread much faster, the shame and pain would have been far greater, and any response would have come years later.

Making sense of the politics of AIDS requires some biological grounding. HIV lives in white blood cells. It is found in those bodily fluids that contain white blood cells. So it's in blood, semen and vaginal fluid. But it's not in saliva or shit, unless they contain blood. That's why kissing is safe. To pass from one person to another, the virus needs to get inside the other person's body. That's why blood spills are not dangerous, nor is getting someone's semen on your hand. It's also why oral sex is relatively safe. Semen is less likely get into the blood stream from the mouth or stomach than it is from the vagina or anus.

This is also why injecting drug users are in particular danger if they share syringes. The needle is not the problem. What happens is that a user fills the syringe with a drug, tries to put the needle into a vein, and then draws back the plunger to make sure they've found the vein. That mixes blood with the drug. Why one person hands the syringe to another, the second person injects the mixture, including the blood. The solution, as most people now know, is to use condoms and not share syringes.

Once HIV is inside the body, the virus slowly multiplies. Over the years, it destroys more and more white blood cells, until the immune system stops working properly. At that point, ordinary illnesses become life threatening.

A person is unlikely to get the virus in any one sexual contact. I worked for four years in an HIV testing service in London. I saw a lot of people who came in for a test because their husband, wife or steady partner had HIV. In the majority of those cases, the person tested negative. Even prolonged unsafe sex does not necessarily pass on the virus. This is because the human immune system is almost, but not quite, adapted to HIV, and confronted with the virus, an immune system often kills it.

But this is less likely to happen when people have a lot of the HIV virus in their bloodstream. This happens in the first few weeks after they first get it, before the immune system kicks in. It also happens later when people are very ill with AIDS. And some strains of the virus are stronger than others.

Crucially, a person in good health can often fight off the virus. But someone with flu, or exhaustion, or a sexually transmitted disease, or a skin infection, or a stomach bug, or malnutrition, has less of a chance to reject the virus. This is why, in the US and every country in the world, HIV is a disease of poor people. Poor people are more likely to already be ill with something when they are exposed to HIV. This is because poor people get sick more with everything, and get less treatment.

To return to the politics of HIV, when the first gay men in America started to come down with AIDS in 1981, the cases were concentrated in the two largest gay communities, New York and San Francisco. The first reactions among gay men were, of course, terror and sadness. But in both places the gay liberation movement had been strong. Quite quickly, there were two main political responses.[16] One built on the obvious fact that this was a sexually transmitted disease. The reaction was to say that this was the consequence of promiscuity, the glorious days of the gay scene. It was necessary to close the bathhouses where people had casual sex and to have as few partners as possible.

The other response came from gay men who were furious with the Puritanism about promiscuity. They had changed their whole lives, with great courage, to find themselves in a place and time where they could openly celebrate their sex lives. Now they were being told, they felt, to go back in the closet of shame and guilt. There were enough people on the right already saying that AIDS was God's punishment on gay men. If gay men accepted that, they were lost.

Both responses were made more desperate by the scale of death unfolding.

The flaw in the second response was that it was based on identity politics. Identity politics said that the most important thing was to have pride in yourself and your group, and to insist that only you, and people like you, had any right to express opinions on a specific mater. That meant that as a group with a claim to special knowledge you isolated yourselves from everyone else. Separating yourselves out also meant you could not afford to face the weaknesses in your position, the real material facts that stabbed you in the face. To maintain a strong group identity, you had to deny anything that could wrong or ambiguous about it.

So professional African Americans ignored the reality of the lives of women on welfare and men in prison. Professional women ignored working-class women. But gay men couldn't ignore AIDS. It wouldn't go away. And they didn't want to be ashamed and alone as they tried to deal with it.

The solution the gay movement found was safe sex. This was not the creation of any single person or of doctors, though individuals were important, and one was a gay doctor. It was not discovered in a lab and no one had a grant. The idea of safe sex came from the gay liberation movement. It built on one of the movement's strengths: it's celebration of sexuality. Use a condom, safe sex meant, and have as many partners as you want. The condom was built into sex play. They made posters of one beautiful naked man sucking another, and the words said: 'HIV? SUCK.'

The first wave of safe sex education took place in gay bars. There were no paid workers, no public heath specialists, no mission statements and no business plan. There were just men, with a political answer to the problem they all faced. The argument for safe sex didn't say protect yourself. It said, if you value your lovers, protect them. It was one of the most successful public health campaigns in human history. Safe sex was the second achievement of the gay liberation movement, and it was a gift to the world.

But safe sex came too late for many. And people took risks still, fewer risks but some, because they were in denial about the disease, because they were married and in the closet, because they wanted to feel another man's skin inside them at the moment of love.

The government was still doing nothing by 1985. In eight years in office, Ronald Reagan could not bring himself to say the word AIDS once. When a dozen men came down with Legionnaire's Disease, it was national news. When thousands died of AIDS, there was silence. A cure, or some treatment that stabilised the disease, was desperately needed. That meant serious research and research money. Gay men and their AIDS organisations lobbied Congress each year, and got them to allocate pitifully small amounts. The Reagan administration, year in and year out, failed to spend most of the money that had been allocated.

Gay activists decided that Reagan wanted them to die. They said, and it wasn't really a joke, that they desperately wished this was a disease of boy scouts. Because if boy scouts got it, something would have been done.

In the late 1980s, it finally looked as if the drug corporations – Big Pharma – were beginning to come up with useful drugs. But the federal approval process for drugs took six, eight or ten years. So gay activists formed ACTUP, a political organisation to harry the government into spending research money and speeding the drug approval rules.[17] ACTUP's slogan was 'Silence = Death'. They were noisy as hell, barging into the St Patrick's Day parade in New York, lying down imitating death outside the cathedral, shouting and storming the platforms at scientific meetings, following George Bush the elder on the campaign trail. And they won. They got the new drugs manufactured and approved. This was gay liberation's third achievement.

The new drugs did not cure HIV. They acted by stopping the virus from growing, or preventing it moving from one cell to another. They slowed down the virus, turning HIV into a disease like diabetes, so people might have 20 or 30 years – a life. Some people's bodies can't tolerate the drugs, and no one knows how long they will go on working. But they're better than nothing.

If you can afford them.

There was a fourth achievement too, which came not from the activists, but from the daily lives of millions. From the beginning of the epidemic, gay communities founded groups to help the sick, to provide food, and buddies for the lonely. But it went further than that, because of the way gay men died. From 1981 to 1994, there were treatments for the particular illnesses men with AIDS got, like pneumonia and thrush. But there was no drug to arrest the collapse of the immune system. People died slowly, getting better, then getting worse, on the edge of death, recovering again.

It was a hard, long, painful way to die. Hundreds of thousands of gay men in the US, Latin America, Europe and the rest of the world did it with great dignity. I worked as an HIV counsellor in London for the last six years before the drugs became available, two years on the telephone and four years in a clinic. I watched and learned how to die well. It is a common thing and very difficult. The men I knew died for the sake of the living. They knew there were gay men coming behind them to face the same death. They tried to live a real life. They tried to cry, to be open and to model dying without shame. Even though they hated their bodies at times, and always hated that thing, the virus, within them.

The metaphor people used, over and over, was that they were in a war. They were soldiers and they might have to die. But they were fighting for the others. The other gay men reacted with millions of small acts of kindness. People visited bedsides, dropped by, went out on picnics, tried not to talk about it, tried to listen, held men while they cried. In the early days of gay liberation the 'gay community' was something people talked about, but it was a political fiction. Now the community had become a reality. It was what people did for each other.

It was crucial to gay men that this was not a gay disease. Anyone could get it. Moreover, if gay men were to get through this in any way at all, they would need help. Politically, they would need help with getting drugs. Gay men with HIV had jobs. They needed the tolerance and kindness of co-workers. They needed time off sick. Always, gay men reached out beyond the ghetto. In every novel and movie about gay men and AIDS, there are the relatives who love and accept them. Not all mothers or fathers or sisters did that. But the ones who did made all the difference. And an army of lesbians came to the bedside, because they understood the men were suffering because of the same prejudices they faced.

Gay men with AIDS reached out because they had to, and because their politics did not require them to blame themselves. The reaching out transformed American politics. Reagan could pretend gay men weren't there. But by 1994 almost everyone in America had known someone with HIV. They mostly believed that person should have medical treatment and human dignity. Eventually even President Bush the elder had to say the word AIDS in public. The Ryan White Act that went through Congress in 1994 was named for a white teenager who died of AIDS from a blood transfusion. That was a cop-out. But the act provided money to give drugs and treatment to the large majority of people with HIV. There are only two diseases in America that is true for – renal failure and AIDS.

The steady love and care among gay men also meant that, in contrast to the other movements, the gay and lesbian movement was much stronger at the end of the 1980s than at the beginning. Prejudice was still there, but it was steadily eroding. In October 1987 roughly 500,000 people marched for gay and lesbian rights in Washington, DC.[18] They put the people with AIDS at the front of the march.

None of that makes the epidemic worth it. And most people with HIV weren't gay men. In the US, injecting drug users and an increasing number of common or garden heterosexuals also had AIDS. Elsewhere around the world, HIV is a disease of cities and of the poor. And the numbers keep increasing. At the end of 2001, the UN guessed there were 40 million people with HIV in the world. Of these 28.5 million were in sub-Saharan Africa, 6.6 million in Asia and a million in the US.[19] That includes 5 million people in South Africa, a fifth of the adult population. The proportion is probably so high because South Africa is such an urban nation. The number for Asia is almost certainly an underestimate, as both the Indian and Chinese governments are trying to conceal the extent of the epidemic. A reasonable guess for India at the moment would be 4 to 5 million people. China is harder to estimate, because HIV is more hidden still. There may be between half a million and 2 million people with HIV.

In 2001, Africa south of the Sahara accounted for 40 per cent of the world's desperately poor and 70 per cent of people with HIV. But this is changing. India and China have over two billion people between them and neither government is doing anything to stop the virus spreading. The UN guesses there will be 10 to 15 million people in China with HIV by 2010, and 20 to 25 million in India.[20] It is likely that 100 million will die before the epidemic is finished, and maybe more.

Many will have hard deaths. All are dying unnecessarily. It's happening for two reasons. The WTO and Washington are trying to make sure people can't afford the drugs. And the national politicians have made safe sex impossible for most people.

Let me take safe sex first. Safe sex was invented by gay men and based on a celebration of human sexuality. It paid attention to biology and said: 'use a condom'. Then you can have as many partners as you want. The point of safe sex, after all, is that it's safe if one of you has HIV.

This approach was unacceptable to the Christian right, and other guardians of heterosexual morality. In the US, the messages for heterosexuals on the television and in the schools said: use a condom and have as few partners as possible. AIDS kills, they said. It has changed everything. The time for promiscuity is over.

That was lethal advice, because it didn't make sense.[21] People said to themselves, if a condom works, why do I need fewer partners? If it doesn't work, why should I use one? People could tell they were being lied to, something they were used to at school and on the TV. But they couldn't tell which part was the lie: condoms or promiscuity? So by and large they had sex and didn't use condoms.

The response of African-American politicians, church and community leaders, was equally unfortunate. Injecting drug users were particularly at risk, especially in New York, and many of them were black. The New York police did not enforce the law against heroin and crack effectively. But they did enforce the law against pharmacists selling syringes. By 1987, HIV prevention workers understood the consequences. And they knew addicts only shared syringes because they had to. Since it was politically impossible for pharmacists to provide every user with their own syringe, public health workers in New York tried to set up a city-funded 'needle exchange' in 1987 to do the same thing.

This was at the height of the War on Drugs, and it presented African American politicians and church leaders with a problem.[22] They could support a campaign for clean syringes and save tens of thousands of lives in New York, among users and their lovers. That would weaken the War on Drugs. It would imply that many African Americans took drugs, that black politicians felt compassion and fellowship with such people and that saving human life was more important than punishing drug users. So African American politicians, editors and preachers attacked the needle exchange in vitriolic terms. When the liberal African American David Dinkins was elected Mayor of New York in 1989, he closed the needle exchange.

Drug treatment workers, and some users, continued covert illegal distribution of syringes, keeping up the pressure. By 1995 they had won the argument, and New York had needle exchanges. The delay had killed tens of thousands of people.

By 2000, 57 per cent of people testing positive for HIV in the US were African Americans. One cause was the concentration of HIV in specific places, particularly New York. Everywhere, HIV is found in big cities and among the poor. Another cause was the lack of needle exchanges. Still another was the fact that many black men, like white men, are also gay or bisexual. Church leaders knew this, but found it uncomfortable to admit it. Finally, there was the failure of safe sex in the black community. This was not chance. The leadership of the community had insisted, from early on, that AIDS was a gay and therefore a white disease. Much of the leadership also came from the church or was part of a professional class obsessed with respectability. Given the strong white prejudices about black sexuality in America, the last thing the black leadership could bring themselves to do was participate in campaigns that celebrated the sexuality of black teenagers.

In all this the leadership of black America was no different from the white leaders, and the US response set a tone for conservative establishments globally.[23] Across Africa and Asia, almost all governments first tried to conceal the extent of infection. Where governments in Africa and Asia did respond to HIV, at best they followed the US line: use condoms and reduce your number of partners. At worst, the influence of the Catholic Church meant they were against condoms as well. Almost no governments provided condoms free. The exception was Thailand, where the upper classes sensibly moved to protect themselves and everyone else through a national campaign that seriously encouraged prostitutes to use condoms. Ruling-class and middle-class Thai men were open with themselves and others about their exploitation of women. They wanted clean prostitutes.

More generally, what was necessary to save tens of millions of lives were national campaigns based on the American gay model. That meant people mobilising at the grass roots for safe sex as part of fighting their other oppressions. It meant a festival of sexuality, with bishops, businessmen and presidents saying use condoms, because I do.

But the routes along which HIV spread most quickly were precisely in the places where people were most lonely, oppressed and desperate. In clinical prose that only accentuates the loneliness, researcher Catherine Campbell describes the transaction between a sex worker and a migrant worker in a South African mine:

> During the day, women commonly gathered in groups of four or five and waited to be approached by clients. Clients would generally approach the group and point or beckon to the sex worker of their choice. She would walk up to him, with a fairly typical interaction proceeding as follows:
> Sex worker: Can I help you?
> Client: Can you help me?
> Sex worker: Do you have money? It will be R20.
> Client produces the money and hands it over. Sex worker gives the money to a colleague for safekeeping. Both client and worker move a little distance away, behind bushes if they are available, but often within sight of colleagues if there are no bushes. Sex worker removes her panties and lies down on her back, client takes his trousers down to just above his knees. Penetrative sexual intercourse takes place (usually lasting about 3 minutes). Thereafter they both stand up, dress and the client walks away. Verbal communication, apart from the initial negotiation of money, is rare.
>
> It was important to have a colleague standing by, given that a man might pull out a knife after the encounter and demand the money back, or that [an] unemployed man might lie in wait to attack and rob the couple during sexual intercourse.[24]

These men were migrant workers, often from neighbouring countries, living in dormitories. They had come this far because someone had to earn for their families. Contact with sex workers was their only physical love. They were reluctant to show emotion, and the fear of HIV, they told Campbell, was no greater than their fear of the mine. Men died down there all the time. The first time they got into the cage that would take them three kilometres down, other men would comfort them. Campbell asks a miner:

> How did they console you when you entered the cage?
> They told me that in this situation you must know that you are on the mines and you are a man and you must be able to face anything without fear ... To be called a man served to encourage and console you time and again ... You will hear people saying, 'a man is a sheep, he does not cry.' I mean, this is the way to encourage or console you at most times.
> [Campbell asks why men are sheep.]
> No matter how hard you hit a sheep or slaughter it you will not hear it cry. The animal that can cry is a goat. So, that is a comparison that whatever pain you inflict on a man you will not see him cry.[25]

Most of these women were unmarried, one reason they had to do this work. Most of the miners had wives. One day they would take HIV home. All were trapped by the fact they couldn't speak. Shame made them silent.

And silence, as ACTUP said, is death. Campbell worked with the miners and sex workers on a small local HIV-prevention scheme. They had some success. But to make a real difference they needed a mass movement that would change attitudes across the whole society. The scheme Campbell worked for was similar to many run by NGOs in the poor countries. They don't challenge power. They stay within the limits of what the local government and their funders, the UN and the US and the EU, will allow. Neither the African state, nor the UN, nor European and American donors will allow a celebration of safe sex and promiscuity.

There was treatment for most people in the US, but not in Africa. The reason was the WTO and the US government. The WTO was about many things. In two ways, it moved beyond the plan of globalisation. First, it was about protecting international investment not just in industry, but in services. These were a growing proportion of the economy everywhere. They were also areas where the rate of profit could be pushed up, because there was less fixed-capital investment. So the WTO rules were progressively tightened to take away the rights of national governments to regulate their own service industries. Instead, there would be arbitration by the WTO in Geneva, which would usually rule in favour of the international corporation.

The WTO had a set of rules called GATS, the General Agreement on Trade in Services (not the same thing as the old GATTS).[26] The GATS said that if a country allowed any private activity in any sector of services, it must allow international and local businesses to bid for all government work in that sector. So if a country allowed some private schools or a few private hospitals, then it had to allow businesses to bid to run all schools or hospitals. This provision has not been used much yet, but it's there, and the plan is to enforce it.

Secondly, the WTO has rules to protect patent rights. These rules for 'intellectual property' are called TRIPS.

The gay movement in the US had fought for the production and government approval of the new AIDS drugs. Those drugs cost $15,000 for treatment for a year in the US, and about $10,000 a year in Britain. Almost no one in Africa could afford that. Nor could African governments. It would cost $50 billion a year to treat 5 million South Africans. But by the mid-1990s a pharmaceutical company in India was making the drugs needed at a cost of $300 a year. South Africa, the richest country south of the Sahara, could afford that. Other African countries could not, but there was enough money in the world to give Africa the drugs easily.

The international pharmaceutical companies were deeply hostile to the idea. The Indian drugs were so cheap because they were 'generic drugs' – exact chemical copies of the drugs protected by patent in rich countries. Until the 1990s, all the poor countries had used generic drugs. The thinking behind this was that poor people could not afford Western-patented drugs. If they were to live, they needed cheap drugs. Until the 1990s and the WTO, this was widely regarded as a matter of common human decency. Jonas Salk, the inventor of the polio vaccine in the 1950s, was once asked who owned the patent on it. He said, 'No one. Why? Could you patent the sun?'[27]

TRIPS, the rules for 'intellectual property', now say that patent rights on medicines, software and every other invention will apply not just in rich countries but in every country. In the past, countries had industrialised by copying the processes used in economically more advanced countries. This was how the US and Germany, for instance, caught up with Britain. And how South Korea and Japan were catching up with the US. These new patent and copyright rules stop that. They give a monopoly to the corporation – almost always in the rich countries and usually in the US – that develops the process or just is first to get the patent. In theory, a patent on a medicine only lasts for ten years, but there are several tricks for prolonging it.

Patents are particularly important to 'Big Pharma', the international pharmaceutical companies, for several reasons. Each corporation gets most of its income from a small number of 'blockbuster drugs', usually three to ten. These are not drugs for acute illnesses, because people get better and stop taking those. Some blockbusters are drugs for chronic conditions, like diabetes, asthma and high blood pressure. Others are anti-depressants, lifestyle drugs like Viagra, and ones that help you lose weight or grow hair on the top of your head. The minimum cost of developing a drug is now $1 billion. So there is no economic point in developing drugs for acute diseases found in tropical countries.

Doctors Without Borders, the activist health NGO, found that Big Pharma developed 1,200 molecules to market between 1975 and 1997. Of those, 13 went into trials for treating tropical diseases. Of the 13, five were veterinary drugs already used on animals, and four were developed by the US army for the Vietnam War. That leaves four out of 1,200 developed by the pharmaceutical companies themselves.[28]

To take only a few examples, sleeping sickness kills 150,000 Africans a year:

> The only drug currently available to treat it is a seventy-year-old mixture of melarsen oxide and propylene glycol that has been likened to arsenic in antifreeze. The treatment itself kills 5 per cent of the people who are injected with it.
>
> There used to be alternatives, made by Aventis and Bayer, but both companies are backing away from producing them. In the meantime, one strain of sleeping sickness is becoming resistant to that only drug left on the market and no major pharmaceutical company reports new research on the disease …
>
> Bacterial meningitis was once treated cheaply and easily with something called 'Choramphenicol in oil'. The drug was manufactured by Roussel Uclaf … but in 1995 Roussel stopped making it. Now, no one does.
>
> A disease called leishmaniasis comes from a parasite and causes severe skin lesions and, sometimes, death. The treatment for it is said to exist in a drug company laboratory. None of the companies suspected of holding the cure will admit to it.[29]

There is little or no research on malaria and TB drugs, either. And then there's river blindness, a West African disease caused by a parasitic worm. Roy Vagelos became CEO of Merck, an American drug corporation, in 1985. Merck had a drug that was used to treat heartworm in dogs. Mohammed Aziz, a scientist with Merck, discovered the dog drug could cure river blindness. Vagelos was a decent man. He decided to manufacture the drug, even though the people who needed it 'lived in mud huts and couldn't possibly ever pay for it'. According to the writer Jeffrey Robinson, who interviewed Vagelos years later:

Vagelos heard from the legal staff that they had apprehensions about corporate exposure to liability if the drug caused unexpected adverse reactions.

He heard from his people dealing with Wall Street and shareholders that this might upset the investment community ... He heard from his finance people, who felt this could set a precedent that would make Merck look terrible if it didn't give away other drugs to people who needed them.

And he heard from other Big Pharma CEOs, who complained that, if Merck made a habit of this, they might be expected to follow suit ... They warned that one alternative, if Merck continued to put them in such an awkward position, was simply to stop doing the research.[30]

Vagelos went ahead anyway. But he couldn't use Merck's money. He needed $20 million to give the drug to 100,000 people for a year. He went to the World Health Organization, part of the UN. They said no. The African governments said they didn't have any money. Vagelos went to Washington. Because he was a CEO, powerful administration figures saw him. Vagelos said:

We weren't asking for a lot of money. Everyone kept telling me, this is good and we need to do it. I met with Don Regan at the White House, he was Ronald Reagan's chief of staff, who said this was something we ought to do and that he wanted to do it. But as soon as we walked out of his office, the fellow I'd been in there with from the Agency for International Development said we'd love to do it but we have no money. I went to the State Department and had exactly the same experience. The Deputy Secretary of State said he wanted to do it but as soon as I stepped out of his office, his guy said, yes we'd love to do it but we're broke. Can you imagine that?[31]

Vagelos thought river blindness wasn't high on their list of priorities. He didn't really get it. The government wanted to make sure drugs were not given away. They were just ashamed to admit it to a decent man. Eventually, Vagelos spent his company's money giving the drug away. One hundred thousand people took it the first year. But his decision is unusual.

The reason for not giving the drugs away is simple. It isn't that profits will be made selling drugs in Africa. North America, Western Europe and Japan are 80 per cent of the market for pharmaceuticals. Africa is one per cent. That includes all the government and foreign aid spending in Africa. No one was going to make any money that counted from selling the new AIDS drugs in Africa, either.

The problem was that if drugs were sold cheaply in Africa, Americans might hear about it. They already know that drugs are cheaper in Canada, and American doctors are advising their patients to buy Canadian drugs over the internet.

Americans buy 40 per cent of the global market in pharmaceuticals. But the US provides 60 per cent of the global profits of the industry. This is because private medicine dominates in the US, and there is no national health service or regulator to bid down the price. The patents are a bonanza too. Big Pharma makes three to four times as much profit as the average corporation. Twenty of the 25 best-selling drugs in the world are owned by American multinationals.

There are even bigger reasons for denying Africans AIDS drugs. The US spends 14 per cent of its Gross National Product on health. That's the largest percentage any country spends, because so much of American medicine is private. Private medicine is expensive and inefficient. That makes health the biggest industry in the biggest economy in the world. The principle of private medicine is central to the profits of the American economy. Through the WTO, the corporations want to make private medicine central to the world. They're prepared to kill for it.

To put it into perspective, the US spends more on the military than the next nine countries combined. American military spending is less than half of US public and private spending on health.

When they do get a drug, Big Pharma justifies the high price by the cost of development. A survey by the *Boston Globe*, however, found that '45 of the 50 top-selling drugs in the world were discovered, developed and/or tested with the tax-payers' money.'[32]

For years, no one in Africa got the new AIDS drugs aside from a few very rich people. Then, in South Africa, people finally began to organise.

Nelson Mandela's African National Congress came to power in 1994.[33] For 30 years, the ANC had promised social justice. The deal that ended apartheid was brokered by the US government. It allowed an elected black government in return for keeping business white. A small number of black politicians and union leaders were offered places on the boards of major corporations. In power, the ANC then adopted all the policies of globalisation. Unemployment increased and public spending fell. The ANC had promised millions of new homes for working people. Instead, the ANC began evicting unemployed people from public housing for not paying their rent. They privatised electricity, raised the rates and cut off people who couldn't pay. They did the same with water. People who shared their water with those who had been cut off were cut off themselves. Many people began to drink poisonous water from the ponds and ditches. Factories paid far lower electricity rates than householders.

Almost all the leaders of the freedom struggle had been bought off. Still people re-elected the ANC. It had carried all their hopes for so long. The alternative was the old white opposition. In the late 1990s, though, a new movement developed in the African, Indian and coloured working-class townships. 'Struggle electricians' began reconnecting electricity. 'Struggle plumbers' did the water. Whole neighbourhoods turned out to fight the police when they came to evict people. The police replied with tear gas and rubber bullets.

The Treatment Action Campaign (TAC) was part of this new movement. The founder was an AIDS worker, Zaki Achmat. His mother and his aunt had been union shop stewards. Achmat was gay. He caught HIV while in prison for organising for the ANC.

Gay liberation, the freedom struggle and the unions came together in Achmat's person. On founding TAC, he announced that he could afford the new drugs. But he wouldn't take them until ordinary South Africans could get them from the hospital.

TAC's goal was to get access to the generic AIDS drugs. In a country where people had been bitterly ashamed, TAC members marched in T-shirts that said HIV positive. They lobbied, they demonstrated and they took the government to court. There they argued that the South African constitution guaranteed the right to health, and that meant people with HIV should have generic drugs. The South African government looked as if they might support the TAC court case. Then the US government reacted:

> In February 1999, the State Department reported to congress that it was 'making use of the full panoply of leverage in our arsenal' to take on the South Africans. That included, the report said, the Vice President's office, with Al Gore himself putting the problem at the top of his agenda in his meeting with the man who would become South Africa's president [after Mandela], Thabo Mbeki. At that point the industry lobby, PhRMA, admitted it was pushing the administration to label South Africa a 'priority foreign country' in order to establish a deadline, after which trade sanctions would come into effect.[34]

Al Gore again, the scourge of social security. Mbeki, the new South African president, backed down. It wasn't only American pressure, of course. The whole strategy of the new South African government, like globalisers everywhere, depended on taking away what rights to social benefits people already had. They wanted to cut public spending. The government could afford the new drugs, yes. But they would cost substantial money. How would the budget balance then? If you admitted the government could provide AIDS drugs, why couldn't they let unemployed people have clean water?

Yet these were all things Mbeki and his ministers couldn't possibly admit. And 5 million people in South Africa, one adult in five, had HIV. That meant most people would bury someone they loved. Many already had. Everyone was afraid. Before Achmat and TAC, people hadn't talked about that much. It hadn't been understood as a political issue. Now it was. Mbeki was going to face a whirlwind if he simply denied people what they desperately needed.

So he came out with a left-wing justification. Mbeki said HIV does not cause AIDS. That's a white imperialist myth. Poverty causes AIDS. So people don't need the drugs. In effect, Mbeki and the South African government did what Gore told them to, and then went even further. TAC was campaigning for the government to give a short course of AZT, one of the new AIDS drugs, to every baby born to a mother with HIV. Studies in Europe proved that this reduced the baby's chance of getting HIV by 80 per cent. The South African government could easily afford those few pills. Mbeki refused that too.

Brazil was running into US pressure as well. Brazil managed to give the new AIDS drugs to every patient who needed them by threatening Big Pharma with generic drugs if they didn't lower the price. The US government took Brazil to the WTO disputes procedure in Geneva. If Brazil didn't back down, their exports would be banned from the US.

Then came Seattle.

10 | Seattle and Afghanistan

In the spring of 2003 an editorial in the *New York Times* said there are now two superpowers, the United States and world public opinion. This chapter and the next are about the contest between the two since the protests against the WTO in Seattle. So they're also about Genoa, Bush, 9/11, Afghanistan, Iraq, the anti-war movement and climate change.

Early in 1999, activists in Seattle, on the north-west coast of the US, learned that the next world conference of the WTO would be held in their town.[1] They were delighted. Seattle had been a radical union city for a century. The movement against Vietnam had been strong there. It was still a centre for the environmental and anti-nuclear movements. Now the local activists planned to demonstrate and shut down the WTO if they could. They began meeting in the Labor Temple, the headquarters of the Seattle unions. The unions were involved from the beginning, and the majority of demonstrators would come as part of a union contingent. John Sweeney, the leader of the AFL-CIO, came. The unions who came in strength, the Steelworkers and the Teamsters, were not left wing. For the unions to demonstrate against the president of the United States, against government foreign policy, in alliance with the left, was something quite new. Following Seattle, the same new alliance would appear on the streets of other countries.

The unions came because their members had been bitter for a long time. The defeats of the 1980s and 1990s had left people feeling helpless. The politicians, the media and the academics had all said American unions couldn't fight because globalisation was unstoppable. The corporations had threatened to move their factories, and NAFTA and the WTO set that in stone. It made sense to union people that if the WTO was the problem, protest there.

A sea change was happening in the structure of feelings that lies beneath political activity. A generation of cuts and inequality had left people pretty clear that the corporations were their enemies. I lived in the US for most of 1999. I have never lived in a country that was not a dictatorship where the gap between what was publicly said and what people privately thought was so great. Michael Moore summarises the opinion polls around the turn of the century:

> Fifty-seven per cent of the American public believes that abortion should be legal in all or most cases ... A solid 53 per cent think the legalization of abortion was a good thing ... compared to just 30 per cent who think it was bad ...
>
> A whopping 86 per cent ... say they 'agree with the goals of the Civil Rights movement' ... Seventy-four per cent disagree with this statement: 'I don't have much in common with people of other ethnic groups and races' – which puts us ahead of Great Britain, France, Germany, and Russia, when the same question is asked in those countries ...
>
> Seventy-seven per cent of us would adopt a child of another race, and 61 per cent say they have a friends or family members who are dating or married to someone of another race ...
>
> Eighty-three per cent ... say they are in agreement with the goals of the environmental movement ... Ninety-four per cent ... want federal safety regulations enacted on the manufacture and use of all handguns ... Only 25 per cent . ... own a gun.
>
> Eight in ten Americans believe that health insurance should be provided equally to everyone in the country ... Sixty-two per cent ... support changing current laws so that fewer nonviolent offenders are sent to

prison ... Seventy-four per cent prefer treatment and probation [to prison] for nonviolent drug offenders.

Eighty-five per cent ... support equal opportunity in the workplace for gays and lesbians. And sixty-eight per cent want laws enacted to punish anyone who would discriminate against homosexual employees ... Half of us have no problem with gay and lesbian couples adopting children ...

[In 2002] 58 per cent thought labour unions were a good idea ... while only 32 per cent were opposed ... 72 per cent believe that Washington gives too little consideration to working Americans. ... Eighty-eight per cent have little or no trust in corporate executives ... and 74 per cent think the problems in Corporate America are due to greed and lack of morality.[2]

Moore is emphasising these figures because they fly in the face of what most Americans believe that other Americans believe. Until 2004, if you read the newspapers, watched TV or listened to radio in America, it seemed almost the whole country was right wing.

Another sea change was happening on the left. People were turning away from identity politics, and beginning to call themselves 'activists'. Canadian Naomi Klein put the change this way in her 2000 bestseller, *No Logo*:

What is striking in retrospect is that in the very years when PC [political correctness] politics reached their most self-referential peak, the rest of the world was doing something very different: it was looking outward and expanding. At the moment when the field of vision among most left-wing progressives was shrinking to include only its most immediate surroundings, the horizons of global business were expanding to encompass the whole globe ... In this new globalised context, the victories of identity politics have amounted to a rearranging for the furniture while the house

burned down ... Though girls may indeed rule in
North America, they are still sweating in Asia and
Latin America, making T-shirts with the 'Girls Rule'
slogan on them and Nike running shoes that will
finally let girls into the game. This oversight isn't simply
a failure of feminism but a betrayal ...

As we look back, it seems like willful blindness. The
abandonment of the radical economic foundations of
the women's and civil rights movements ... successfully
trained a generation of activists in the politics of
image, not action ... We were too busy analyzing the
pictures being projected on the wall to notice that the
wall itself had been sold.[3]

What was new about Seattle, for America, was that people from
many different movements came to town to protest together
against the world system as a whole. They came from all over
the world, but many of the protesters and most of the organisers
were local. Ben White was one of the organisers.

In his time, White had been active around civil rights, peace,
anti-nuclear, environmentalist and animal rights issues. He went
to the meetings at the Labor Temple from the beginning, and
they made him think about sea turtles. In the late 1980s 'each
year, hundreds of thousands of sea turtles were drowning in
shrimp nets.'[4] For a cost of $50 to $400, a shrimp boat could
buy a device that allowed the turtles to escape at the opening
to the net. In 1991, under pressure from the environmental
movement, the US passed a law that all shrimp sold in the US
had to be from boats using excluders. In a reversal of the usual
WTO power play, India, Malaysia, Pakistan and Thailand took the
US to a WTO tribunal. In 1998 the WTO ruled that American
regulations protecting turtles were a restraint on free trade.

In Seattle, Ben White learned that all seven species of sea turtle were now endangered. He decided to make 240 cardboard
turtle costumes for the demonstrators. White cut out the patterns,
and then delivered them to turtle-making parties all over
Seattle for assembly.

The WTO was set to open on Tuesday, 30 November 1999. The WTO held such meetings every few years. They approved the outcome of the trade negotiations of the last few years, and began another round. Each meeting was supposed to tighten the rules of globalisation. The meetings of local activists in Seattle decided to try to shut it down. Monday night the ministers and presidents arrived in hotels around downtown Seattle. They included Madelaine Albright, the US Secretary of State. President Clinton was to address the delegates on the second day.

The demonstrators had a plan. In Seattle and the North-west, there was a traditional form of direct action on environmental, peace and anti-nuclear protests. The protesters would form a symbolic picket. Those who did not want to be arrested would stand at the edges. The organisers would notify the police who the 'arrestables' were, and they would be taken off and booked.

It was a good-natured form of protest. The police were used to it. It fitted the demonstrations of middle-class people, who could afford to be arrested and prosecuted. Working-class people might lose their jobs or custody of their children. Many working-class people also had a deep fear of arrest. It meant something different in their world. This was why the civil rights movement had not been built around being arrested, but around large groups of disobedient non-violent protesters. By 1999 many working-class people had reasons to be terrified of the police. The middle-class demonstrators did not share these feelings.

This time the protesters planned to surround the convention centre, allowing a path through the middle of the ring for delegates to arrive. From before dawn the protesters arrived, prepared to sit down or support those sitting down.

While the activists were sitting down, the union people were at a rally in the stadium. For those who attended, it was electric, one of the high points of their lives. There were 30,000 to 40,000 people in the stadium and roughly 20,000 activists downtown, though a few striking steelworkers were already in the city centre too.

It didn't go down as the activists planned. There were too many protesters. The police couldn't arrest token numbers, faced with a crowd like this. Every time someone was arrested, an arresting officer also had to leave the scene. The cops would quickly be heavily outnumbered. The Seattle police did what all police forces do when they have to clear large crowds: they used violence to scare them away.

Meanwhile, the WTO delegates were unwilling to walk from their hotels through the demonstrators. They were men and women of power, and unprepared for such humiliation. Madelaine Albright stayed in her hotel, furious. So Clinton put pressure on the Seattle mayor and police chief to clear the streets, no matter what.

As the morning progressed, the protesters learned that the first day of the WTO had been closed down. They also saw the kind of police violence that African American neighbourhoods knew too well. It was dark visors, Darth Vader riot costumes, tear gas and clubs. The police came up behind people sitting down, and sprayed mace into their faces from inches away. Rubber bullets fired at close range wounded people, broke legs, smashed faces. The mayor wanted to use high-pressure fire hoses, but the firefighters refused. Gradually, over many hours, the police cleared downtown and drove the protesters back into the student neighbourhood. The demonstrators chanted 'This is What Democracy Looks Like'. It meant: They tell us we have democracy, but this is what we really have.

As this was happening downtown, the union members were marching separately. The union stewards tried to keep their members from heading for downtown. A number broke away through the stewards towards the WTO, particularly from the radical dockers and seafarers unions and from the Teamsters, who organise truck drivers and others. The shout went up, 'Teamsters and Turtles Together'.

As the protesters were forced back, some broke the windows of Starbucks, McDonald's and a Nike store. The TV showed the broken windows over and over. The message was the demonstrators were violent. It didn't work. If there was an emotion that united most working Americans, it was a kind of helpless rage. The millions who had worked briefly for McDonald's, lost their jobs to NAFTA or seen their brother to prison didn't care what happened to corporate property. The destruction of property is deeply offensive to many American pacifists, but not necessarily to most Americans.

The next morning the protesters were back for more. This time the police cleared a broad path for the delegates, and Clinton was able to come to town. The WTO delegates had come to Seattle assuming that the US ruled the world, and they had to do what Clinton said. Now all their deep ambivalence about globalisation surfaced. If Clinton can't control his own people, they said to themselves, why do we have to do what he says? The WTO meeting ended with no agreement on anything. The protesters had won.

The result was a new movement that spread rapidly across the world. Many have since pointed out, quite rightly, that the movement didn't start that day, or in the US. Many now insist it began in the poor countries of the global south, with the Zapatista rising in Mexico on the day NAFTA began in 1994. Before that, there had been the IMF riots in Caracas and many other cities. In the rich countries, too, there was the 1995 French general strike in the public sector. Even in Britain the churches had mobilised 50,000 demonstrators in 1998 to protest against Third World debt outside the G8 summit meeting in Birmingham, England.

The sea change in political attitudes in the US was happening all over the world, and more quickly in many places. The point about Seattle though, was that it was the moment when the many global resistances could recognise themselves as one movement.

It is worth insisting on this point; because it is a matter of life and death for activists in the global south to see that class struggle happens in both the north and south. If you can't see it in the north, you also can't see it in the south. If you're an activist in Mexico, you are lost if you don't recognise the importance of American power. But you're also lost if you think the main struggle in the world is between rich countries and poor ones. Then you miss the strength of the Mexican ruling class, and its alliances with the ruling class in Europe and the US. Again and again in the last century, radical Third World nationalists were blindsided by their own ruling classes.

Seeing the working class in the US is also important for activists in the global south because it tells them who their possible allies are. Now, for instance, there is global opposition to the American occupation in Iraq. That involves resistance in Iraq, demonstrations around the world and a peace movement in the US. No one of these three movements can stop the American occupation without the other two. The resistance may be strongest in Iraq, as it was in Vietnam. But before the US occupation ends, the American working class will be crucially involved.

The Seattle protest was small, only 60,000 people. That's much smaller than the demonstrations in Washington for gay rights in 1987, for abortion rights in 1989 and the Million Man March in 1995. It's small compared to the 2004 World Social Forum in India, the G8 protests in Genoa in 2001 or the massive marches against the Iraq war on 14 February 2003.

But Seattle mattered because it was in the United States. I was part of a one-day general strike by 30 million workers in India against globalisation in May 2000. Hardly anyone outside India noticed. The Indian strikers knew about Seattle. What happens at the centre of the world system, in the most powerful country on earth, radiates around the globe.

Seattle also mattered because it was against the organisation that epitomised the 20-year project of globalisation. The demonstrators were confronting the representatives of every power on earth, protesting against everything that was happening to the whole world.

The other reasons Seattle mattered was that the trade unions were central, the protesters were radical, and they won. Around the world many saw that had been done by Americans, of all people. If they could do that, so could we.

The anti-capitalist movement

In the next 18 months there were similar demonstrations at world summits and conventions in Washington, DC, Quebec

City, Prague, Nice, Gothenburg, Naples, Port Moresby, Melbourne, Zurich, Seoul, Durban and many other places.

The new movement went by different names. In Britain it was often called anti-capitalism. In Italy it was called *No Globo*, and in France *Alter-Globalisation*, meaning another globalisation. In all places, people were careful to explain to you that it was not globalisation as such they were against, but the kind currently on offer. The movement adopted one central slogan: Another World is Possible. There was considerable disagreement about what other world and most were uncertain how to achieve it. But the other favourite slogan made it clearer what people were against: Our World is Not For Sale.

Two events were particularly important: the World Social Forum and Genoa. The first World Social Forum was held in Porto Alegre, Brazil, early in 2001. This was a gathering of NGOs, social movement activists and trade unionists from all over the world. It was sponsored by the Brazilian trade unions, the movement of the landless in Brazil, Greenpeace and ATTAC, the main French anti-capitalist group. The forum was a festival of meetings, rather than a march. It was more mainstream: there were more suits and bureaucrats than on street demonstrations. But in some ways this was a strength, for it helped to bring the mainstream into the new movement. Within a year, the WSF was giving rise to continental social forums in Europe and Asia. The WSF linked organisationally, for the first time, the movements in the global south and the rich countries. By the time it moved to Mumbai, India, in 2004, the WSF was a strongly grassroots event, mobilising the downtrodden of the earth.

One striking change in the new movement, in fact, was the relationship between activists in the north and south. For years, many activists in the rich countries had thought that their relationship to the poor countries should be one of solidarity with the most oppressed. Now the focus shifted. Activists in the global north saw themselves as primarily fighting the same forces at home as the movements faced in the global south. The way the plan of globalisation had reshaped the world had made the experiences of working people in both rich and poor countries more similar. Solidarity did not go away, as Iraq was to prove. But it was to a large extent stripped of pity.

The other key event was Genoa.[5] The leaders of the G8 countries – the US, Canada, Britain, France, Germany, Italy, Spain and Russia – held their annual summit there in June 2001. The Italian movement invited activists from all over Europe to attempt to close down the summit. On the first day, 50,000 tried to march to the fence that enclosed the powerful. The police reacted with force, killing one demonstrator, Carlo Guiliani. The leadership of the Italian movement went on television that night live and asked all Italy to come for the big march without direct action the next day. Three hundred thousand responded. As we marched though the streets, we chanted, like Seattle, 'This is What Democracy Looks Like'. We didn't mean the police this time. We meant we were democracy.

That night the police arrested 90 sleeping demonstrators, beat them, tortured them and accused them of conspiracy. The 300,000 people who had been on the demonstration went home and organised marches all over Italy. First in Genoa, and then in Rome, the banners went up all over town, in the public parks, across the streets, in front of police stations. They said: Assassins. They meant the police. The government was forced to release all the imprisoned demonstrators without charge. The Italian government, with the support of Bush and Blair, had tried to break the new movement with violence and had been humiliated.

The European movement was on a high. What was happening in South Africa was at least equally important. There the Treatment Action Campaign for AIDS drugs had been founded just before Seattle. In late 1999, the American government was still supporting Big Pharma. After Seattle, and with a presidential campaign coming up, Al Gore backed away from personal involvement. The South African government had originally brought a court case against Big Pharma, in an attempt to get the court to rule that the import of generic drugs was illegal. Mbeki's government had been refusing to support the court case. The TAC forced him to.

As the case came to court, the TAC appealed for demonstrations around the world. The most important was at Yale. This was an elite Ivy League college in the US. All four main candidates for president and vice-president in 2000 (Bush, Cheney, Gore and Lieberman) were Yale men. So was the elder Bush. Bill and Hillary Clinton met there. One of the AIDS drugs involved in the South African court case had been developed at Yale. The scientist who did the work wanted the drug copied for free. The Pfizer corporation, who made it, did not. But students at Yale demonstrated in solidarity with TAC.

The global campaign would not have happened that way without Seattle. It forced Big Pharma to drop their opposition to the case. A few months later, the US withdrew its case at the WTO against Brazil. That didn't mean Africans got the AIDS drugs. Despite the court case, Mbeki refused to let his health service give the AIDS drugs. He was still under pressure from the US, and even generic drugs would mean expanding the budget.

Big Pharma promised drugs at reduced prices for Africa that Africans still could not afford. They promised to give some of the drugs for free. This was to avoid South Africa using generic drugs. A gift of drugs was a short-term affair. Generic drugs would be permanently available. In any case, the promised gifts did not arrive. Kofi Annan and the UN tried to set up a $10 billion fund to treat TB, malaria and AIDS in the poor countries, but not using generic drugs. No one came up with the money.

In 2003 the South African government finally rolled out a programme for gradually giving generic drugs to any South Africans who needed them, with the proviso that it would take years before it reached the whole country. In 2004 the first patients began receiving the drugs at a few centres. This was an enormous victory. In the rest of Africa, except Botwsana, almost everyone was still dying.

9/11 and George Bush

Three months after the Genoa demonstration, on 11 September 2001, 19 men, most of them middle-class Saudis, flew two civilian airliners into the World Trade Center in New York and one airliner into the Pentagon. Outside the US, the world watched on the television, with complex feelings.

There was sympathy. For many watching on TV, this was the first time they had seen a bombing in all its horror. We watched people jump to their deaths. We saw ordinary working people, interviewed on the street, in their grief, fear and confusion. It was easy for your heart to go out to them.

That feeling was strongest in the US. It went with a question, however. Why? The media and politicians had kept Americans in systematic ignorance of what their country did in the Middle East. September 11 was in fact one more, particularly awful, set of deaths in a war that had been going on for a long time. Yet to most Americans, it seemed literally to come out of the sky.

Many people around the world also thought, 'Now you know what it feels like.' Few were proud of that feeling, but it was there.

The American administration spent 11 September in chaos. The next day they met in the White House to decide what to do. Some wanted to bomb and invade Afghanistan. Some wanted to go straight for Iraq.

To understand the decisions the Bush administration made, we have to start by being clear about what George Bush represented. Many see him as a fool or a madman. He is neither. Bush represents the American ruling class at their most confident, after 20 years of victories.[6] George W. Bush is a child of the ruling class. His family has been part of Wall Street finance for three generations, with close connections to national politics and the CIA. His father, George Bush the elder, moved to Texas and went into the oil business. Young George grew up there, and kept the accent. But he went to an elite private high school in the East, and from there to Yale and Harvard Business School. He was not the smartest student there, but not the dumbest either. When his father ran for president, George was the man who did the ugly stuff. He was in charge of the racist attack ads. And when someone had to be fired, it was George who did it.

At the same time, he went into business in Texas, first in oil and then in baseball. Both careers owed everything to the patronage and investments of men who needed to be close to the president's son. Then in 1994 George W. Bush was elected governor of Texas. He was widely regarded, by Texas legislators and corporate businessmen, as doing the job well.

When he began to put himself forward for the presidency, though, Bush had a problem. He's a bully, a cynic and a cruel man. When he opened his mouth, what came out was likely to be unacceptable to most Americans. His advisers trained him how to come across as a 'compassionate conservative'. But for a long time it was hard for him, so he just sort of garbled his words.

After 9/11 he came into his own. Now he was the president for revenge. Cruelty was in fashion. Bush addressed to crowds of soldiers, under orders to cheer, but he talked informally too, off the cuff. He spoke of hunting down the terrorists in their caves. He talked of other men like they were animals and made clear his pleasure in killing. The words flowed and everything he said made sense.

In much of the world, though, people asked themselves why had Americans voted for such a man. The simple answer was that they hadn't. He didn't win a majority of the popular vote. The Republican machine in Florida – and the governor, his brother Jeb Bush – tried to fix the election for him, and the Supreme Court finally elected him: 5 to 4.[7]

That's all true, but what it glides over is that Bush very nearly won the popular vote. He could so easily have been elected fairly. One reasons is that Americans mostly don't vote. In 2000 about half of adult Americans voted, though it was a larger proportion of registered voters. This was not untypical of the presidential elections, which are every four years. There are also 'off-year' elections every two years between the big races, which elect many governors, senators, congressional representatives and local politicians. Less than a third of adults vote in these elections. In all the elections, a solid majority of the richest fifth of the population vote. A majority of the working class, four-fifths of the population, do not. The poorer workers are, the less likely they are to vote. The exception is old people, who still think it matters and who want to defend social security.

So the actual electorate is richer and more privileged than the average American, and more right wing. Still, in other countries, with more voters, the right often wins too. America is just a more extreme version of something that is happening around the world. The traditional parties of the left and the labour movement have lost their nerve as they enforce capitalism themselves. In response to this betrayal, a rising proportion of working-class voters stay home. And when they do vote, they often simply vote against the government. Bush didn't win the election. Gore lost it. People didn't know what Gore had tried to do social security or AIDS drugs. But they could sense what he was.

And if Bush now seems a warmonger, that wasn't how it seemed at the time of the election. Clinton had supervised wars in Somalia, Haiti and Kosovo, and insisted on the sanctions on Iraq. Bush, by contrast, said he was against too much intervention.

The response to 9/11

George Bush, in short, is no fool, and the American people are mostly not rabid right-wingers. So how do we understand the policy that came out of the White House after 9/11?[8] (911 is the emergency phone number in America, just as 999 is in Britain.)

First, the terrorist attacks represented an opportunity for the American ruling class. For the first time since Vietnam, the American people might permit their children to die for American foreign policy. Ground troops were suddenly possible. And if the US government didn't seize the opportunity and use troops now, they would never be able to in future.

There was also the blow to American power. In much of the world the US dominated with at least some popular consent – in Britain and much of Europe, for instance. But there were places, particularly in the Middle East, where American power rested on fear of US might and of local dictators supported by

Washington. The sight of the Pentagon, the centre of that military power, in flames showed the US was vulnerable. Fear had to be restored. If it wasn't, US control over oil was in jeopardy. The public humiliation of 9/11 would have to be hidden by a much larger act of revenge.

There were other considerations, too. The global economy, and the US, was in recession. Throughout the 1990s, the American economy had expanded. The rate of growth had been half that of the 1960s, but the expansion had been real. Unemployment was down to 4 per cent. Industrial profits in the US had recovered some, regaining between a quarter and a half of what they had lost in the 1960s. The stock market had soared, driven by yet another bubble, this time based on fantasies about the internet. The Federal Reserve had backed that bubble, and so had the stockbrokers' analysts and the media. There had been an air of vainglorious triumph on Wall Street. It was said that recessions had come to an end, that the American economy was now unstoppable.[9]

Just as Bush became president, this all came crashing down. This was a political problem for him. It was a deeper problem for the ruling class and the corporations. They had justified the system to their workers by claiming it would go on growing forever. Now the market was partly discredited.

The recession produced a series of business failures. The most prominent of these was Enron. An energy trading firm in Houston, Enron specialised in complex futures trading and derivatives – gambling on what would happen in the market.[10] Enron's CEO, Ken Lay, had been a major financial backer for Bush in Texas. Other administration figures had close ties with Enron as well. These meant, paradoxically, that when Enron ran into trouble the administration didn't dare save it, for fear of being brought down too. For Enron had in effect been cheating other, more powerful corporations. It had claimed to be one of the ten largest corporations in the world. It was not. What they had been doing was counting all the transactions they arranged as if they were sales. It was as if a firm of stockbrokers count-ed all the stocks they sold as income. The real income of the stockbroker, though, would be the small percentage commission they made on the sales. So it was possible to let Enron go without threatening the whole system of debt.

But the administration, sensitive to the widespread hatred of CEOs in the country, arrested several executives of Enron and other failing companies. They were made to do the 'perp walk'. The police arrived at the perpetrator's place of work, put him in handcuffs and marched him out in front of the cameras.

The recession also exacerbated the tensions with Western Europe and China. Although American profits had recovered somewhat, European profits had not. When the US economy was sweeping all before it, the economic rivalries between the different powers mattered less. Now that the world economy was in recession again, competition intensified. The US economy depended on large, and constant, foreign investment to balance the fact that the US bought far more from abroad than it exported. There was always the possibility that the European Union might be seen as a safer home for capital investment. If that investment started to shift to Europe, the Euro would then become the world currency, instead of the dollar. Then the American economic empire, and the domestic economy, would come crashing down.

The Middle East was a particular worry. The regimes and the rich of the Middle East invested a great deal of their money in the US rather than in productive investment at home. As hostility to the US increased in the Middle East, the American ruling class started to worry about this money shifting from dollars to Euros. So when Saddam Hussein in Iraq started asking for payment for oil in Euros, he angered Washington. It was crucial for the US to continue to appear to the Arab ruling classes as the dominant world power.

There was another worry, too. It was not entirely accidental that George Bush was such a bully. He represented, in his person, a change in relations at work over much of the world. Bullying was rampant, as a result of the pressures of globalisation, speedup, privatisation and subcontracting. Middle managers and line managers were under constant pressure to increase profits. In the public sector, and in newly privatised companies, they were under pressure to restructure the whole world of work. This was particularly acute in sectors like health and education, where workers and professionals were used to putting the patients or the students first. In areas that were not already driven by the clock and the production line, the changes required constant personal bullying, every day. Bullies were more likely to become managers, and existing managers found themselves turning into bullies. As with prison guards and police in the US, this opened a space for personal cruelty. In the UK, where I have seen it up close, I know many people now who have gone home from work and cried themselves to sleep, or lain awake with fantasies of violent revenge.

The bully in George Bush also represented the confidence of the American ruling class. They had defeated the American unions, won the Cold War, imprisoned the black working class, put their stamp on the world economy. Their personal experience for 20 years had been of victory. They felt, now, like masters of the universe.

On the other side, the constant attacks, and the generation of defeats, were producing a global resentment that was feeding an increasing global resistance. This resistance was meeting American ruling-class power at its most confident and arrogant. The ruling class hoped the reaction to 9/11 would bury the new anti-capitalist movement without trace.

All these considerations meant that 9/11 presented George Bush and his team with a tremendous opportunity. They also meant that if their response didn't work, American dominance of the world would be in serious trouble. So would the power of the ruling class inside America. And so would the dominance of the ideas of globalisation and the 'free market' in every country, for those ideas were closely linked to American power. Every bully at work in the world would be weakened. There was everything to play for. And George Bush and his team had to do something. The question was: What?

Iraq or Afghanistan?

The people who gathered in the White House on 12 September 2001 debated whether to invade Afghanistan or Iraq. Many in the administration had wanted to 'do' Iraq for years. The obvious reason was oil. The countries of the Persian Gulf – Saudi Arabia, Iraq, Iran, Kuwait and the Emirates – controlled 65 per cent of the world's oil reserves. Control of that oil meant power in all the industrialised world. It also made it possible to keep the price down. These considerations had long been important.

There were two new factors, however. The American ruling class had expected their policy of sanctions would provoke a military coup in Iraq that would throw up a dictator they could work with. This had not happened, and international opposition to the sanctions was rising. Russian and French companies, not American ones, were getting oil contracts in Iraq. The Iranian regime, already hostile to the US, was also doing oil deals with other countries. And the Saudi regime was in danger.[11]

Saudi Arabia was America's strongest ally in the region. It had a quarter of the world's oil reserves, but the price of oil had been falling for some years. Saudi statistics are useless, but a reasonable guess is that income per person has fallen to a third of what it was 20 years ago.[12] The Saudi population had long held their tyrannical rulers in contempt. The widespread sympathy for Osama bin Laden was only one sign of the growing support for Islamist solutions.

Saudi Arabia, Iraq and Iran were not just important for the sake of controlling the world. They were the countries in the world most resistant to privatisation and globalisation. The Middle Eastern governments had taken ownership of the drilling and production of oil away from the transnational corporations in the 1960s and 70s. Though Russian oil has recently been privatised, the large majority of the world's oil production is still in government hands. Middle Eastern oil was the last holdout, the only manufacturing or extractive industry where this was true.

Iraq, Iran, Saudi Arabia and the Gulf kingdoms were also welfare states. Even under sanctions, Iraq was still using the

UN-run oil for food programme to provide cheap rations to the majority of its people. The Iranian Islamists had stayed in power by giving more generous subsidies and benefits than the previous regime, the Shah's. Saudi Arabia provided free schools, health care, pensions and all sorts of subsidies to native Saudis, although not to migrant workers. The Saudi government was under constant pressure from the US Treasury, the IMF, the World Bank and mainstream economists to 'reform'.[13] The Saudi royal family were still powerful enough economically to refuse. They were also aware that such reforms would probably cause the Saudi people to hack them to pieces.

Oil and the Middle Eastern welfare states were the last big challenge for the globalisers. The Bush administration had a particular interest in oil. Bush, Cheney, Rice, Rumsfeld and Wolfowitz had all been oil company executives. Rice even had a Chevron oil tanker named after her. The older men remembered the nationalisation of Middle Eastern oil. They knew in their bones it could be undone. When they finally invaded Iraq, they arrived with detailed plans for selling off Iraqi oil to themselves and their friends.

If Bush himself was sometimes lightweight, the advisers around him were intelligent people, experienced in world affairs. They knew the Middle East the way they knew the Permian Basin in West Texas. And they were more inclined than any previous government to think globally. That's how oil business people think, because that's how they operate. They weren't ignorant – they knew what had to be done. And if there were risks for other American corporations, for the oil companies it was a magnificent chance.

So Rumsfeld, Cheney and Wolfowitz arrived in office gunning for Iraq from day one. Paul O'Neill, Bush's treasury secretary at the time, has said so at length.[14] However, they were not allowed to do it. There were powerful arguments against it, the same ones that had prevented George Bush the elder from invading Iraq in the 1991 Gulf War.

Before 9/11, the US would have been internationally isolated had they attempted an invasion of Iraq. They would not have been able to use bases in Saudi Arabia, Turkey, Bahrain or probably even Kuwait. Without these bases, they couldn't have done it. O'Neill, the former CEO of Alcoa Aluminum and a spokesman for corporations as a whole, spoke against it. So did secretary of state Colin Powell, who represented the career military, the foreign service and the interests of the ruling class. American workers wouldn't have tolerated it either. So Rumsfeld backed down.

In this sense, 9/11 did not provide the hard right in the administration with a pretext for doing what they would have done anyway. Rather, it gave them a chance to do what they couldn't have done otherwise.

But even then, they couldn't do it immediately. Rumsfeld came to the National Security meeting on 12 September arguing for Iraq. Powell said no, do Afghanistan now. Powell won.

The reason was that any invasion had to be backed by the American people. There was a plausible case for arguing that Osama bin Laden, who was in Afghanistan under the protection of the Taliban government, had been involved in 9/11 in some way, if not as an organiser, then as a mentor. Americans were willing to go to war after 9/11, but it couldn't be any old war. And the US still needed support from other countries.

So Bush decided to wait. Nine days later, on 20 September, he told Tony Blair they would be going for Iraq after Afghanistan. Plans got under way. The calculation was that a victorious Afghan war would cure the Vietnam syndrome and scare the other governments of the world. Then Iraq would be doable.

In public, though, the administration concentrated on Afghanistan. It was another moment, as with the War on Drugs, when the whole American ruling class came together to back the plan. When congress voted for war, only one woman voted no, the representative from Berkeley, the most liberal constituency in the country.

Afghanistan

Afghanistan had two advantages as a stage for the drama of

revenge. One was that bin Laden was there. The second was that it was one of the most helpless places on earth. The Afghans had lived through 23 years of war. They longed for peace, and the Taliban government had little support.

The Russian occupation had failed in 1988.[15] The Americans then withdrew all aid to the Islamist resistance groups, the Mujahedin, who they had previously supported. The Muhajedin leaders then fell out with each other. Kabul, the capital, had been spared Soviet carpet bombing. Large areas of the city were now reduced to rubble as competing Mujahedin leaders fought for control. Mujahedin commanders also established regional power bases, often with connections to the opium trade, which Afghan farmers still needed to survive. The Afghans had resisted the Soviets in the name of Islam. Now they were appalled by the corruption of the Mujahedin and longed for peace and safety.

In 1995 the old alliance of the American government, the Pakistani military and Saudi intelligence stepped in. On the Pakistani border the allies created a new army of Taliban. The word means students, and many of the soldiers were boys from religious schools in the refugee camps in Pakistan. The officers were mullahs, serving Pakistani army officers and former Afghan communists.

The prize for the US was oil and gas from Central Asia. The Muslim provinces of the Soviet Union were now all independent states. All but one of them sat on considerable petroleum reserves. Russia, China and America were competing for control of this oil. The American weakness was that they had no nearby military bases, and no way of getting the oil and gas out of Central Asia. The existing pipelines all ran to Russia, enabling the government there to take a large share of the proceeds. The Americans had plans to build a long network of pipelines that ended in the Mediterranean. This network would pass through, or close to, several theatres of conflict – Azerbaijan, Georgia and Turkish Kurdistan. The easier, safer and much cheaper way for the Central Asian regimes to get their oil to the world market was a pipeline down through Iran to the Persian Gulf. But Iran was America's enemy. French, German and Russian corporations would predominate.

The solution was a pipeline straight south through Afghanistan, a bit of Pakistan, and then to the sea. An American corporation, Unocal, had plans to build it. With Afghanistan dominated by competing local commanders, this would be impossible. Washington hoped that the Taliban would impose order and make the pipeline possible.

At first, it worked. The Taliban troops swept north from the southern border, meeting little opposition. The local commanders knew the Americans were backing the Taliban. But almost all the Taliban came from the Pashtuns, the largest language group in Afghanistan, who lived mainly in the south and east. The official Taliban ideology was a form of pious right-wing Islam, modelled on Saudi Arabia. Beneath that, though, was Pashtun chauvinism. For 30 years Afghan politics had been divided on ideological, not ethnic lines. Now Afghans had lost faith in both communism and political Islam. The only remaining way to mobilise was ethnicity. The coming of Taliban power to the north would mean that many local commanders, and their followers, would lose their land to the new Pashtun fighters. The ethnic minorities in the North resisted the Taliban. Within a year, the Taliban had control of most of the major towns in the North, but the Northern Alliance of non-Pushtun groups – led by ex-Mujahedin – controlled enough of the countryside to make the plan for a Central Asian pipeline impossible. Clinton withdrew support from the Taliban. The Taliban provided a refuge for Osama bin Laden.

Then, in September 2001, the US decided on invasion. The Taliban began negotiating to turn bin Laden over to the Americans. Washington was not interested. This time they would restore order and build the pipeline.

The Americans didn't invade directly. Instead, they sent some CIA and special forces, they bombed heavily from the air, and they used the Northern Alliance troops as their local ally. The Vietnam syndrome was still alive. Washington was also aware that Afghans, with memories of the Russian invasion, might react badly. And the US government had to keep Pakistan on side. Pakistan was a military dictatorship, but there was strong popular feeling against the Afghan war. As the war began, there were demonstrations all over Pakistan. A massive American invasion would stoke those protests.

Without substantial invasion troops, however, the US plan quickly ran into trouble. The few thousand Northern Alliance troops, like all Afghans, were weary of war. They didn't want to fight. The bombs kept falling, but the American backed advance on Kabul stalled.

Meanwhile, the protests were increasing in Pakistan, Britain and the US. Washington felt they had to break the logjam. With the help of Pakistani intelligence they negotiated a deal with the Taliban. The Taliban would leave power and Kabul. Those who wanted could go home to their towns and villages in the south and east, where their influence would not be challenged. Others chose to be ferried to the tribal Pashtun areas of Pakistan along the border. The Pakistani army and police did not dare venture there and the Taliban would be safe. Osama bin Laden was also allowed to escape there. This deal has been largely observed. No senior Taliban leaders have been taken into custody, except for one man who was ambassador in Pakistan. Several thousand rank and file Taliban fighters were cut off in the north. Among them were a few hundred foreign volunteers who had come to help the Taliban. Many of them were massacred on Donald Rumsfeld's orders. The rest of the foreigners were sent to Guantanamo Bay, the American controlled base on the Cuban coast.

They were sent there to shield them from the protection of American law and appeals to American courts. Pictures of men being humiliated and carried to torture on stretchers were disseminated around the world media. These pictures were taken by the Pentagon or with their permission. The intention, clearly, was to induce fear, both in the Middle East and in the US itself. The detainees would be charged in special military tribunals without the normal rights enjoyed by American soldiers at courts martial. Despite that, there have been almost no trials.

These people are nobodies and cannot go to trial. The reason is that the Americans agreed to let all the Taliban and Al Qaida ringleaders go.

That was generally understood in Afghanistan. On the world stage, however, the fall of Kabul appeared as a complete American victory. The US came out of the war with bases in Pakistan and in all but one of the oil states of Central Asia to the north. Work began in earnest on a massive deep-water port in Gwadar, in Pakistan, close to the Iranian border. Gwadar would be the end point for the new pipeline, and give the US a massive military base on the Iranian border. The port is being funded by the World Bank and built by the Chinese government under contract.

In Afghanistan itself, the USA installed Hamed Karzai as president. Karzai was an Afghan from a family of Pushtun landlords. It was widely believed in Afghanistan that Karzi was also a career CIA agent. He ruled in uneasy partnership with the Northern Alliance. To shore up his power, Karzai and the Americans turned increasingly to the politics of Pashtun chauvinism. This strained the partnership with the northerners.

Twenty thousand NATO troops occupied Kabul and about 15,000 US troops patrolled the south and east. They enjoyed very little popular support. Resistance, led by the Taliban and some ex-Mujahedin, began. Within a year, the NATO troops in Kabul evacuated the city every night at five and did not return until eight the next morning. Attacks on Americans and their bases were running at an average of two a day. Some parts of the country were controlled by the old local commanders and some by the insurgents. Karzai could no longer trust any Afghans and all his bodyguards were American mercenaries. The US had been expected to spend large sums of money on reconstructing the country. Washington, however, had never promised such a thing and didn't do it.

The world media had left Afghanistan. The hollowness of the US victory was not apparent. The Bush administration, after the fall of Kabul, felt supremely confident. Now they could do Iraq.

11 | Iraq and the Planet

The dividends of the Afghan war for the American ruling class were seen most clearly at the WTO meeting in Doha in November 2001, the first big conference since Seattle. Doha was selected because it was in the Persian Gulf kingdom of Qatar, and the dictatorship would ensure that protests were impossible. Qatar was close to the Afghan War, and the delegates were only too aware of American fury. They did what Washington told them to do. The defeat of Seattle was, for the moment repaired.[1]

George Bush effectively announced his intention to invade Iraq in his annual State of the Union speech to congress in January 2002. He linked Iraq with Iran and North Korea in an 'axis of evil'. North Korea was thrown in so it would not seem the US was only after Muslims. The North Korean regime had nuclear weapons, and the Chinese government had made it clear to the Americans they would react to any invasion so close to their borders. But Iran was a real target, and Iraq would be first.[2]

Congress applauded Bush's speech, and the media agreed. But there was a serious problem. Bush had declared a 'War on Terror', the name taken from the War on Drugs. Many people, of many different political persuasions, had sympathised with the demand that the perpetrators of 9/11 be brought to justice. There had been protests at the Afghan war, notably in London, where I was one of 100,000 marchers. But the view that this was simply a war for American empire was in a minority.

However, Bush's switch to invade Iraq could not be justified by the War on Terror. The Bush administration persuaded some Americans and much of the American media. In the rest of the world, people who had supported the Afghan war out of sympathy began to feel that their decency had been used.

The US administration argued on several fronts. In a covert way, they implied to Americans that bin Laden and Saddam were both Muslims, both enemies, and therefore the same. In a more open way, they argued that Saddam was a tyrant whose people would welcome liberation, just as Eastern Europeans had welcomed the end of their dictatorships. And they argued that Saddam possessed weapons of mass destruction which threatened the world.

This last argument was particularly important to Tony Blair in Britain. His government was backing Bush all the way. Partly this was because the alliance with the US had been the cornerstone of foreign policy for every British government since 1945. Britain had lost its empire, and was no longer strong enough to fight militarily in its own right. They could do a minor war like the Falklands, but nothing serious. British corporations and banks were still important international investors, and Britain was the fifth largest economy in the world. The British ruling class needed the American umbrella. Britain was big economically, so had a lot to lose, but not *big enough* to protect itself.[3]

There was another reason Blair backed Bush. Outside of the US, the rich countries where privatisation, globalisation and the cuts in the welfare state have gone furthest are Britain and New Zealand. Inequality has risen sharply in Britain. Margaret Thatcher's defeat of the miners strike in 1985 was the single largest humiliation for any labour movement in Europe since 1980. From 2000 on, the unions and anti-capitalist movement in Germany, France, Italy, Spain and Greece were fighting against major 'reforms', almost all of which had already been introduced in Britain. These had begun under conservative governments, but been continued under Blair's 'New Labour'.

Tony Blair, in his person, like Bush, expressed a similar triumph of the right and the ruling class. He had been elected and remained head of the Labour Party because its leaders believed now that there was no alternative. The shift in power that had happened at the base of society was reflected at the top. Britain stood shoulder to shoulder with the US because they were similar places.

However, not all of the British ruling class was happy with the close alliance. British investment went to both Europe and the US, while the majority of exports went to Europe. It was important to industrial corporations to keep the European link. If the US and Europe split, they would want to go with Europe.

That split began to happen. What pushed it was the rising international movement against war. This was something Bush and company had not expected, because nothing on the same scale had ever been seen before. The size of the demonstrations makes it hard to estimate numbers. Above about 200,000 it becomes difficult even for experienced journalists to guess. For many years activists had used a simple formula. They took the police estimate and the organisers' estimate and averaged them. But the police were now choosing ridiculously low numbers. The only check we have had on any of the numbers was the protest on 15 February 2003 in London. On the day, the organisers guessed two million. The next day a national opinion poll included an extra question: was there a person from your household on the demonstration? Extrapolating the poll to the nation, 1,200,000 households participated. As many people came with family or housemates, this suggests the guess of two million was right.

In most places, the anti-war movement was started by activists and organisations already part of the anti-capitalist movement.[4] They went to their diaries, mobiles and email lists and started contacting people. The attitude of the established parties of the far left also made a considerable difference. The Socialist Workers Party in Britain, for instance, and Communist Refoundation in Italy were both at the heart of the anti-war movement. In some countries, like France and Germany, the established left was hostile to Islamist politics, and so did not mobilise against the Afghan war. In these countries the demonstrations against the Iraq war would also be smaller, but still significant.

In the US and most countries in Europe the anti-war movement was soon stronger than the anti-capitalist movement had
been and the marches were much bigger. In the spring of 2002,
anti-capitalists in Barcelona called a demonstration 'Against War
and Global Capitalism'. In a city of three million, 500,000
people, mainly locals, demonstrated. The anti-war coalitions were
also usually much wider than the anti-capitalists had been. In
Britain, for instance, the movement was large for four reasons.
One was Tony Blair and the fact that Britain was also going to
war. The second was that the Stop the War Coalition had campaigned hard against the whole War on Terror, had gone to the
mosques in every city and involved the large Muslim community. This increased the numbers and it also cut against the
anti-Muslim prejudice the right was using to justify the war.

The third reason the movement was large was that most of
the trade union leaders supported the campaign, spoke at rallies
and marched in the streets. The fourth reason was that the largest
far left organisation in Britain, the Socialist Workers Party,
was very active in the coalition from the start. SWP members –
I'm one myself – brought to the movement both a roots and
branch opposition to American imperialism and an insistence
on bringing together the left, the Muslims and the unions.

The movements in Italy and Spain, though, were as large. As
in Britain, much of the anger at the war was fed by a deeper
dissatisfaction, of long standing, at what had happened to people's
lives. This was not obvious in the official propaganda, but quite
clear in every conversation I had.

From 2001 to 2003 the anti-capitalist movement was also
spreading into the unions. The rejection of globalisation gave
union activists heart. For too long they had stepped back because
they were unable to imagine an alternative to capitalism. Now
they said, 'Another World is Possible'. The idea that you did not
have to accept things as they were was spreading quickly.

Meanwhile, recession and competition were piling on the
pressure for globalisation at the top. In Italy, Spain, Greece and
India, the governments proposed 'reforms' that attacked long
cherished employment and pension rights. The unions replied

with one-day general strikes. The anti-globalisation and anti-war movements had mobilised large numbers of individuals. The unions were now mobilising majorities in most of the big workplaces. In France, too, there were big public-sector strikes in the summer of 2003. In China there were now tens of thousands of local demonstrations every year against the cuts in employment and pensions that go with membership of the WTO.

The movement in Latin America, though, was the biggest, and seemed closest to challenging for power. In Venezuela Hugo Chavez had taken power in a military coup, declared himself on the side of the poor and won a massive majority in an election.[5] In practice, he did little to help the poor, and privatisation continued, though at a slower pace. But his foreign policy defied Washington. Venezuela was an oil producer, America's biggest foreign supplier. Chavez attempted to strengthen OPEC, the Organization of Petroleum Exporting Countries, and drive up the price of oil by rationing supply. The lack of real change on the ground seemed to leave Chavez vulnerable, however. The Venezuelan ruling class, encouraged by the CIA, went for a military coup. The workers poured out of the neighbourhoods on the hills around Caracas to surround the military. The soldiers had already refused to kill Chavez – he was released, triumphant, back in power, a humiliation for the US. A similar operation in Haiti was, however, successful early in 2004.

In Brazil, which has a third of the population of Latin America, Lula and his Workers Party were elected in 2002. Lula himself had begun as a car worker, influenced by liberation theology, organising in the factories under the dictatorship in the 1980s. That workers' movement had broken the dictatorship. Now, finally, it seemed that the working class had some sort of power. Washington waited to see what happened. Lula had promised the US that he would carry out the cuts the IMF had already imposed. He did so, and publicly supported the US invasion of Iraq. For the moment, Washington relaxed.

In Argentina, the currency crashed in December 2001. The immediate cause was that the IMF had persuaded the government to scrap the national pension scheme and replace it with a private one. The government had to pay out to established pensioners without getting any contributions in, and public finance collapsed. The longer-term cause, though, was that Argentine industry was uncompetitive in a globalised world. When the banks closed, 2 million people turned out all over Buenos Aires. Their fury removed four governments in quick succession. The main forces in the movement were the unemployed and middle-class people who had lost their savings. The unions, though, remained under the control of 'Peronists' allied to the government. When an election was finally permitted, the mass movement voted in a left Peronist still largely prepared to do what the IMF said.

The same pattern was repeated in Peru, Bolivia and Ecuador. Uprisings or general strikes produced new governments who then continued the policies of globalisation. The new movements had no idea of how to get to 'Another World'. In practice, they found themselves supporting politicians who tried, once again, to make one national economy profitable in a global capitalist world. The movement so far knew how to protest, but not how to take power. Their strength, of course, was that the new movements were now powerful enough to remove governments, where 15 years before IMF riots had exploded into angry defeat.

The challenge to American, and corporate, power was escalating. As the troops gathered on the borders of Iraq, the anti-war movement grew too. In September 2002, 400,000 people demonstrated against the war in London, the largest demonstration in British history. The World Social Forum in Porto Alegre had given birth to continental social forums. The first European one was to held in Florence, Italy, in November 2002. The British march inspired the loose international organising committee for the forum to call a demonstration against the war and the forum. The Italian anti-capitalist movement responded enthusiastically. A million people marched in Florence. The forum organisers, with the support of the great majority present, called for a demonstration against the Iraq war in every European capital on 15 February 2003. The anti-capitalist movement and the anti-war movement had fused.

The European activists took the call for an international protest to the World Social Forum in Brazil in January 2003. At the start of the week the leaders of most Latin American movements were saying the real war was against poverty in Latin America, not Iraq. By the end of the week people were ready to organise demonstrations in many cities of Latin America, and more widely.

On 15 February, 2 million people marched in London and the same number in Rome. Three to four million joined marches in cities across Spain. In New York, in Manhattan, where 9/11 had happened, half a million people joined an illegal demonstration. Worldwide, roughly 15 million people marched in more than a hundred countries. A few months later a Norwegian environmentalist at the European Social Forum in Paris explained to me that he had counted more than 80 different demonstrations in Scandinavia. He said it was not true that there was only one protest at a scientific research station in Antarctica. There were two.

The threat to American dominance was suddenly very real. Before 15 February the UN Security Council had approved, with no votes against, a resolution effectively allowing the US to invade Iraq, but not saying that in so many words. Now Tony Blair, under pressure from the 2 million, and fearing a parliamentary revolt, insisted Bush go back to the Security Council. The conservative president of France, Jacques Chirac, and the social democrat chancellor of Germany, had both supported the Afghan war. Both countries had voted for the first UN resolution. After the demonstrations, they calculated that the weight of public opinion at home was such that they could not do so. The second resolution fell, with support from only the US, Britain and Spain.

The French and German governments also took some pleasure in defying the US. The economic competition between Europe and the US had been building for some time. Now it was taking a political form.

Demonstrations began in the Middle East as well. In Lebanon and Turkey, relatively free countries, these were large. The Turkish protests encouraged parliament to vote to refuse transit for American troops. In the dictatorships of the region demonstrations were smaller and illegal. In Egypt a few thousand demonstrators in Cairo were met with police brutality, mass arrests and torture. But the feeling in the country was such that the dictator, President Mubarak, had to appear on television and condemn the American war.

The US and Britain had to go war, effectively, alone. Bush could not back down. The very size of the global opposition meant that any retreat into peace would be a decisive defeat for American power. It also meant Bush had to win the war and hold the occupation that followed. And it meant the latter would be very difficult.

The advance on Baghdad was swift and successful. The gaze of world opinion meant the bombing could not be on the scale of the Gulf War of 1991. This time perhaps less than 20,000 Iraqis, troops and civilians died and most of the infrastructure was left untouched. On taking Baghdad, the US troops rounded up a few hundred Iraqis to topple a statue of Saddam Hussein for the world's cameras. The camera angles served to hide the fact that the square was largely empty.

Donald Rumsfeld, the Pentagon and Dick Cheney had expected public support for the American invaders. There was almost none, except in the Kurdish north. What there was, in many quarters, was deep relief that Saddam had gone.

Resistance to the American occupation began with demonstrations. In the town of Falluja, American troops opened fire on a march and killed 13. Falluja has been at the centre of the armed resistance ever since.

The Shia majority had been largely excluded from power under Saddam, as had the Sunni minority. The American occupiers tried to divide Shia, Sunnis and Kurds. This was now standard operating procedure in any American occupation. In part their experience at home caused the American ruling class to see racial segregation and hostility as natural. It was also because there were only three possible ways local politics could be polarised. People could split along class lines, as parties did in Europe, Latin America and South Asia. This was anathema to the occupiers. People could also split along the lines of opposition to the occupation, as they increasingly did in Afghanistan and Iraq. Or they could split on ethnic and religious lines. The US authorities preferred the latter. They explained every political situation in the occupied world in terms of tribal, sectarian or ethnic rivalries.

In Iraq, for a time and to a limited extent this worked. The senior religious leadership of the Shia community cooperated with the American-nominated provisional government. But the pressure from below to cease doing so grew. The Sunni areas were already in open revolt. The mass death of children during UN sanctions meant that a large proportion of Iraqis were united in their hostility to Western invaders.

The American generals faced several problems because of the scale of the anti-war movement internationally. First, the demonstrations across the world, and particularly in the Middle East, had been shown on independent Arab satellite television. The Iraqis had seen it. That gave the Iraqi resistance a spirit and confidence they otherwise would not have had. They knew the world was on their side.

Second, the extent of resistance by the Iraqi Army to the invasion had convinced Washington they could not rely on indirect rule. Left intact, the Iraqi Army might turn on them. So the soldiers were sent home with a promise of a one-off payment of $35, which was then mostly not paid. The American troops couldn't stop the Iraqi soldiers taking their arms home with them. Any American can imagine what US GIs would do if they lost their jobs and pensions and were sent home to mass unemployment, carrying machine guns and rocket launchers. Many Iraqi ex-soldiers did the same.

Third, the depth of opposition to the American occupation is combined with the US not having enough soldiers on the ground. The US is commonly said to have the world's largest military. What it actually has is the world's most expensive military. The numbers were cut after the Cold War from 2.1 million to 1.4 million. Most of these are support forces, or Navy, or Air Force, or already in garrison somewhere else.

Unlike Vietnam, and all American wars since, half the American troops in Iraq are now National Guard or reservists. They are largely untrained for such work. They want out and their families are saying so publicly. Even with these troops, the US now has only 135,000 troops in Iraq, a country of 20 million people. They had 500,000 in Vietnam. The US troops are supported by a small British force, and token forces from other countries, who do not expect their soldiers to die in large numbers. There are also large numbers of mercenaries for battle and privately-contracted support staff.

The US, however, will probably find it impossible to increase the number of troops substantially because of the domestic opposition it would arouse. The 600 Americans officially dead in the war is already a large enough number to trouble the Pentagon. The Vietnam syndrome has not gone away.

Without more troops, however, the US cannot protect Iraqi police or collaborators. That means they have no one to work through. Any occupation requires a network of local supporters, administrators, informers and interrogators. That is absent.

Fourth, outside of Kurdistan in the North, the American occupation has a partnership with no real social force on the ground. When the NATO troops leave Kabul at five every afternoon, the soldiers of the Northern Alliance remain. In South Vietnam, the US had the support of landlords, safe refuges in the cities, and the South Vietnamese Army. In Iraq, the US has no such local support.

Fifth, the world's press, including Arab television stations, are still in Iraq. What happens in Afghanistan is now hardly noticed, yet every American death in Iraq is reported. That is because of the effect of the demonstrations on 15 February.

Sixth, the anti-war movement has not gone away. This limits what the occupying troops can do. An army of occupation faced with armed and widely-supported resistance usually reacts with massive force. The aim is to frighten the local population so badly they insist the resistance stops. This is what the German occupiers tried to do in Europe and what the Americans did in

Vietnam. The American generals are increasingly tempted to do the same in Iraq. However, US bombers killed something like 2 million people in North and South Vietnam. Nothing on that scale is possible in Iraq.

Seventh, the cost of the occupation is escalating. The US plan was to take over Iraqi oil. In the short term, they would have used the proceeds to fund the occupation. In the long term, American corporations would control the oil. The resistance, however, continuously blows up the pipelines. Oil production has not recovered to the low levels permitted to Saddam under UN sanctions. Contractors like Bechtel had expected to walk into Iraq. But their foreign employees cannot move safely in the country. Without the oil, the bill for the occupation is escalating. Bush had to go to Congress in 2003 for $87 billion and will be back for more. This is a strain on the American economy. In a recovery from recession that has produced few jobs, it is also unacceptable to working America. The opinion polls show a very large majority of Americans opposed the congressional vote for the $87 billion.

Finally, the scale of Iraqi opposition means that the American government cannot permit Iraqis to vote. Any democratically-elected government would take back control of the oil and ask the Americans to leave. But the refusal to allow elections only stokes opposition. And if elections cannot be allowed, strikes must also be broken and demonstrations fired upon. That too increases the resistance.

The American occupation is now caught in an escalating spiral. Unable to control the country, they must reply with brutal violence. When that does not work, because their forces are too small, they reply with greater violence. Backed in a corner, they can make no new allies in the country. The escalating killing alienates almost all Iraqis, which means there is more opposition to be crushed and more people to be killed. The main lie that Tony Blair told British people was about weapons of mass destruction. But the main lie George Bush told Americans was about the American troops being welcomed. Americans are rapidly turning away from supporting the war.

For all these reasons, it looks like George Bush made a mistake. On one level, the sensible thing would be for the American ruling class to throw its support to John Kerry and withdraw. As I write this, in the spring of 2004, the opinion polls say that voters are evenly divided. Since so many Americans do not vote, pollsters do not provide the numbers who actually answer their questions. Instead, they modify the numbers to reflect the likelihood that particular respondents will vote. As working people and Democrats are less likely to vote, evenly balanced numbers in the polls reflect a solid majority for Kerry among Americans.

Many things are possible. Elections are full of accidents. Kerry's election would not necessarily end the occupation. Kerry has long been a 'New Democrat', like Clinton and Gore. They supported American business interests abroad and at home, and Kerry will probably do the same. He voted for the wars in Afghanistan and Iraq, supports the occupation, has called for more troops to be sent there and telephoned the new Spanish prime minister in April 2004 to ask him to leave his troops in Iraq. Parts of the American ruling class, and much of the media, are supporting Kerry in the hope that he will be a safe pair of hands. The past, the thinking goes, could then be dumped on Bush, and Kerry could manage the present. On the other hand, many in the ruling class also fear a defeat for Bush would be seen globally as a defeat for American power.

Many in the US ruling class now favour a compromise where the UN is brought in. This won't work. The hostility to the UN is still very high because of the sanctions. Most Iraqis will only accept the UN if American troops leave. That would be a major problem for the American ruling class. For them, withdrawal from Iraq is full of danger whether Bush or Kerry is in charge. Iraq has become the world's biggest political issue in 50 years. American withdrawal would be a victory for the Iraqi resistance and the global anti-war movement. There would be several probable consequences. The US would likely be asked also to withdraw its troops from Saudi Arabia. The opposition in Saudi Arabia, Egypt and Jordan might take heart and overthrow their dictators. The US would probably lose control of Middle Eastern oil to corporations from other countries, the people of the Middle East, or some alliance of both. The regimes in Pakistan, Afghanistan and Israel would be in grave trouble.

The consequences would be more serious than that, however. American dominance as a whole would come under question. The American people would be unlikely to tolerate another invasion for a long time to come. They would suffer from 'Iraq syndrome'.

The emerging European economic and political alliance would also be strengthened. This would not necessarily be a good thing for humanity. The US is not a uniquely evil empire. The ruling classes of Britain, France, Germany, Russia, China and Japan have all shown in the past that they are capable of equal evils. For the first 89 years of the 20th century, the world lived under competing superpowers. The wars of that time were, if anything, worse than the present ones. This applies not just to the World Wars, but to the hot proxy wars fought during the long Cold War. And European patriotism could soon be as dangerous for Europeans as American patriotism is now for Americans.

That said, American power over the poor countries would also be threatened by a withdrawal from Iraq. The Doha meeting of the WTO was a walkover for the US. The next was held in Cancun, Mexico, in the autumn of 2003, with the resistance in Iraq growing. This time there were only a few thousand demonstrators outside, because the Mexican left and unions did not mobilise. But inside, the delegates of the poor countries, effectively led by right-wing regimes in China and India, refused any agreement. This too was a consequence of the Iraq resistance.

An American defeat in Iraq would threaten 25 years of increasing inequality in the US. Every American opposition movement would take heart from the humiliation of George Bush. Increasing European power and the loss of control of Middle Eastern oil would at least threaten the dollar and American debt.

It is likely that only some of these possibilities would come to pass. But all of them must worry the American ruling class. This is why George Bush and John Kerry are saying America must stay the course in Iraq.

But this doesn't touch another consideration, which worries ruling classes everywhere. The project of globalisation has linked American power with the restructuring of the world to drive up profits. The two have been presented as a package deal. If American power is enfeebled, everyone opposed to the rest of globalisation will take heart. The drive for profits has depended on the idea that there is no alternative. The great strength of this drive has been its rigidity and its all-encompassing claims. But a rigid system of ideas and power has trouble bending, and can break. If the occupying forces are driven out of Iraq, then French, German and Russian corporations will have to worry about their own overseas interests, and their own workers at home. The ruling classes of France, Britain and Russia have all said they support the American occupation in Iraq. It may have been wrong to go to war, they say, but we don't want to see the US withdraw. They mean it.

If the US leaves, people all over the world will say to each other, if the Iraqis can do that, maybe we can stand up to our supervisor.

I will end, not with Iraq, but with the planet.

Climate change

There have been many years of controversy among scientists about climate change.[6] The jury is now in. All scientists who know anything about the subject, regardless of their politics, are now convinced global warming is happening and it's serious. The only exceptions are a few who take money from the oil companies. The scientists have convinced the rest of us. All of us, rich and poor, now know something has to be done. Nothing is being done. The reason is globalisation and profits. Let me explain.

Global warming is caused by 'greenhouse gases'. The most important is carbon dioxide, but they all work in much the same way. Carbon dioxide acts as a sort of one-way blanket over the earth. It allows the heat from the sun to get through, but stops some of the heat from the earth rising into space. As the proportion of carbon dioxide in the air rises, the earth gets warmer.

That proportion is increasing mainly through the burning of fossil fuels like oil, natural gas and coal. These were originally made from carbon life forms. So when they burn, the carbon mixes with oxygen. Two ways of using fossil fuels account for the majority of global warming. One is burning fuels to make electricity for industry and homes. The other is petrol in cars, trucks and planes. Because carbon dioxide stays in the air a long time, the effect of emissions is cumulative. Trees absorb carbon dioxide out of the air, but the great forests are being cut down. This factor, however, is not as important as fossil fuels. There are also other greenhouse gases, but carbon dioxide accounts for 80 per cent of global warming.

It is clear that the world's temperature has been increasing lately, especially near the poles. This is beginning to melt the artic ice. When this happens to a marked extent, the oceans will rise. Water will cover the low-lying islands, the coastal plains of New York, Washington, Boston, Holland, Belgium, London, Bangladesh, Calcutta, Hong Kong, Shanghai, and much of the world's agriculture.

The shift in temperature will also destabilise the world's weather system, leading to fierce floods, droughts and storms. This has already begun to happen in a small way. Recent floods in Bangladesh have already killed hundreds of thousands.

In time, the majority of the world's species will be exterminated as their habitat changes around them. The other trouble will be the inequality. Hundreds of millions of people will lose everything to storms or rising water. Insurance will not cover that. It is possible to imagine a world where they would be welcomed in a new home, given a warm drink, a house, some new clothes, a job, a future and respect. That is not the world we live in. Our world produces famine, plague and war in such circumstances.[7]

And the consequences, the scientists keep reminding us, may be worse than that. They pick their words with care, because they don't want to seem foolish, they don't want to make mistakes and they aren't sure of the future. They worry about several feedback mechanisms, none of them certain to happen, but all of them possible. Any one of them could create a spiral where the earth heats out of control.

So we have to cut the amount of carbon dioxide going into the air massively. The solutions are pretty clear to most scientists. These solutions need to be applied not just in the US and Europe, but in China and every other poor country in the world. We need public transport on buses, trains and trucks, instead of cars and planes. Houses and work buildings need to be comprehensively insulated, so less electricity has to be produced. This could only be done on the scale needed as a programme of free public works. We need to plant more trees. We need to use the available technology for wind, solar and water power to make electricity. And we need to do all these things at once.

If we do all this seriously, we can reduce the level of carbon dioxide emissions to less than half. And we can do it without reducing the population. This point is important. We are often told there are too many people in the world and they consume too much. In fact, the rate of population increase in every country in the world is falling. In the most developed countries, the population is not replacing itself. This means the world's population should continue to grow until it about doubles, and then will start to fall.

There is a real argument to be had about whether there are too many people for the world's resources. I belong to the group that, with some qualifications, thinks not. But that argument is a red herring when it comes to climate change. If the world population doubles and the way we use fossil fuels remains the same, then we will cook the world. But we will also heat the world if the population remains the same and nothing basically changes. And if we stop using fossil fuels, try alternative power sources and plant forests, we can double the world's population.

It is also often said that controls on carbon dioxide would mean the poor countries could never catch up. But new factories and electricity plants without fossil fuels can be built in poor countries just as easily as anywhere else. If the problem is that it takes more labour, well, they have labour.

In other words, it can be done. But the present economic system stands in the way. Reducing global warming would mean getting rid of oil and cars. Sixteen out of the 40 largest corporations in the world sell oil or cars. That is an enormous chunk of power in the global system. The health of an industrial economy is often measured by new car sales for the last month. Whole national economies have become dependent on oil, in the Middle East, Russia, Nigeria, Central Asia and Venezuela. US power rests on control of oil.

There is also the question of regulation. The whole thrust of globalisation and profit for 25 years has been to reduce regulation, including environmental regulation, in every country to increase profits. The whole thrust of international negotiations has been to impose controls on the poor countries and lift controls on the rich. In every aspect of our lives, those with power have argued for the rule of market, not human need.

Two recent books describe the negotiations of the WTO in Doha and the negotiations that led to the Kyoto treaty on climate change.[8] Both are written by activists who were trying to lobby the governments. Both tell the same story of late night negotiations, Third World delegates in fury and tears, US manipulation in special rooms. In both, the striking thing is that the US delegations allow representatives of the American corporations to sit at the table. The people from industry write the clauses of the draft agreement. Big Oil and Big Pharma do not trust or respect American civil servants. The lobbyists from the industry stay up late into the night, pecking away at their laptops, making sure no one from Kenya or some low-lying Pacific atoll sneaks in a clause.

As it is, businesses try every way possible to avoid environmental regulation. Collective agreements on global warming would work in the opposite direction. Governments would be bound to make major changes in the structure of the economy because people and the planet needed the changes. That would rehabilitate regulation. It would set a precedent for massive agreed change that could then apply to AIDS, TB, housing and everything else. Alternative power sources would require immense public works. That would mean taxes. If the price of energy went up, it wouldn't be terrible for people. They would get jobs. But it would squeeze profits.

Even people in the ruling classes recognise that climate change is a serious threat. It's just that in practice they can't make the changes necessary. So all the governments in the world sent representatives to a conference in Rio and then to one in Kyoto. At Kyoto they finally agreed a treaty that would reduce the level of increase in emissions. The agreement was full of holes and had no provisions for enforcement. Some environmentalists said the treaty was useless, but at least it was a start. Others said it was worse than useless.

The Clinton administration agreed to the Kyoto treaty, but did not actually sign it. That refusal to sign allowed George Bush, when elected, to say publicly he would refuse to sign it. That in turn permitted President Putin of Russia to say he wouldn't sign either, and Kyoto was finished.

The powers that be can't retreat from Iraq, because it would threaten the drive for globalisation and profits. They can't regulate global warming for the same reason. They stay in Iraq so that they can burn oil that increases global warming.

As they say in Seattle: Teamsters and Turtles Unite. I have argued that what's wrong with America is what's wrong with the world. Many millions are now debating how we could make another world. The global crisis of profits that has brought us all to this place has not gone away. So the pressure from the top, from the ruling classes, is growing too.

As pressure and resistance both grow, the future becomes hard to predict. Much is at stake. Do what you can.

References

I **Profits**

1 An easy short introduction to Marxist economics is Harman, 1995. To really get to grips with Marxist economics, though, you need to read the first volume of Marx's *Capital* (Marx, 1976). This is not as hard to read as often claimed. The most difficult bits are at the beginning, where Marx is wrestling with his background as a philosopher. The book gets steadily more concrete and easier as you go along. The easiest way to read it is to start at Chapter 4, read to the end, and then go back to the beginning. If you have trouble, Baran, 1973, is a good introduction to *Capital*, making the same arguments in a way that is easier to understand.

2 For this argument, start with Harman, 1999, who builds on the idea of the 'permanent arms economy' developed in Kidron, 1970 and 1974.

3 Rees, 1994, p 71.

4 Rees, p 7.

5 Most of the figures that follow are taken from Brenner, 2002, the most detailed and reliable source I can find. Economists will notice that I have rounded percentages to the nearest whole number, so 13.6 per cent becomes 14 percent. This makes the figures less precise, but the gain is that non-specialists find it easier to understand the numbers. And the figures aren't really that precise anyway. Brenner, 2002, is also the best place to begin reading about the fall in the rate of profit and its consequences. This can be supplemented by Brenner, 1998. Harman, 1999, has a more convincing explanation of the reason that profits fell, but is harder to understand for the beginner. Harvey, 1982, is also useful. After that, try the technical discussions in Shaikh and Tonak, 1994, Mosely, 1991, and the articles in *Historical Materialism*, 1999, especially the ones by Anwar Shaikh, Chris Harman, Fred Mosely, and Ben Fine et al. Many of these writers are basing themselves on Marx's theory of the tendency of the rate of profit to fall in volume 3 of *Capital* (Marx, 1981, Chapters 1–15).

6 Brenner, 2002, p 21. The figure for the 1970s is in fact 1969–1979, and for the 1990s it is in fact 1979–1990.

7 Brenner, p 8.

8 Different accounting systems in different countries give rather different rates of profit. Statistics were gathered and analysed in different ways in

different countries. None of the statisticians were counting exactly the same thing as I mean by 'gross profits'. For the problems with the US accounts alone, see Shaikh and Tonak, 1994. The point, though, is that within each country the numbers were collected and analysed in much the same way from year to year. It is true that in the 1990s American companies began to change their accounting systems, and also to lie outright, in order to inflate their recorded profits and thus drive up their share prices. But this tended to overstate the rate of profit, not understate it.

9   Brenner, 2002, p 33.

10 Brenner, p 47.

11 At the time they had no idea why. Recently, many of them have adopted the idea of long waves of productivity and stagnation, with new technologies producing a surge in the economy for a generation, and then a fallow period until another technology arrives. This idea comes originally from the early 20th-century economist Kondratiev, and was introduced into mainstream economics, oddly enough, by the Marxist economist Ernest Mandel (Mandel, 1978). This explanation does not seem to me to be very helpful, and does not really explain why profits crashed when they did. In any case, the important points are that in the 1970s and 80s, mainstream economists had no explanation. They were trying to fix something without knowing why it was broke.

12 Harman, 1999, Brenner, 1998 and 2002, Harvey, 1982. There have been other radical explanations as well, but these are the arguments that have stood the test of time.

13 The best guide to these policy changes in the US is Meeropol, 1998, and for the world as a whole, Whitfield, 2001.

14 Brenner, 2002, pp 59–78, particularly 68–73.

15 Brenner, 1998 and 2002.

16 Bond, 2000a, is the easiest place to start. Then try Harvey, 1982 and 2003.

17 Harman, 1995 and 1999.

2 Class in America

1   For more on this way of thinking about class, see Zweig, 2000, on the US, and Callinicos and Harman, 1987, and German, 1996, on Britain.

2   Zweig, 2000, p 30, defining the working class quite narrowly, gets a figure of 62 per cent of the workforce.

3   Zweig, p 31.

4   Mishel, Bernstein and Boushey, 2003, p 398.

5   This is based on data in Mishel et al, pp 120, 128, and 395–432.

6   Mishel et al, pp 425.

7   Mishel et al p 244.

8   Mishel et al, p 405.

9   For the American ruling class, start with Zweig, 2000. Domhoff 1967 and 1983, Munkirs, 1996, and Mintz and Schwartz, 1985, are good on the networks that bind the ruling class together. For how the ruling

class actually rule in particular situations, there are good cases from a liberal perspective on Vietnam War policy by Halberstam, 1986, from a ruling class perspective on economic policy by Woodward, 1994, from a radical perspective on strikes by Franklin, 2001, and from a Marxist perspective on economic policy by Meeropol, 1998.

10   There are many books on this. You can start with Palast, 2003.
11   For this world, see the delightful Aldrich, 1998.
12   On the New American Century, see particularly Callinicos, 2003, and Harvey, 2003.
13   Zweig, 2000, p 58.

3 The Opposition

1   For the CIO, start with Dubofsky and Van Tine, 1977, pp 181–279, and then Preis, 1964, pp 3–85, Fine, 1969, Milton, 1982, Bernstein, 1971, and Honey, 1993.
2   See Preis, 1964, pp 257–86.
3   For this business backlash, see Lipsitz, in Bergin and Garvey, 1983, Fones-Wolf, 1994, and Harris, 1982.
4   For anti-communism, the best place to start is Schrecker, 1998. After that Caute, 1978, and Navasky, 1980.
5   For this analysis of the communist countries and the Cold War, see Cliff, 1987, on what happened to the Russian revolution, Harman, 1988, on Eastern Europe, Harris, 1978, and Hore, 1991, on China, and Neale, 2003a, on Vietnam.
6   For good accounts of the communists in the 1930s, see Keeran, 1980, Naison, 1983, and Hudson, 1979.
7   For the civil rights movement, see Garrow, 1993, Clayborne, 1995, Halberstam, 1998.
8   Garrow, 1993, p 249.
9   Garrow, 1993, p 250.
10   For the northern riots see Fogelson, 1971.
11   Clayborne, 1995, is good on the Black Power split.
12   For both the Vietnam War and the anti-war movement, start with Neale, 2003. Then see Kolko, 1985, Appy, 1993 and 2003, Wells, 1994, and Halstead, 1978.
13   Caputo, 1977, p xvii.
14   Wells, 1994, p 23.
15   For the anti-war movement among the armed forces see Cortright, 1975, Moser, 1996, Neale, 2003a, pp 149–184, and Lutz, 2001, pp 131–70.
16   Neale, 2003a, pp 157–58.
17   See Stacewicz, 1997, Kovic, 1976, Moser, 1996, and Nicosia, 2001.
18   Moser, 1996, pp 113–14.
19   Moser, 1996, p 49.
20   O'Brien, 1973, pp 113–14 and 173.
21   For 1968 start with Harman, 1988, and then Ali and Watkins, 1998.

22   Wells, 1994, p 395.
23   George and Sabelli, 1994, pp 41–42.
24   On the early days of women's liberations, see Evans, 1980.
25   Gorney, 2000, pp 21–22.
26   Gorney, p 15
27   For Stonewall and gay liberation, see Duberman, 1993.
28   Coles, 1971, pp 133–34.
29   For DRUM see Geschwender, 1997.

4 Strikes and Taxes

1   This account of the air traffic controllers' strike is based on Norlund, 1998.
2   Norlund, 1998.
3   Parenti, 1999, p 39.
4   For a general view of union struggles in the 1980s and 1990s, Franklin, 2001 is a beautifully written case study of wider relevance. Moody, 1988, provides a good survey of the early years. Rosenblum, 1994, Lendler, 1997, Erem, 2001, and Sacks, 1988, are particularly good case studies.
5   Pollin, 2003, p 55.
6   Franklin, 2001, pp 80–81.
7   Geoghegan, 1991, pp 4–8.
8   Woodward, 2000, p 168.
9   For what these jobs are like, see Ehrenreich, 2001.
10   For the joys and difficulties of this sort of organising see Erem, 2001.
11   Zweig, 2000, pp 68–69.
12   Based on Mishel, Bernstein and Bushey, 2003, p 128.
13   Based on Mishel et al, p 128.
14   Based on Mishel et al, p 130.
15   For Carter's economic policies and their electoral consequences see Meeropol, 2000, pp 52–56 and 70–79.
16   Meeropol, pp 55–56.
17   Brenner, 2002, p 54.
18   The gross profit includes the net profit the company declares for tax. But it also includes interest payments, rent payments and the money the company reinvests on new plant, all of which go down on the books as losses, not profit. It's a bit more complicated than this, of course, because the corporations were not paying any tax on the portion of gross profits they paid out in new investment. The new investment went down on the books as a loss, and so did not count as taxable profit.
19   Meeropol, 2000, p 107.
20   See the table in Meeropol, p 334.
21   Meeropol, p 19.
22   For the analysis of Clinton's economic policy I rely on Meeropol, and for the details of the day-to-day arguments on Woodward, 1994.
23   Woodward, 1994, p 91.
24   Woodward, pp 141–43.

25   Woodward, p 93.
26   For the iniquities of the American health system, see Abraham, 1993, Himmelstein, Woolhandler and Hellander, 2001, and Woolhandler, 2003.

5 Race and Prison

1   My account of the war on drugs and imprisonment in this chapter relies particularly on Parenti, 1999, Abramsky, 2002, Cole, 1999, Baum, 1996, Prashad, 2003, Bergner, 1998, Tonry, 1995, and Mauer and Chesney-Lind, 2002.
2   Quoted in Baum, 1996 p 13.
3   Parenti, 1999, p 7.
4   Jim Dwyer, 2002, p 161.
5   Parenti, 1999, p 50.
6   Moore, 2001, pp 59–60.
7   Parenti, 1999, pp 55–56.
8   Parenti, pp 56 and 57.
9   Lusane, 1991, p 45.
10 Abramsky, 2002, pp 192–93.
11 Abramsky, pp 13 and 119.
12 Prashad, 2003, p 90.
13 Abramsky, 2002, pp 14 and 73–74.
14 Abramsky, p 11.
15 Abramsky, p 11.
16 Western, Pettit, and Geutzkow, 2002, p 169.
17 Western at al, p 170. People with GED certificates are counted as having finished high school.
18 Abramsky, 2002, p 90.
19 Hallinan, 2003, pp 5–6.
20 Hallinan, p 8.
21 Bergner, 1998, p 83.
22 Abramsky, 2002, p 90.
23 Quoted in Parenti, p 182.
24 Quoted in Parenti, p 182.
25 Quoted in Parenti, p 64.
26 Mishel, Bernstein and Boushey, 2003, pp 138–39.
27 Braman, 2002, pp 129 and 134.
28 Braman, p 130.
29 Braman, p 132.
30 Callinicos, 1993, p 53. For the riots as a whole, see Callinicos, pp 52–57, and Davis, 1992.
31 Callinicos, p 53.

6 Family Values

1   Kelley, 1991.
2   Mishel, Bernstein and Boushey, 2003, p 232.
3   The figures that follow are based on Mishel et al, pp 130 and 132.

4   Mishel et al, pp 208–09.
5   Faludi, 1999.
6   Faludi, p 112.
7   Faludi, p 121.
8   Faludi, p 121
9   For abortion politics start with Gorney, 2000, a humane and gripping epic that also manages the difficult job of telling both sides of the story fairly. Then see Ginsburg, 1989, and Saletan, 2003.
10 Quoted in Gorney, 2000, p 337.
11 Quoted in Gorney, pp 472–73. I have decided not to put dots where I have made cuts in the poem.
12 Gorney, pp 476–77.
13 The analysis of feminism that follows owes much to German, 1998 and 2003, and Lindisfarne, 2001 and 2002.
14 Ehrenreich, 2002, pp 87–93. See also the account of cleaning work in Ehrenreich, 2001, pp 51–120.
15 For the politics of welfare see Prashad, 2003, and Gans, 1995. For what it's like to live on welfare, see the wonderful Leblanc, 2003.
16 Quoted in Prashad, 2003, p 142.
17 Quoted in Prashad, p 147.
18 Prashad, p 146.
19 See Gans, 1995.
20 Newman, 1999, pp 164–65 and 190–91.
21 LeBlanc, 2003, p 32.
22 Prashad, 2003, p 151.
23 Quoted in Prashad, pp 154–55.
24 Prashad, p 146.
25 The arguments on mental illness that follow are based partly on my experience as a counsellor in Britain. For different aspects of the changes in therapy in the US in the 1980s and 1990s, see Luhrman, 2000, Rhodes, 1991, Breggin, 1991, and Young, 1995. Shem, 1999, is a funny, wise novel that explains much through exaggeration.
26 Norwood, 1985. See also the critique in Faludi, 1999, pp 347–56.
27 Gray, 1993.

7 Globalisation

1   For globalisation, start with Neeraj, 2001, for the poor countries and Whitfield, 2001, for Europe. Next try several outstanding case studies: Bond, 2000a, on South Africa, Green, 2003, on Latin America, Collins, 2003, on clothing companies in the US and Mexico, Monbiot, 2000, on Britain, de Waal, 1997, on Sudan. Also useful are Bond, 2000b, Garson, 2001, and Bello, Cunningham, and Rau, 1994. On the World Bank, see George and Sabelli, 1994, and Caulfield, 1997. Stiglitz, 2002, is very good on the IMF but very soft on the World Bank, his old employer. On foreign aid and NGOs start with Maren, 1997. Good studies of the

effects of globalisation on ordinary people are Desai, 2002, on South Africa, Nazpary, 2002, on Kazakhstan, and Scheper-Hughes, 1992, on Brazil.
2 The best-known exposition of these ideas is in Hardt and Negri, 2000. For critiques of their work, see Callinicos, 2001, Nimitz, 2002, and especially Petras, 2003, Chapters 1, 4 and 5.
3 Anderson, Cavanagh, and Lee, 2000, p 68.
4 For the miners' strike see Callinicos and Simons, 1985, and for the Bombay textile strike van Wersch, 1992.
5 Green, 2003, pp 46–49.
6 Green, p 87.
7 Green, pp 87–89. The quotes are from Green's summary of Moser's work, rather than Moser, 1993, herself.
8 Turshen, 1999, p 14.
9 Turshen, p 10.
10 Ferguson, 1994, p 5.

8 War

1 Chomsky, 1999, pp119–20 and note 3, p 180.
2 Lembcke, 1998.
3 For star wars see Grossman, 2001.
4 Kissinger, 1999, pp 803–08 and 829–32.
5 For Nicaragua, see Gonzalez, 1985, and Gonzalez, 1990.
6 A good way to get a feel for liberation theology is Kidder, 2003, a magnificent biography of American activist Paul Farmer. For liberation theology on the ground in Brazil, see Scheper-Hughes, 1992, and Wilentz, 1994, for Haiti.
7 For El Salvador, see Bonner, 1984.
8 Cockburn and St Claire, 1998. For the links between the CIA and drugs in general, see McCoy, 1991, and Naylor, 1987.
9 For how the economic blockade affected one working class neighbourhood, and the gradual erosion of support for the Sandinistas, see Lancaster, 1992.
10 For Afghanistan, see Neale, 1981, 1988, 2001b, and 2003b.
11 For Afghan communists, see Anwar, 1988.
12 For the Islamist resistance, see Bonner, 1987, Roy, 1986, and Kakar, 1995.
13 For Washington politics and CIA support for the rebels, see Crile, 2003, a fascinating, and quite fun, account of the inner workings of the agency.
14 For Grenada see O'Shaughnessy, 1984, and Ferguson, 1990.
15 For Panama see Johns and Johnson, 1994, and Woodward, 1991.
16 For a good introduction to Middle Eastern politics, see Aburish 1996 and 1997. After that, see Ali, 2002, Aburish, 1999 and 2000, and Batatu, 1979.
17 Anderson, Cavanagh and Lee, 2000, p 68.
18 Klare, 2001, p 55.
19 For Islamism see Alexander, 2000, Ali, 2002, Lindisfarne, 2002.
20 For the Iranian revolution, see Marshall, 1988, and Bayat, 1987.

21 For Lebanon see Fisk, 1992.
22 For Iraq see Aburish, 2000, Batatu, 1979, and Ali, 2003.
23 See Woodward, 1991.
24 George Bush and Brent Scowcroft, *A World Transformed*. Knopf, New York, quoted by Senator Edward Kennedy in 'Iraq, America and Presidential Leadership', a speech to the Center for American Progress, January 14, 2004.
25 For the effect of sanctions see Arnove, 2000, and Simons, 1998.
26 For Somalia see Maren, 1997, and Simons, 1995.
27 For Haiti start with Goff, 2000, an extremely wise and well written book, and then Ridgeway, 1994, and Wilentz, 1994.
28 For Bosnia and Kosovo see Glenny, 1996, German, 1999, and Hudson, 2003.

9 The WTO and AIDS

1   The importance of the international organisations is sometimes over-stated in the economics literature of the new anti-capitalist movement. Much of this is written by people associated with NGOs, who concentrate attention on the international organisations. The NGOs receive much of their funding from the UN, the US and the UK. The condition of this funding, never stated but very clear, is that they can attack the policies of international organisations, but only rarely the policies of the American government. They must never attack any particular American president by name. Nor should they attack the governments of the Third World countries where they work.
2   For NAFTA, start with MacArthur, 2000. Collins, 2003, Bacon, 2004, and the articles in Wise, Salazar and Carlsen, 2003a are also useful.
3   MacArthur, 2000, p 133.
4   MacArthur, p 281.
5   Wise, Salazar and Carlsen, 2003b, p 4.
6   Wise et al, p 3.
7   Green, p 145.
8   Wise, Salazar and Carlsen, 2003b, p 3, Green, 2003, pp 146–48, Acuna Rodarte, 2003.
9   Quoted in MacArthur, 2000, p 276.
10 For the inner workings of the WTO, see Jawara and Kwa, 2003.
11 For India, see Neeraj, 2001.
12 For Chinese workers in the Cultural Revolution see Perry, 1993, and for now see Pun, 1998.
13 See Collins, 2003.
14 Hooper, 1999.
15 For HIV in the US, start with Shilts, 1987, and then Cohen, 1999, Siplon, 2002, and Neale, 1991.
16 For the debates in the gay movement in the early days and the invention of safe sex, see Shilts, 1987, and then Bayer, 1989, Berkowitz, 2003, Kramer, 1990, and Silverside, 2003.

17 For ACTUP see Kramer, 1990, Crimp and Rolston, 1990, and
    Stockdill, 2003.
18 Silverside, 2003, p 126, gives the official police estimate as 200,000 and
    the optimistic estimate as 600,000.
19 Irwin, Millen and Fallows, 2003, p 14.
20 Irwin et al, p 6.
21 The explanation I am giving here is based on six years of work as an HIV
    counsellor, a job that involved giving a lot of safe sex advice to heterosexuals.
22 For 1989 in New York, see Perrow and Guillen, 1990. For the response
    of African-American politicians more generally, see the important
    book by Cohen, 1999. Stockdill, 2003, is also interesting.
23 For HIV in the poor countries see Dube, 2000, Beyer, 1998, Barnett
    and Whitside, 2002, Campbell, 2003, Hooper, 1990, Farmer, 1999,
    Farmer, 2003, Kidder, 2003, Irwin, Millen and Fallows, 2003, Neale,
    1991, Neale, 2003, pp 73–88, Robinson, 2001, and the Treatment
    Action Campaign website at www.tac.org.za. The argument that follows
    builds on all of these, but is my own.
24 Campbell, 2003, pp 66–67.
25 Campbell, p 32.
26 Sexton, 2003.
27 Robinson, 2001, p 46. The discussion of Big Pharma that follows is
    based on Robinson.
28 Robinson, pp 19–20.
29 Robinson, pp 17 and 19.
30 Robinson, p 117.
31 Robinson, p 118.
32 Robinson, p 121.
33 For South Africa after 1994 start with Bond, 2000a, then Desai, 2002,
    Peter Dwyer, 2002, and Bond, 2000b.
34 Robinson, p 96.

10 Seattle and Afghanistan

1   The best way to get the feel of the new movement for another world is
    to read three books by grassroots activists of very different politics:
    Thomas, 2000, on Seattle, Neale, 2002, on the Genoa protests and the
    European movement, and Desai, 2002, on the South African move-
    ment. For general views also try Bircham and Charlton, 2001, and
    Callinicos, 2003a. For Seattle see Thomas, 2000, Charlton, 2000, and
    Cockburn and St Claire, 2000.
2   Moore, 2003, pp 168–74.
3   Klein, 2000, pp 122–24.
4   Thomas, 2000, p 19. For Ben White and the turtles, see Thomas, pp 18–24.
5   See Neale, 2002.
6   For Bush, see Hatfield, 2002, Ivins and DuBose, 2002, and Philips, 2004.
7   See Philips, 2004, pp 97–108.

8   The analysis of Bush's War on Terror that follows relies partly on a close
     reading since 2001 of the *International Herald Tribune*, the *Financial Times*,
     the London *Guardian*, the London *Independent*, the London *Socialist Worker*
     and *Channel 4 News* in Britain. I have not footnoted the coverage, as I
     was not clipping it. For more general analyses and details, I have also
     found Callinicos, 2003b, Harvey, 2003, Koshy, 2003, Ahmed, 2004,
     Prashad, 2002a, Chomsky, 2003, Rees, 2001, Alexander, 2000 and 2001,
     and Susskind, 2004 particularly useful. For the anti-war movement and
     global justice movements, I have relied on what I learned from meetings
     and private conversations during daily activism. I have also leaned heavily
     on conversations with people from the Middle East, especially Afghanistan.
     Much of what follows is my own attempt to synthesise all these sources
     into an analysis that makes sense on the balance of probabilities.

9   For different aspects of the bubble and how it burst, see Frank, 2000,
     Brenner, 2002, Cruver, 2003, and Krugman, 2003

10   For Enron see Cruver, 2003, and Prashad, 2002b.

11   Champion, 2003, is a very useful account of recent Saudi economics,
     from a largely neoliberal point of view. Aburish, 1996, remains the best
     book on the Kingdom as a whole up to 1996.

12   That's Aburish's figure, and he is a reliable judge. Champion is good on
     the weakness of Saudi statistics.

13   A recurring theme in Champion, 2003, who reflects a much wider consensus.

14   Susskind, 2004.

15   For more detail on Afghanistan, see Neale, 2001b and 2003b, Rashid,
     2000, Griffin, 2001, Lindisfarne, 2002, and Maley, 1988.

11 Iraq and the Planet

1   See Jawara and Kwa, 2003.

2   The following account of the Iraq war relies on the same range of
     sources cited in note 8 in Chapter 10.

3   See Curtis, 2003.

4   Ashman, 2003.

5   See Gott, 2000.

6   For global warming see Lynas, 2004, Houghton, 1997, Godrej, 2001,
     and Leggett, 1999. The argument that follows builds on all of these, but is
     my own.

7   [For a harrowing description of the way environmental problems can
     become social nightmares see Davis, 2001.

8   Jawara and Kwa, 2003, and Leggett, 1999. For a striking example of
     how NAFTA prevented environmental regulation see Bejarano
     Gonzalez, 2003.

Bibliography

Laura Kaye Abraham, 1993, *Mama Might Be Better Off Dead: The Failure of Urban Health Care in America*. Chicago University Press, Chicago.

Sasha Abramsky, 2002, *Hard Time Blues: How Politics Built a Prison Nation*. Thomas Dunne, New York.

Said Aburish, 1996, *The Rise, Corruption and Coming Fall of the House of Saud*. St Martin's Press Press, New York.

Said Aburish, 1997, *A Brutal Friendship: The West and the Arab Elite*. Orion, London.

Said Aburish, 1999, *Arafat: From Defender to Dictator*. Bloomsbury, London.

Said Aburish, 2000, *Saddam Hussein: The Politics of Revenge*. Bloomsbury, London.

Olivia Acuna Rodarte, 2003, 'Towards an Equitable, Inclusive and Sustainable Agriculture: Mexico's Basic Grain Producers Unite'. Wise, Salazar and Carlsen, 2003a.

Aijaz Ahmed, 2004, *Iraq, Afghanistan and the Imperialism of Our Time*. Left Word, Delhi.

Nelson Aldrich, 1998, *Old Money: The Mythology of America's Upper Class*. M. E. Sharpe, New York.

Anne Alexander, 2000, 'Powerless in Gaza: The Palestinian Authority and the Myth of the "Peace Process"'. *International Socialism* 89.

Anne Alexander, 2001, 'The Crisis in the Middle East'. *International Socialism* 93.

Tariq Ali, 2002, *The Clash of Fundamentalisms: Crusades, Jihads and Modernity*. Verso, London.

Tariq Ali, 2003, *Bush in Babylon*. Verso, London.

Tariq Ali and Susan Watkins, 1998, *1968: Marching in the Streets*. Verso, London.

Sarah Anderson and John Cavanagh with Thea Lee, 2000, *Field Guide to the Global Economy*. The New Press, New York.

Raja Anwar, 1988, *The Tragedy of Afghanistan*. Verso, London.

Christian Appy, 1993, *Working Class War: American Combat Soldiers and Vietnam*. University of North Carolina Press, Chapel Hill.

Christian Appy, 2003, *Patriots: the Vietnam War Remembered from All Sides*. Viking, New York.

Antony Arnove, editor, 2000, *Iraq Under Siege: The Deadly Impact of Sanctions and War*. Pluto, London.

Sam Ashman, 2003, 'The Anti-capitalist Movement and the War'. *International Socialism* 99.

David Bacon, 2004, *Children of NAFTA: Labor Wars on the U.S./Mexico Border*. University of California Press, Berkeley.

Paul Baran, 1973, *The Political Economy of Growth*. Monthly Review Press, New York, first published 1957.

Tony Barnett and Alan Whiteside, 2002, *AIDS in the Twenty-first Century*. Palgrave Macmillan, London.

John Batatu and Hanna Batatu, 1979, *The Old Social Classes and the Revolutionary Movements of Iraq*. Princeton University Press, Princeton.

Assaf Bayat, 1987, *Workers and Revolution in Iran: A Third World Experience of Workers' Control*. Zed Books, London.

Dan Baum, 1996, *Smoke and Mirrors: The War on Drugs and the Politics of Failure*. Back Bay Books, Boston.

R. Bayer, 1989, *Private Acts, Social Consequences: AIDS and the Politics of Public Health*. Macmillan, London.

Fernando Bejarano Gonzalez, 2003, 'Investment, Sovereignty, and the Environment: The Letalcald and NAFTA's Chapter 11'. Wise, Salazar and Carlsen, 2003a.

Walden Bello, Shea Cunningham and Bill Rau, 1994, *Dark Victory: The United States and Global Poverty*. Pluto, London.

Daniel Bergner, 1998, *God of the Rodeo: The Quest for Redemption in Louisiana's Angola Prison*. Ballantine Books, New York.

Richard Berkowitz, 2003, *Stayin' Alive: The Invention of Safe Sex, a Personal History*. Westview, Boulder.

Chris Beyer, 1998, *War in the Blood: Sex, Politics and AIDS in Southeast Asia*. Zed Books, London.

Emma Bircham and John Charlton, editors, 2001, *Anti-Capitalism: A Guide to the Issues*. Bookmarks, London.

Patrick Bond, 2000a, *Elite Transition: From Apartheid to Neoliberalism in South Africa*. Pluto, London.

Patrick Bond, 2000b, *Against Global Apartheid: South Africa Meets the World Bank, IMF and International Finance*. University of Cape Town Press, Lansdowne, South Africa.

Arthur Bonner, 1987, *Among the Afghans*. Duke University Press, Durham.

Raymond Bonner, 1984, *Weakness and Deceit: U.S. Policy and El Salvador*. Times Books, New York.

Donald Braman, 2002, 'Families and Incarceration'. Mauer and Chesney-Lind, 2002.

Peter Breggin, 1991, *Toxic Psychiatry*. St Martin's Press, New York.

James Brennan, 1994, *The Labor Wars in Cordoba, 1955-1976: Ideology, Work and Labor Politics in an Argentine Industrial City*. Harvard University Press, Cambridge.

Robert Brenner, 1998, 'The Economics of Global Turbulence'. *New Left Review* 229.

Robert Brenner, 2002, *The Boom and the Bubble: The USA in the World Economy*. Second edition, Verso, London.

Alex Callinicos, 1993, *Race and Class*. Bookmarks, London.

Alex Callincos, 2001, 'Toni Negri in Perspective'. *International Socialism*, 92.

Alex Callinicos, 2003a, *An Anti-Capitalist Manifesto*. Polity, Cambridge.

Alex Callinicos, 2003b, *The New Mandarins of American Power*. Polity, Cambridge.

Alex Callinicos and Chris Harman, 1987, *The Changing Working Class: Essays on Class Structure Today*. Bookmarks, London.

Alex Callinicos and Mike Simons, *1985, The Great Strike; The Miners' Strike 1984–5 and its Lessons*. Bookmarks, London.

Catherine Campbell, 2003, *Letting them Die: Why HIV/AIDS Prevention Programmes Fail*. James Currey, Oxford.

Philip Caputo, 1977, *A Rumor of War*. Ballantine, New York.

Catherine Caulfield, 1997, *Masters of Illusion: The World Bank and the Poverty of Nations*. Macmillan, London.

David Caute, 1978, *The Great Fear: The Anti-Communist Purge Under Truman and Eisenhower*. Simon and Schuster, New York.

Daryl Champion, 2003, *The Paradoxical Kingdom: Saudi Arabia and the Momentum of Reform*. Columbia University Press, New York.

John Charlton, 2000, 'Talking Seattle'. *International Socialism*, 86.

Noam Chomsky, 1999, *The New Military Humanism: Lessons from Kosovo*. Pluto, London.

Noam Chomsky, 2003, *Hegemony or Survival: America's Quest for Global Dominance*. Hamish Hamilton, London.

Carson Clayborne, 1995. *Struggle: SNCC and the Black Awakening of the 1960s*. Harvard University Press, Cambridge, Mass.

Tony Cliff, 1987, *Revolution Besieged: Lenin, 1917–1923*. Bookmarks, London.

Alexander Cockburn and Jeffrey St. Claire, 1998, *Whiteout: The CIA, Drugs and the Press*. Verso, London.

Alexander Cockburn and Jeffrey St. Claire, 2000, *Five Days that Shook the World: Seattle and Beyond*. Verso, London.

Cathy Cohen, 1999, *The Boundaries of Blackness: AIDS and the Breakdown of Black Politics*. University of Chicago Press, Chicago.

David Cole, 1999, *No Equal Justice: Race and Class in the American Criminal Justice System*. The New Press, New York.

Robert Coles, 1971, *The Middle Americans: Proud and Uncertain*. Little Brown, Boston.

Jane Collins, 2003, *Threads: Gender, Labor and Power in the Global Apparel Industry*. University of Chicago Press, Chicago.

David Cortright, 1975, *Soldiers in Revolt: The American Military Today*. Anchor, Garden City, New York.

George Crile, 2003, *My Enemy's Enemy: The Story of the Largest Covert Operation in History: The Arming of the Mujahideen by the CIA*. Atlantic Books, London.

Douglas Crimp with Adam Rolston, 1990, *AIDS Demo Graphics*. Bay Books, Seattle.

Brian Cruver, 2003, *Enron: Anatomy of Greed*. Arrow, London.

Mark Curtis, 2003, *Web of Deceit: Britain's Real Role in the World*. Vintage, London.

Mike Davis, 2000, *Magical Urbanism: Latinos Reinvent the U.S. Big City*. Verso, London.

Mike Davis, 2001, *Late Victorian Holocausts: El Niño Famines and the Making of the Third World*. Verso, London.

Ashwin Desai, 2002, *We Are the Poors: Community Struggles in Post-Apartheid South Africa*. Monthly Review Press, New York.

G. William Domhoff, 1967, *Who Rules America?* Prentice-Hall, Englewood Cliffs, NJ.

G. William Domhoff, 1983, *Who Rules America Now? A View for the 1980s*. Prentice-Hall, Englewood Cliffs, NJ.

Sidarth Dube, 2000, *Sex, Lies and AIDS*. HarperCollins, Delhi.

Martin Duberman, 1993, *Stonewall*. Dutton, New York.

Melvyn Dubofsky and Warren Van Tine, 1977, *John L. Lewis, A Biography*. Quadrangle, New York.

Jim Dwyer, 2002, 'Casualty in the War on Drugs'. Mike Gray, editor, 2002, *Busted: Stone Cowboys, Narco-Lords and Washington's War on Drugs*. Thunder's Mouth Press, New York.

Peter Dwyer, 2002, 'South Africa under the ANC: Still Bound to the Chains of Exploitation'. Leo Zeilig, editor, *Class Struggle and Resistance in Africa*. New Clarion, Cheltenham, UK.

Barbara Ehrenreich, 2001, *Nickel and Dimed: On (Not) Getting By in America*. Henry Holt, New York.

Barbara Ehrenreich, 2003, 'Maid to Order'. Barbara Ehrenreich and Arlie Russell Hochschild, editors, *Global Woman: Nannies, Maids and Sex Workers in the New Economy*. Granta, London.

Suzan Erem, 2001, *Labor Pains: Inside America's New Union Movement*. Monthly Review Press, New York.

Sara Evans, 1980, *Personal Politics: The Roots of the Women's Liberation Movement in the Civil Rights Movement and the New Left*. Random House, New York.

Susan Faludi, 1991, *Backlash: The Undeclared War Against American Women*. Anchor, New York.

Paul Farmer, 1999. *Infections and Inequalities: The Modern Plagues*. University of California Press, Berkeley.

Bibliography

Paul Farmer, 2003, *Pathologies of Power: Health, Human Rights and the New War on the Poor*. University of California Press, Berkeley.

James Ferguson, 1990, *Grenada: Revolution in Reverse*. Latin America Bureau, London.

James Ferguson, 1994, *Venezuela: A Guide to the People, Politics and Culture*. Latin America Bureau, London.

Sidney Fine, 1969, *Sit-Down: The General Motors Strike of 1937–1937*. University of Michigan Press, Ann Arbor.

Robert Fisk, 1992, *Pity the Nation: Lebanon at War*. Second edition, Oxford University Press, Oxford.

Robert Fogelson, 1971, *Violence as Protest: A Study of Riots and Ghettos*. Doubleday, New York.

Elizabeth Fones-Wolf, 1994, *Selling Free Enterprise: The Business Assault on Labor and Liberalism, 1945–60*. Illinois University Press, Urbana.

Thomas Frank, 2000, *One Market Under God: Extreme Capitalism, Market Populism and the End of Economic Democracy*. Doubleday, New York.

Stephen Franklin, 2001, *Three Strikes: Labor's Heartland Losses and What They Mean for Working Americans*. Guilford Press, New York.

Herbert Gans, 1995, *The War Against the Poor: The Underclass and Antipoverty Policy*. Basic Books, New York.

David Garrow, 1993, *Bearing the Cross: Martin Luther King, Jr. and the Southern Christian Leadership Conference*. Vintage, London, first published 1986.

Thomas Geoghegan, 1991, *Which Side Are You On? Trying to be for Labour When It's Flat on its Back*. Farrar, Straus & Giroux, London.

Susan George and Fabrizio Sabelli, 1994, *Faith and Credit: The World Bank's Secular Empire*. Westview, Boulder.

Lindsey German, 1996, *A Question of Class*. Bookmarks, London.

Lindsey German, 1998, *Sex, Class and Socialism*. Bookmarks, London.

Lindsey German, editor, 1999, *The Balkans: Nationalism and Imperialism*. *Bookmarks*, London.

Lindsey German, 2003, 'Women's Liberation Today'. *International Socialism* 101.

James Geschwender, 1997, *Class, Race and Worker Insurgency: The League of Revolutionary Black Workers*. Cambridge University Press, Cambridge.

Faye Ginsburg, 1989, *Contested Lives*. University of California Press, Berkeley.

Barry Glassner, 1999, *The Culture of Fear: Why Americans are Afraid of the Wrong Things*. Basic Books, New York.

Misha Glenny, 1996, *The Fall of Yugoslavia: The Third Balkan War*. Third edition, Penguin, London.

Dinyar Godrej, 2001, *The No-Nonsense Guide to Climate Change*. Verso, London.

Stan Goff, 2000, *Hideous Dream: A Soldier's Memoir of the US Invasion of Haiti*. Soft Skull Press, New York.

Mike Gonzalez, 1985, *Nicaragua: Revolution Under Siege*. Bookmarks, London.

Mike Gonzalez, 1990, *Nicaragua: What Went Wrong?* Bookmarks, London.

Cynthia Gorney, 2000, *Articles of Faith: A Frontline History of the Abortion Wars*. Second edition, Simon and Schuster, New York.

Richard Gott, 2000, *The Shadow of the Liberator: Hugo Chavez and the Transformation of Venezuela*. Verso, London.

John Gray, 1993, *Men are from Mars, Women are from Venus: A Practical Guide for Improving Communication and Getting What You Want in Relationships*. Thorsons, London.

Duncan Green, 2003, *Silent Revolution: The Rise and Crisis of Market Economies in Latin America*. Monthly Review Press, New York.

Michael Griffin, 2001, *Reaping the Whirlwind: The Taliban Movement in Afghanistan*. Pluto, London.

Karl Grossman, 2001, *Weapons in Space*. Seven Sisters Press, London.

David Halberstam, 1986, *The Best and the Brightest*. Random House, New York, first published 1972.

David Halberstam, 1998, *The Children*. Random House, New York.

David Halberstram, 2002, *War in a Time of Peace: Bush, Clinton and the Generals*. Bloomsbury, London.

Joseph Hallinan, 2003, *Going up the River: Travels in a Prison Nation*. Second edition, Random House, New York.

Fred Halstead, 1978, *Out Now! A Participant's Account of the American Movement against the Vietnam War*. Pathfinder, New York.

Michael Hardt and Antonio Negri, 2000, *Empire*. Harvard University Press, Cambridge.

Chris Harman, 1988a, *Class Struggles in Eastern Europe, 1945–1983*. Third edition, Bookmarks, London.

Chris Harman, 1988b, *The Fire Last Time: 1968 and After*. Bookmarks, London.

Chris Harman, 1995, *Economics of the Madhouse*. Bookmarks, London.

Chris Harman, 1999, *Explaining the Crisis: A Marxist Reappraisal*. Bookmarks, London, first published 1987.

Howell Harris, 1982, *The Right to Manage: Industrial Relations Politics of American Business in the 1940s*. University of Wisconsin Press, Madison.

David Harvey, 1982, *The Limits to Capital*. Basil Blackwell, Oxford.

David Harvey, 2003, *The New Imperialism*. Oxford University Press, Oxford.

James Hatfield, 2002, *Fortunate Son: George W. Bush and the Making of an American President*. Vision Paperbacks, London.

David Himmelstein, Steffi Woolhandler and Ida Hellander, 2001, *Bleeding the Patient: The Consequences of Corporate Health Care*. Common Courage Press, Monroe, Maine.

Historical Materialism, 1999 4: 'Special issue on the falling rate of profit'.

Michael Honey, 1993, *Southern Labor and Black Civil Rights: Organizing Memphis Workers*. University of Illinois Press, Urbana.

Ed Hooper, 1990, *Slim: A Reporter's Own Story of AIDS in East Africa*. Bodley

Head, London.

Edward Hooper, 1999, *The River: A Journey Back to the Source of HIV*. Penguin, London.

Charlie Hore, 1991, *The Road to Tiananmen Square*. Bookmarks, London.

John Houghton, 1997, *Global Warming: The Complete Briefing*. Second edition, Cambridge University Press, Cambridge.

Hosea Hudson, 1979, *The Narrative of Hosea Hudson: His Life as a Negro Communist in the South*. Edited by Nell Painter, Harvard University Press, Cambridge.

Kate Hudson, 2003, *Breaking the South Slav Dream: The Rise and Fall of Yugoslavia*. Pluto, London.

Alexander Irwin, Joyce Millen and Dorothy Fallows, 2003, *Global AIDS: Myths and Facts*. South End Press, Cambridge.

Molly Ivins and Lou Dubose, 2002, *Shrub: The Short But Happy Political Life of George W. Bush*. Second edition, Vintage, New York.

Fatoumata Jawara and Aileen Kwa, 2003, *Behind the Scenes at the WTO: The Real World of International Trade Negotiations*. Zed Books, London.

Christine Johns and P. Ward Johnson, 1994, *State Crime, the Media, and the Invasion of Panama*. Praeger, Westport.

M. H. Kakar, 1995, *Afghanistan: The Soviet Invasion and the Afghan Response, 1979–1982*. University of California Press, Berkeley.

Roger Keeran, 1980, *The Communist Party and the Auto Workers Unions*. Indiana University Press, Bloomington.

Kitty Kelley, 1991, *Nancy Reagan: The Unauthorized Biography*. Simon and Schuster, New York.

Tracey Kidder, 2003, *Mountains Beyond Mountains*. Random House, New York.

Michael Kidron, 1970, *Western Capitalism Since the War*. Second edition, Penguin, London.

Michael Kidron, 1974. *Capitalism and Theory*. Pluto, London.

Henry Kissinger, 1999, *Years of Renewal*. Simon and Schuster, New York.

Michael Klare, 2001, *Resource Wars: The New Landscape of Global Conflict*. Henry Holt, New York.

Naomi Klein, 2000, *No Logo: Taking Aim at the Brand Bullies*. Flamingo, London.

Gabriel Kolko, 1985, *Anatomy of a War: Vietnam, the United States and the Modern Historical Experience*. Pantheon, New York.

Ninan Koshy, 2003, *The War on Terror: Reordering the World*. LeftWord, Delhi.

Ron Kovic, 1976, *Born on the Fourth of July*. Simon and Schuster, New York.

Larry Kramer, 1990, *Reports from the Holocaust: The Making of an AIDS Activist*. Penguin, London.

Paul Krugman, 2003, *The Great Unraveling: From Boom to Bust in Three Scandalous Years*. Allen Lane, London, 2003.

Roger Lancaster, 1992, *Life is Hard: Machismo, Danger and the Intimacy of*

What's Wrong with America?

Power in Nicaragua. University of California Press, Berkeley.

Adrian Nicole LeBlanc, 2003, *Random Family: Love, Drugs, Trouble and Coming of Age in the Bronx.* Flamingo, London.

Jeremy Leggett, 1999, *The Carbon War: Global Warming and the End of the Oil Era.* Penguin, London.

Jerry Lembcke, 1998, *The Spitting Image: Myth, Memory and the Legacy of Vietnam.* New York University Press, New York.

Marc Lendler, 1997, *Crisis and Political Beliefs: The Case of the Colt Firearms Strike.* Yale University Press, New Haven.

Nancy Lindisfarne, 2001, *Thank God We're Secular: Gender, Islam and Turkish Republicanism* (in Turkish). Iletism, Istanbul.

Nancy Lindisfarne, 2002, 'Starting From Below: Fieldwork, Gender and Imperialism Now'. *Critique of Anthropology* 22:4.

George Lipsitz, 1982, *Class and Culture in Cold War America: A Rainbow at Midnight.* J. F. Bergin, New York.

T. M. Luhrmann, 2000, *Of Two Minds: An American Anthropologist Looks at American Psychiatry.* Vintage Books, New York.

Clarence Lusane, 1991, *Pipe Dream Blues: Racism and the War on Drugs.* South End Press, Boston.

Catherine Lutz, 2001, *Home Front: A Military City and the American 20th Century.* Beacon Press, Boston.

Mark Lynas, 2004, *High Tide: News from a Warming World.* Flamingo, London.

John MacArthur, 2000, *The Selling of 'Free Trade': NAFTA, Washington and the Subversion of American Democracy.* University of California Press, Berkeley.

Alfred McCoy, 1991, *The Politics of Heroin: CIA Complicity in the Global Drug Trade.* Lawrence Hill, Brooklyn.

William Maley, editor, 1998, *Fundamentalism Reborn? Afghanistan and the Taliban.* Hurst, London.

Ernest Mandel, 1978, *Late Capitalism.* Verso, London.

Michael Maren, 1997, *The Road to Hell: The Ravaging Effects of Foreign Aid and International Charity.* Free Press, New York.

Phil Marshall, 1988, *Revolution and Counter-Revolution in Iran.* Bookmarks, London.

Karl Marx, 1976, *Capital, Volume One.* Penguin, London.

Karl Marx, 1981, *Capital, Volume Three.* Penguin, London.

Marc Mauer and Meda Chesney-Lind, editors, 2002. *Invisible Punishment: The Collateral Consequences of Mass Imprisonment.* The New Press, New York.

Michael Meeropol, 1998, *Surrender: How the Clinton Administration Completed the Reagan Revolution.* University of Michigan Press, Ann Arbor.

David Milton, 1982, *The Politics of U.S. Labor from the Great Depression to the New Deal.* Monthly Review Press, New York.

Beth Mintz and Michael Schwartz, 1985, *The Power Structure of American Business.* University of Chicago Press, Chicago.

Lawrence Mishel, Jared Bernstein and Heather Boushey, 2003, *The State of*

Working America, 2002/2003. Cornell University Press, Ithica.

George Monbiot, 2000, *Captive State: The Corporate Takeover of Britain.* Macmillan, London.

Kim Moody, 1988, *An Injury to All: The Decline of American Unionism.* Verso, London.

Michael Moore, 2001, *Stupid White Men and Other Sorry Excuses for the State of the Nation.* Regan Books, New York.

Michael Moore, 2003, *Dude, Where's My Country?* Warner, New York.

Fred Moseley, 1991, *The Falling Rate of Profit in the Postwar United States Economy.* Macmillan, London.

Caroline Moser, 1993, 'Adjustment from Below: Low-Income Women, Time and the Triple Role in Guayaquil, Ecuador'. Sarah Radcliffe and Sallie Westwood, editors, *Viva: Women and Popular Protest in Latin America.* Routledge, London.

Richard Moser, 1996, *The New Winter Soldiers: GI and Veteran Dissent During the Vietnam War.* Rutgers University Press, New Brunswick.

John Munkirs, 1996, *The Transformation of American Capitalism: From Competitive Market Structures to Centralized Private Sector Planning.* M. E. Sharpe, Armonk.

Mark Naison, 1983, *Communists in Harlem during the Depression.* University of Illinois Press, Urbana.

June Nash, 1979, *We Eat the Mines and the Mines Eat Us: Dependency and Exploitation in the Bolivian Tin Mines.* Columbia University Press, New York.

Victor Navasky, 1980, *Naming Names.* Viking, London.

R. T. Naylor, 1987, *Hot Money and the Politics of Debt.* Unwin, London.

Joma Nazpary, 2002, *Post-Soviet Chaos: Violence and Dispossession in Kazakhstan.* Pluto, London.

Jonathan Neale, 1981, 'The Afghan Tragedy'. *International Socialism* 12.

Jonathan Neale, 1988, 'Afghanistan: The Horse Changes Riders'. *Capital & Class* 35.

Jonathan Neale, 1991, 'The Politics of Aids'. *International Socialism* 53.

Jonathan Neale, 2001a, *The American War: Vietnam, 1960–1975.* Bookmarks, London.

Jonathan Neale, 2001b, 'The Long Torment of Afghanistan. *International Socialism* 93.

Jonathan Neale, 2002, *You Are G8, We Are 6 Billion: The Truth Behind the Genoa Protests.* Vision Paperbacks, London.

Jonathan Neale, 2003a, *A People's History of the Vietnam War.* The New Press, New York, second edition of Neale, 2001a.

Jonathan Neale, 2003b, 'Afghanistan', Farah Reza, editor, *Anti-imperialism: A Guide to the Issues.* Bookmarks, London.

Neeraj (Jain), 2001, *Globalisation or Recolonisation?.* Alaka Joshi, Pune.

Katherine Newman, 1999, *No Shame in my Game: The Working Poor in the*

Inner City. Vintage, New York.

Gerald Nicosia, 2001, *Home to War: A History of the Vietnam Veterans' Movement.* Crown, New York.

August Nimitz, 2002, 'Class Struggle Under 'Empire': In Defense of Marx and Engels'. *International Socialism*, 96.

Willis Norlund, 1998, *Silent Skies: The Air Traffic Controllers' Strike.* Praeger, Westport.

Robin Norwood, 1985, *Women Who Love Too Much: When You Keep Wishing and Hoping He'll Change.* Pocket Books, New York.

Tim O'Brien, 1973, *If I Die in a Combat Zone, Box Me Up and Send Me Home.* Delacorte, New York.

Hugh O'Shaughnessy, 1984, *Grenada: Revolution, Invasion and Aftermath.* Sphere, London.

Greg Palast, 2003, *The Best Democracy Money Can Buy: An Investigative Reporter Exposes the Truth about Globalisation, Corporate Cons and High-Finance Fraudsters.* Robinson, London.

Christian Parenti, 1999, *Lockdown America: Police and Prisons in the Age of Crisis.* Verso, New York.

Charles Perrow and Mauro Gillen, 1990, *The AIDS Disaster: The Failure of Organizations in New York and the Nation.* Yale University Press, New Haven.

Elizabeth Perry, 1993, *Shanghai on Strike: The Politics of Chinese Labor.* Stanford University Press, Stanford.

James Petras, 2003, *The New Development Politics: The Age of Empire Building and the New Social Movements.* Ashgate, Aldershot.

Kevin Phillips, 2004, *American Dynasty: How the Bush Clan Became the World's Most Powerful and Dangerous Family.* Allen Lane, London.

Robert Pollin, 2003, *Contours of Descent: U.S. Economic Fractures and the Landscape of Global Austerity.* Verso, London.

Colin Powell with Joseph Persico, 1995, *My American Journey.* Random House, New York.

Vijay Prashad, 2002a, *War Against the Planet: The Fifth Afghan War, Imperialism, and other Assorted Fundamentalisms.* LeftWord, Delhi.

Vijay Prashad, 2002b, *Fat Cats and Running Dogs: The Enron Stage of Capitalism.* Zed Books, London.

Vijay Prashad, 2003, *Keeping Up with the Dow Joneses: Debt, Prison, Workfare.* South End Press, Cambridge.

Art Preis, 1964, *Labor's Giant Step: Twenty Years of the CIO.* Pathfinder, New York.

Pun Ngai, 1998, *Becoming Dagongmei: Body, Identity and Transgression in China.* SOAS PhD Thesis, University of London.

Ahmed Rashid, 2000, *Taliban: Islam, Oil and the New Great Game in Central Asia.* Yale University Press, New Haven.

John Rees, 1994, 'The New Imperialism'. Alex Callinicos and others,

Marxism and the New Imperialism. Bookmarks, London.

John Rees, 2001, 'Imperialism, Globalisation, the State and War'. *International Socialism* 93.

Lorna Rhodes, 1991, *Emptying Beds: The Work of an Emergency Psychiatric Unit.* University of California Press, Berkeley.

James Ridgeway, editor, 1994, *The Haiti Files: Decoding the Crisis.* Essential Books, Washington.

Jeffrey Robinson, 2001, *Prescription Games: Money, Ego and Power inside the Global Pharmaceutical Industry.* Simon and Schuster, London.

Jonathan Rosenblum, 1994, *Copper Crucible: How the Arizona Miners' Strike of 1983 Recast Labor-Management Relations in America.* Cornell University Press, Ithica.

Olivier Roy, 1986, *Islam and Resistance in Afghanistan.* Cambridge University Press, Cambridge.

Karen Sacks, 1988, *Caring by the Hour: Women, Work, and Organizing at Duke Medical Centre.* University of Illinois Press, Urbana.

William Saletan, 2003, *Bearing Right: How Conservatives Won the Abortion War.* University of California Press, Berkeley.

Nancy Scheper-Hughes, 1992, *Death Without Weeping: The Violence of Everyday Life in Brazil.* University of California Press, Berkeley.

Ellen Schrecker, 1988, *Many are the Crimes: McCarthyism in America.* Little Brown, Boston.

Kasturi Sen, editor, 2003, *Restructuring Health Services: Changing Contexts and Comparative Perspectives.* Zed Books, London.

Sarah Sexton, 2003, 'Trading Healthcare Away: the WTO's General Agreement on Trade in Services (GATS)'. Sen, 2003.

Anwar Shaikh and E. Ahmet Tonak, 1994, *Measuring the Wealth of Nations: The Political Economy of National Accounts.* Columbia University Press, New York.

Samuel Shem, 1999, *Mount Misery.* Black Swan, London, first published 1997.

Randy Shilts, 1987, *And the Band Played On: Politics, People and the AIDS Epidemic.* Penguin, New York.

Ann Silverside, 2003, *Aids Activist: Michael Lynch and the Politics of Community.* Between the Lines, Toronto.

Anne Simons, 1995, *Somalia Undone: Networks of Dissolution.* Westview, Boulder.

Geoffrey Simons, 1998, *The Scourging of Iraq: Sanctions, Law and Natural Justice.* Macmillan, Basingstoke.

Patricia Siplon, 2002, *AIDS and the Policy Struggle in the United States.* Georgetown University Press, Washington, D.C.

Richard Stacewicz, 1997, *Winter Soldiers: An Oral History of the Vietnam Veterans.* Twayne, New York.

Joseph Stiglitz, 2002, *Globalization and its Discontents.* Penguin, London.

Brett Stockdill, 2003, *Activism Against AIDS: At the Intersections of Sexuality,*

Race, Gender and Class. Lynne Reiner, Boulder.

Ron Susskind, 2004, *The Price of Loyalty: George W. Bush, the White House, and the Education of Paul O'Neill.* Simon and Schuster, New York.

Janet Thomas, 2000, *The Battle in Seattle: The Story Behind and Beyond the WTO Demonstrations.* Fulcrum, Golden, Colorado.

Michael Tonry, 1995, *Malign Neglect: Race, Crime and Punishment in America.* Oxford University Press, Oxford.

Meredith Turshen, 1999, *Privatizing Health Services in Africa.* Rutgers University Press, New Brunswick.

Hubert van Wersch, 1992, *Bombay Textile Strike, 1982–83.* Oxford University Press, Bombay.

Alex de Waal, 1997, *Famine Crimes: Politics and the Disaster Relief Industry in Africa.* James Currey, Oxford.

Dexter Whitfield, 2001, *Public Services or Corporate Welfare: Rethinking the Nation State in the Global Economy.* Pluto, London.

Tom Wells, 1994, *The War Within: America's Battle over Vietnam.* University of California Press, Berkeley.

Bruce Western, Becky Petit and Josh Guetzkow, 2002, 'Black Economic Progress in the Era of Mass Imprisonment'. Mauer and Chesney-Lind, 2002.

Amy Wilentz, 1994, *The Rainy Season: Haiti Since Duvalier.* Vintage, London.

Peter Winn, 1986, *Weavers of Revolution: The Yarur Workers and Chile's Road to Socialism.* Oxford University Press, Oxford.

Timothy Wise, Hilda Salazar and Laura Carlsen, 2003a, *Confronting Globalization: Economic Integration and Popular Resistance in Mexico.* Kumarian, Bloomfield.

Timothy Wise, Hilda Salazar and Laura Carlsen, 2003b, 'Introduction: Globalization and Popular Resistance in Mexico,' in Wise, Salazar and Carlsen, 2003a.

Bob Woodward, 1991, *The Commanders.* Simon and Schuster, New York.

Bob Woodward, 1994, *The Agenda: Inside the Clinton White House.* Simon and Schuster, New York.

Bob Woodward, 2000, *Maestro: Greenspan's Fed and the American Boom.* Simon and Schuster, New York.

Steffie Woolhandler, 2003, 'The Sad Experience of Corporate Health Care in the USA'. Sen, 2003a.

Allen Young, 1995, *The Harmony of Illusions: Inventing Post-Traumatic Stress Disorder.* Princeton University Press, Princeton.

Michael Zweig, 2000, *The Working Class Majority: America's Best Kept Secret.* Cornell University Press, Ithica.

Index

Index

586477

About the Author

Jonathan Neale was born in New York, grew up in Connecticut, Texas, and India, and settled in London in the 1970s. He has written 11 plays, mostly for young people, and nine books. His most recent books are *A People's History of the Vietnam War*, *Tigers of the Snow*, about Sherpa climbers, and *Lost at Sea*, a novel for children.

Jonathan studied anthropology at the London School of Economics, doing fieldwork in Afghanistan, and social history at the University of Warwick, writing a thesis on mutinies in the 18th-century navy. He worked in clinics and hospitals in London as a porter, occupational therapy technician, abortion counsellor and HIV counsellor. He is now a part-time senior lecturer in creative writing at Bath Spa University College.

Jonathan has been a socialist and trade union activist for many years. More recently he has been active in Globalise Resistance and the anti-war movement. He was one of the organisers of the Genoa Social Forum and the European Social Forums in Florence and Paris.